Practical Feelings

Practical Feelings

Emotions as Resources in a Dynamic Social World

MARCI D. COTTINGHAM

UNIVERSITY PRESS

OXFORD
UNIVERSITY PRESS

Oxford University Press is a department of the University of Oxford. It furthers
the University's objective of excellence in research, scholarship, and education
by publishing worldwide. Oxford is a registered trade mark of Oxford University
Press in the UK and certain other countries.

Published in the United States of America by Oxford University Press
198 Madison Avenue, New York, NY 10016, United States of America.

© Oxford University Press 2022

Library of Congress Cataloging-in-Publication Data
Names: Cottingham, Marci D., author.
Title: Practical feelings : emotions as resources in a dynamic social world
/ Marci D. Cottingham.
Description: New York : Oxford University Press, [2022] |
Includes bibliographical references and index.
Identifiers: LCCN 2021058978 (print) | LCCN 2021058979 (ebook) |
ISBN 9780197613696 (paperback) | ISBN 9780197613689 (hardback) |
ISBN 9780197613719 (epub)
Subjects: LCSH: Emotions—Social aspects. | Emotions—Sociological aspects.
Classification: LCC BF531 .C597 2022 (print) | LCC BF531 (ebook) |
DDC 152.4—dc23/eng/20220203
LC record available at https://lccn.loc.gov/2021058978
LC ebook record available at https://lccn.loc.gov/2021058979

DOI: 10.1093/oso/9780197613689.001.0001

1 3 5 7 9 8 6 4 2

Paperback printed by Marquis, Canada
Hardback printed by Bridgeport National Bindery, Inc., United States of America

Contents

Acknowledgments

With the research reported in this book spanning more than a decade, I am in the privileged position of having many to thank. I want to thank my advisors and mentors from Indiana University of Pennsylvania: Val Gunter, Kay Snyder, and Tom Nowak. Each of you provided crucial guidance during my formative time there and, perhaps most importantly, showed me that there are many ways to be a scholar. My expert informant on fandom, "Kevin," was generous with his time, enthusiasm, and in gifting me a Terrible Towel. I'm grateful for his help in connecting me with other Steelers fans and answering my many questions.

I want to especially thank Becky Erickson for her mentorship over the years, her invaluable feedback on prior drafts, and generosity in allowing me to use data from the CARMA project. I am also grateful to the nurses who detailed their experiences for that project and the team members who assisted with data collection, including Jamie Chapman, Mike Steiner, and Tiffany Wade. Other colleagues kindly read and provided feedback on my work at various stages, including Christian Bröer, Jan Willem Duyvendak, Jill Fisher, Monique Kremer, Giselinde Kuipers, and Danny de Vries.

The research on nursing was financially supported by a grant from the National Science Foundation ("Identity and Emotional Management Control in Health Care Settings," SES-1024271, awarded to Dr. Rebecca J. Erickson, PI, and Dr. James M. Diefendorff, co-PI). The research on mediated emotions during the Ebola outbreak was financially supported by a grant from the Fund for the Advancement of the Discipline, in association with the American Sociological Association and the National Science Foundation, and a grant from the Amsterdam Young Academy. Additionally, dedicated time for research and writing was made possible by a fellowship at the Hanse-Wissenschaftskolleg Institute for Advanced Study in Delmenhorst, Germany, and through Aspasia funding from Sarah Bracke's Vici grant, funded by the Dutch Research Council (NWO, project number 016.Vici.185.077). Thank you, Sarah, for this and much more.

I also want to thank my research assistants, Ariana Rose and Christopher Zraunig, for their assistance with the Viral Fear project.

An earlier version of Chapter 3 was published as "Interaction Ritual Theory and Sports Fans: Emotion, Symbols, and Solidarity," *Sociology of Sport Journal* 29, no. 2 (2012). An earlier version of Chapter 2 was published (with Rebecca J. Erickson) as "The Promise of Emotion Practice: At the Bedside and Beyond," *Work and Occupations* 47, no. 2 (2020). I gratefully acknowledge Human Kinetics and Sage Publications for their permission to use brief excerpts from those articles.

Introduction

Practical Emotions, Emotion Practices

Emotions well up, spill over, and burst out in inconvenient places, making messes even as they help us make sense. They also dissolve, dissipate, and fizzle out even when we feel them with extreme intensity just moments before. We do not usually think of our emotions as practical—often they are nuisances to overcome, momentary mysteries to solve, or fleeting sensations to savor before getting back to the business of living. But emotions are very much interwoven into the practical elements of daily life. In seeing emotions as practical engagements with the world, this book argues for a new conceptualization of emotion as *practical resources*. Seeing emotions as a form of practice draws on recent theoretical work in the social sciences in which emotions straddle the conscious and nonconscious, emerging from a mindful body constantly calibrating itself to future practical demands. By integrating the sociology of emotion with practice theory, a practice approach helps us to see before, beneath, and beyond individual feelers and discrete emotions, to more fully comprehend the social worlds that shape our personal feelings.

Emotions often connote irrational, base impulses and all that seems mystical about the human experience (Barbalet 1998; Lutz 1998). They have long been the purview of poets, philosophers, and psychologists. Social scientists have recently worked to understand emotions as inherently social, examining the social roots and consequences of even fleeting sensations (McCarthy 1989; 2017). Important scholarship has examined heightened moments of fear, anger, and euphoria in the context of social movements, politics, and romantic love (Glassner 1999; Gould 2009; Hochschild 2016; Illouz 1997). Emotions have increasingly moved from the fringes of the social sciences to become centrally important outcomes and catalysts of social life. Sociological studies of emotion highlight how negative emotions are often framed, in line with lay conceptions, as barriers or problems to manage (Hochschild 1983; Lois 2010). Framing negative emotions as barriers to overcome might be a

Practical Feelings. Marci D. Cottingham, Oxford University Press. © Oxford University Press 2022.
DOI: 10.1093/oso/9780197613689.003.0001

fundamental feeling rule—one so thoroughly engrained in Western thinking that it pervades our lives as workers, consumers, and as members of families and communities. Meditation apps promise to help us cope with workplace stress, moms manage the emotional demands of twenty-first-century parenting with wine and book clubs, social media serves up both anxiety-provoking news updates and opinion pieces on the need to digitally disconnect for the sake of managing our emotional well-being.

This focus on regulating, managing, and coping with emotions overlooks one key point: emotions are useful. Rather than seeing emotions as problems or barriers, we can instead see them as just the opposite, as *practical resources*. An *emotion practice approach*—the approach I develop in this book—promises to get us back to the "signal function" of emotion that Hochschild (1983), building on Freud, argued was dangerously missing from contemporary conceptualizations of emotion. Taking an emotion practice approach allows us to appreciate emotions as practical engagements with a dynamic social world—a world in which mundane feelings, including fatigue and energy, comfort and discomfort, anxiety and relaxation, exist alongside heightened feelings of anger, fear, and happiness. The peaks and valleys traversed in prior research are certainly important, and the daily ebbs and flows are rarely as spectacular—yet mundane emotions hum us along in the well-worn rhythms of work and family life, in our leisure activities and in our digital pursuits (pursuits that, at times, seem to pursue us). It is these well-worn habits of the everyday that this book centrally examines.

Thinking of emotions as practical aligns with developments in a number of different disciplines, including psychology (Barrett 2017; Holbrook and Hahn-Holbrook 2022), neuroscience (Damasio 1994), history (Scheer 2012), and anthropology (Scheper-Hughes and Lock 1987). Seeing emotions as practical fits with recent neuroscientific research in which the brain's primary function is prediction. In developing her theory of constructed emotion, Lisa Feldman Barrett summarizes the state of neuroscientific advances and how they overturn outdated beliefs about emotions:

> In the theory of constructed emotion, however, the dividing line between brain and world is permeable, perhaps nonexistent. Your brain's core systems combine in various ways to construct your perceptions, memories, thoughts, feelings, and other mental states. [. . .] interoceptive predictions produce your feelings of affect, influence every action that you perform, and determine which parts of the world you care about in the moment.

Without interoception, you wouldn't notice or care about your physical surroundings or anything else, and you'd be unlikely to survive long. (Barrett 2017, 153)

Caring about our surroundings is key for our survival—individually and collectively—and emotions, as indicators of our values, attention, and care, are practical resources for identifying and overcoming problems both in our social relationships and physical environment.

In this book, I develop an emotion practice approach by drawing on two prominent sociological theories of emotion: emotion management theory and interaction ritual theory. Both frameworks have accumulated an impressive body of theoretical and empirical research over the years, yet each provides a different set of concepts for making sense of emotions in social life. Emotion management theory (Hochschild 1979; 1983) focuses on what we do with emotions—the effort (or the labor, if paid a wage) we expend to mask, repress, fake, or work to authentically cultivate emotions to match situational expectations. The demands placed on service workers to provide service with a smile go far beyond the hospitality industry, with emotion norms shaping all our social interactions both professionally and personally. Interaction ritual theory (R. Collins 2004), by contrast, emphasizes emotion as energy that emerges from successful interaction rituals, fostering solidarity and collective effervescence in groups of varying sizes. In this theory, positive emotions emanate from successful interactions, imbuing symbols with meaning and groups with insider and outsider demarcations.

Certainly there are many other sociological approaches to emotion in addition to the two I draw from here (Stets and Turner 2014). I focus on these two in developing an emotion practice approach because they have each been especially prominent in shaping the development of the field and have gained notable traction in other disciplines, including psychology and organizational studies.[1] They offer, as I will argue, complementary views of emotion as the product of *effort* and shared social rules about feeling and expression, as well as a view of emotion as *energy*—the product of shared social bonds that seems to spread with little intentional effort. Both emotion management and interaction ritual theory have been critiqued for their interactionist focus. In privileging how interactions with others shape what we feel, the interface with broader social structures—enduring patterns at the macro level—are less developed. In Chapter 1, I detail the contributions and limitations of Hochschild's and Collins's two approaches and the benefits of integrating them with concepts from a different strand of sociology—social practice theory. Through their shared lineage (linked to the traditions of symbolic interactionism and pragmatism), Hochschild's emotion management theory and Collins's interaction ritual chains are especially compatible with a social practice approach to emotion.

A practice approach to emotion promises to overcome lingering dualisms in social theory and commonsense thinking. These include demarcations between the mind and body, between subjective and objective, and most relevant to arguments in this book, the dualism that sees emotion and reason as mutually exclusive. The dominance of Western Enlightenment thinking has framed emotion and reason as separate, with reason seen as the ideal mode for practical action. A practice approach to emotion aims to overturn this division, and while it is not alone in this effort (other approaches take a similar aim; see Barbalet 1998; Damasio 1994), I believe seeing emotions as practical engagements with the world gets at the heart of this issue and provides a set of key concepts for challenging the subtle ways that these dualisms remain entrenched in scholarly and commonsensical approaches to emotion. A practice approach to emotion attends to the social roots of felt emotions often overlooked in a focus on emotion management (Burkitt 2017; Theodosius 2006), while also addressing the "matters of taste" and "dispositions of actors" that are missing from an interaction ritual framework (Barbalet 2006, 448–50).

Practices are acts that can be *taken up* or *fallen into*—they straddle conscious strategies and unintentional habits. We come to embody past practices as our dispositions and physiology attune to the practical demands of life. Cities with devoted bike lanes do not simply have safer and more numerous cyclists than those without such lanes; they are also more likely to have healthier residents with a muscular development that matches the demands of cycling. Through a cascade of connections, city infrastructure shapes bodily musculature. When cities modify their roads to accommodate cyclists, they also change the uptake of these new embodied practices, and with it the actual bodies of their inhabitants. What we do, what we *practice*, becomes embedded in our physiological and dispositional make-up.

Practices are what link city infrastructure with physiology. Practices are "the building blocks of social reality" (Feldman and Orlikowski 2011, 1241). They are both historic and futuristic, containing within them the traces of past demands as well as the seeds of future adaptations. They are the product of past ways of thinking, feeling, and interacting with the world.

As the "invisible conductor that orchestrates" our lives (Murdock 2010, 64), practices cement into the cluster of what makes us who we are (as "habitus"), while also being open to tweaks, refinements, and adaptations to meet new demands (Bourdieu 1990; Bourdieu and Wacquant 1992). Through practices, collective and individual identities are formed, macro-level patterns are developed and maintained, and social hierarchies are enforced or reformed.

But what does a practice approach to emotion mean for everyday emotions? Being swept up in our emotions is a common human experience. A practice approach pushes us to ask: what lingers in our bodies and our social relationships when overwhelming emotions subside? How can we be both in control of emotions but overcome by them at the same time? How are emotions shared as practices that span time and space? What if thinking of emotions as discrete states doesn't match the complexity of our experiences? This book seeks to tackle such questions by seeing emotions as practical, honed resources that are so deeply embedded in who we are that we forget having learned them. This forgetting (or "misrecognition" as Pierre Bourdieu calls it, 1990) accounts for why we fail to see our habits and nonconscious acts as products of our social context. The individualistic (and psychological) focus of our current age often cuts us off from our social roots, including the social roots that shape our everyday feelings.

To take a practice approach to emotion means to focus on how emotions are rooted in the practicalities of living. Practicality underlies human action, and people manage everyday needs through the resources that are at hand. People are resourceful—filled with economic, social, cultural, and emotional resources, adapted to the particular fields that they traverse. They confront common problems and needs—the need for food, shelter, safety from harm, social connection, and meaning. A sociology of emotion practice starts with a view of individuals as embedded in social connections and shared practical needs, and in this way is similar to an emphasis on cultural "toolkits" aimed at addressing "different kinds of problems" (Swidler 1986, 273). The newborn enters the world already connected intimately to another—the one it emerged from—and through this connection with another it communicates the most basic of feelings, such as comfort or discomfort. The feeling of discomfort can set off a chain reaction of crying, of caregiver response, of sleep deprivation, of family distress, of neighbor resentment, and on and on until discomfort is transformed into comfort through nurturing practices of feeding, burping, cleaning, or soothing. Feeling and acting on discomfort is the only practical act for a tiny, fragile creature. Soon enough, said creature develops new mechanisms for achieving comfort as well as a more fine-grained understanding of (and vocabulary for) the various positive and negative feelings that can be experienced or avoided (Gordon 1989; Russell 1991).

As fully formed adults, we continue to move through the world using our feelings of comfort/discomfort as gauges for action. Certain people, situations, foods, music, and jobs attract or repel us in ways that we cannot always articulate cogently. As research on the social shaping of taste shows (Bourdieu 1996), aesthetic preferences are not simply personal preferences but the result of our upbringing. The social class—working, middle, upper—in which we are raised marks our taste buds as much as our life chances. Thus, each individual's effort to calibrate comfort and discomfort is connected to our past experiences and exposures. While seemingly quite distant from our example of the newborn seeking comfort, we can see practices that emphasize connection and comfort in the deep emotional attachments found among groups of sports fans. Beyond the excitement and thrill of watching a game in a stadium or arena, sports symbols become invested with the feelings of connection between family members, communities, and a city. Fans can draw on these emotions in celebrating special events, mourning the loss of family and friends, and it can be especially emotionally painful when they are cut off from fan activities altogether (as we saw in the context of the COVID-19 pandemic; Kilgore 2020). Individual fans rely on the shared, common resources of sports logos and merchandise to forge connections. Wearing team merchandise on the body, they put these resources to use in an act that is simultaneously nostalgic, practical, and embodied: nostalgic of past emotional highs, practical in solidifying connections with others, and worn on and felt in the body.

While past social experiences radically shape our tastes and preferences, we can still acquire tastes for new things. New tastes often result from new practical demands. Unemployed, working-class men, for example, might feel a push toward traditionally feminine occupations due to job shortages in the manufacturing or trade vocations that their fathers were more likely to hold. Some are able to make a switch to traditionally feminine professions and develop the emotional skills they require (Cottingham 2015), others are not (Nixon 2009). Economic fluctuations can reverberate into the day-to-day emotional fluctuations of new job demands and occupational climates. The case of nursing is intriguing because it has high emotional demands while being largely performed by women—women who are stereotyped as naturally suited to what are often *unnatural* encounters. Caring intimately for others as a part of paid employment is fraught with complex emotions

(Stacey 2011). Nurses end their shifts exhausted, overwhelmed, and often depleted of the emotional resources they need to meet the practical demands of the job. How do they conserve these resources? And what happens when they fail to conserve them? How do these feelings linger in their bodies shift after shift? An emotion practice approach can help to answer these questions.

The practical is now also digital. Our lives include face-to-face interactions, to be sure. But we increasingly live our lives in spaces abstracted from the material world. Digital spaces provide community and connection, and they transmit information and up-to-date knowledge about the world "out there." This shapes the world "in here"—in minds and bodies not necessarily formed with an intuitive sense of how to navigate these new spaces. Customs, norms, and "feeling rules" (Hochschild 1979)—shared expectations for what to feel and how to express it—might not transfer readily to these new spaces. New feeling rules might emerge that go against the status quo of in-person interactions. In navigating the stream of up-to-date (mis)information online, news consumers and social media users confront a seemingly endless string of bad news: disasters, political upheaval, and public health crises. Disease outbreaks and disasters should be part of the extraordinary, but through the pace and reach of new information, and the emergence of a global infectious pandemic in 2020, these now seem like ordinary parts of the news of the day. How do publics near and far from an unfolding outbreak calibrate their emotions to such uncertainty? How do politicians and world leaders frame emotions in the face of these challenges? Integrating concepts like habitus and emotional capital from a social practice perspective, which I define in Chapter 1, promises to answer some of these questions about what shapes emotions in digital and political spaces.

In this book, I turn to four distinct social contexts in order to draw out the strengths of an emotion practice approach: work, leisure, social media use, and the political sphere. This range of divergent social domains shows the scope and promise of this approach to practical emotions and emotion practices. From nurses at hospital bedsides to sports fans in stadiums, in the seemingly disembodied space of digital life, and in political responses to collective challenges like COVID-19, emotions inform our understanding of the complexity of social life in important ways. This book traces emotions across these disparate social arenas in order not only to understand them more fully but also to fine-tune key concepts within a sociology of emotion practice. In this approach, negative emotions are neither barriers nor irrelevancies, but the individual and collective sensing of a world in need of practical change.

Why These Cases?

Sociologists studying emotion have covered various aspects of social life, including family and marriage (Erickson 2005; Holmes 2015; Lois 2010; 2013; Simon and Nath 2004), work and occupations (Evans 2013; Hochschild 1983; Pierce 1995), health and medicine (Bolton 2001; Lopez 2006; Theodosius 2008), and popular culture and the emerging technologies that mediate social interactions (McCarthy 2017; Recuber 2016). Because emotions have historically been framed as personal and primarily relevant to the private realm, sociological research on emotions has focused on their role in family life. Going back to Talcott Parsons (1951), whose construction of expressive versus instrumental action is just one illustration of the entrenched emotion/reason dualism in sociological theory, we find that he associates women with expressive action because of their need to nurture and support members of the family, particularly children. It is not too surprising then that sociological studies of emotion in connection with the family and intimate relationships have proliferated in the late twentieth century. Yet, in seeing emotions as forms of practice, we can add to this scholarship by tracing how emotions are enacted and experienced in the more public spheres of work, leisure, digital, and political spaces. Of course, these demarcations of social domains (i.e., family, work, leisure, digital sphere) are arbitrary. Our digital lives often interweave work, family, and leisure experiences. And emotions rarely stay contained within a particular domain; rather, they "spill" over and flow across these tidy analytical divides that we as scholars construct (Cottingham, Chapman, and Erickson 2020).

In this book, I cover diverse areas of social life in order to show the utility of an emotion practice approach, illustrate how emotions are put into practice in these divergent spaces, and trace how emotions—as effort, energy, and embodied resource—spill across domains. Nursing, as a key occupation in healthcare, is part of the fastest growing job sector in the United States (Bureau of Labor Statistics 2020). The complex human experiences that nurses confront mean that each nurse must navigate a labyrinth of emotional demands that cannot be reduced to mere strategies of intentional management. A large body of scholarship takes emotions seriously as critical aspects of healthcare and nursing (Erickson and Grove 2008; Lopez 2006; Theodosius 2008). Applying an emotion practice approach can help us better situate nurses' emotional experiences—and not just their conscious management of emotion—in their social relations and practical needs.

Sports fans, in many ways, represent the opposite of nurses in that fans expect to *receive* an emotional payoff (as emotional energy) from their role rather than be drained of it. With some key exceptions (Elias and Dunning 1986; Fine and Corte 2017), leisure pursuits have generally received limited attention from emotion scholars. While soccer is globally the most popular sport in terms of fan base, the National Football League's (NFL) Sunday night football viewership drew over nineteen million viewers in the 2018–2019 season, making it the most watched television show in the United States.[2] Sports spectatorship is a global phenomenon as well as a key American pastime that can only be explained by looking at how an athlete's physical capital is transformed through fan practices into emotionally rich sports symbols. The family and community remain relevant even in this domain as fan emotions move, through symbols, between sports settings and family and civic life. Seeing emotions as practical rather than superfluous means taking seriously the communities and identities built around the flow of excitement, solidarity, and emotional energy drawn from sports-related practices and symbols.

Social media users are relatively new terrain for emotion scholars (Brownlie and Shaw 2019; Recuber 2013). A full appreciation of the emotional payoff and transfer that takes place online between users requires attending to how symbols and humor are harnessed as resources for building solidarity and community. And, finally, political actors have largely been framed by prior scholarship as emotional manipulators (Furedi 2011; Loseke 2009). Understanding the effectiveness of their trade requires us to dig into the subtle ways that they delegitimize others' emotions as impractical. Applying an emotion practice approach to political framings of Ebola and the COVID-19 outbreaks illustrates what is at stake when we *fail* to recognize emotions as powerful, practical resources.

To meaningfully understand the experiences of these different groups, I zoom into a particular context for each—registered nurses in hospitals in the Midwest, sports fans of the Pittsburgh Steelers franchise, and political actors and social media users responding to the public health threats of Ebola and COVID-19. While their contexts are divergent, the details of their cases reveal the limits of prior approaches to emotion and more fully illustrate the utility of an emotion practice approach. From the intimacy of nurses' diaries detailing their daily lives, Steelers fans decorating homes and shops with team symbols, to social media users and political actors responding to a public health threat—emotions tell us something vital about social connections and conflicts across the spectrum of the private and public divide.

Structure of the Book

Chapter 1 focuses on the main theoretical claims of the book and how we might integrate insights from Arlie Hochschild, Randall Collins, and Pierre Bourdieu in order to develop a theory of practical emotions. An emotion practice approach (Scheer 2012) is not entirely at odds with these other theories, but there are some key distinctions in how each conceptualizes emotion and social action. Collins and Hochschild, both American sociologists working in the tradition of symbolic interactionism and microsociology, present a view of emotion as simultaneously socially *emergent* and socially *constrained.* Bourdieu, of the three, is an outsider.[3] But he, too, draws on shared pragmatist roots, a field of social philosophy influential in shaping both American and European sociology. These three theorists respectively see emotion as *effort, energy,* and *embodied resource.* These need not be seen as divergent, contradictory stances; rather, they can be integrated in order to better capture the complexity of emotional experiences and expression. An emotion practice approach sees emotion as all three: emotions are modes of being and acts (*practices*) that activate emotional capital (*resources*), including the emotional *energy,* knowledge, and skills needed to identify and/ or *effortfully* work over our feelings in order to adapt to new situations. Emotions emerge as low and high levels of energy from a body in relation with other people and environments. Yet emotions also act back on the individual to engrain habits of feeling and skills in emotion management that anticipate expected, future encounters.

Chapters 2 through 5 each turn to a specific empirical case where I draw out the strengths of an emotion practice approach by placing it next to contrasting (but ultimately complementary) theoretical lenses (otherwise referred to as "alternative casing" in an abductive approach to qualitative data analysis; Timmermans and Tavory 2012). Spanning the social domains of work, leisure, digital interactions, and the political sphere, the cases that follow focus on divergent actors across the private and public spectrum. While sociologists of emotion have by and large concentrated their empirical focus on the workplace and the family, the empirical cases taken up in this book overlap with, but go beyond, these well-studied spheres of social life. By analyzing nurses, sports fans, social media users, and political actors, I aim to illustrate the utility of an integrated emotion practice approach across the private and public and face-to-face and digital encounters.

In Chapter 2, nurses provide reflections on their day-to-day working lives through audio diaries—recordings of the events, responses, and meanings that inflect their work as nurses. While emotion management concepts have been thoroughly applied to this professional context (Cottingham, Erickson, and Diefendorff 2015; Lopez 2006; Theodosius 2008), a practice approach can theorize blind spots that emotional labor as a construct overlooks. Nurses—characterized as emotional "jugglers" (Bolton 2001)—share their accounts of daily life and, in doing so, show how applying an emotion practice approach can capture their intentional and unintentional conservation of emotional resources, the divergent emotions they confront, and the effects these practices have on the body. From stress and exhaustion to pride and relief, nurses run the gamut of human experience on a nearly daily basis. Focusing only on emotional labor, while ubiquitous in this context, comes up short in illuminating the emotional complexity that hospital nurses experience as they move from bedside to bedside, and from interactions with patients, patients' family members, and physicians. Taking an emotion practice approach can better account for moments when nurses feel as though their emotional resources are depleted, when they only partially manage negative emotions in order to retain the energy they need to enact changes in the workplace, and the ways in which emotions are both cognitively articulated and felt in aching and exhausted bodies.

In Chapter 3, sports fans provide an empirical basis for thinking through the strengths of interaction ritual theory and facets of sports fandom that seem out of reach using this lens—facets that a practice approach can help to explain. In the case of sports fans, seeing emotions as a form of social practice reveals the linkages between peak emotional moments at the stadium, arena, field, or rink and celebrations of family and community life. Sports fans, in this case Steelers fans, use the symbols of their preferred team, player, or sport to make special events more special and mundane events more meaningful. Emotions come to infuse physical objects, like sports logos, and fans can turn to these symbols to enliven mundane objects or events, to cope with grief, and to mark transitions in the life course. This economy of symbols and emotional energy, though, is at its core built on the physical capital of athletes—the majority of whom are African American men (Belson 2019) who take on disproportionate levels of physical risk in American football (Baron et al. 2012; Roberts et al. 2020). In this way, historic and ongoing racial hierarchies are salient in the generation of good feelings inherent to football spectatorship. African American men disproportionately make up the high-risk positions within the sport while a mixed, but majority white fan base accrues the energizing emotional capital or payoff made possible through these risks. In seeing emotions as resources, we can connect the physical capital of athletes with the emotional capital infused in sports symbols—capital that is taken up by fans and corporations in settings far beyond the stadium or sports bar.

Social media users in the context of the 2013–2016 Ebola epidemic provide a third case in which to apply and refine a theory of emotions as practical engagements with the (digital) world. In Chapter 4, I analyze social media responses to the Ebola outbreak and weigh the utility of emotion practice theory's conceptual tools in the emerging space of digital interactions. In the context of a social media platform like Twitter, users are not simply passively manipulated nor are they malicious actors. They playfully use the outbreak to develop sarcastic and humorous responses that are valued in Twitter's economy of likes and retweets. While often transgressing into the irreverent, these responses suggest a habituated resistance to hopelessness that can generate energy and solidarity as resources for online communities. We have seen similar acts of playfulness in online communities during the COVID-19 pandemic (Wamsley 2020). Looking at digital emotions through the lens of practice theory helps us identify *user* practices that spread both information as well as the emotional resources needed for responding to crises. Critiques of social media platforms as hotbeds of misinformation must acknowledge the emotional resources that are circulated and used through these spaces if we are to fully understand the appeal of misinformation on these sites.

Fear of a legitimate threat like a pandemic might be one of the clearest instances in which an emotional response seems wholly practical and even rational. Yet, as I examine in Chapter 5, world leaders were and remain quick to call for calm during such a threat and they tend to portray fear as an impractical barrier to effective action even in the context of a global pandemic. News consumers are faced with an endless string of disasters, outbreaks, and catastrophes around the world at any given moment. Disasters and outbreaks, unfortunately, increasingly intrude on our everyday lives. In both the case of Ebola and COVID-19, debates about what actions were "rational" or driven by "panic" were at the fore of public discussion during these outbreaks. News coverage of Ebola presents multiple interpretations of personal protective equipment as a source of both comfort and fear. Through mimicry of healthcare practices, they also fostered role-taking and empathy for healthcare workers rather than Ebola victims. In the case of COVID-19, the "panic buying" of toilet paper and debates about face masks in public pointed to the enduring belief of political leaders that public panic was a central problem to manage—a barrier to effectively containing the outbreak. Yet this view is not in line with research on how people actually respond in disaster scenarios (Quarantelli 2001). Calls to avoid panic simultaneously delegitimize emotion as a resource and affirm long-standing myths that panic underlies the inexplicable behaviors of the public (Tierney, Bevc, and Kuligowski 2006). In devaluing emotions and reaffirming a core Western cultural tenet that negative emotions are themselves problems, political actors attempt to enact a stoic, rational disposition (habitus) that focuses our attention on managing inner feelings rather than addressing external threats.

In the final chapter, I distill the theoretical claims and empirical findings that make up a sociology of emotion practice. This approach integrates Hochschild, Collins, and Bourdieu, bridging the sociology of emotion with practice theory. In that final chapter, I more fully detail the role of homophily and affective affinity (Threadgold 2020) for linking emotions with social inequalities, and understanding emotions as practical engagements with an unjust world. The flows of emotions traced in this book are only surprising when we fail to see the social roots that connect emotions with our social positions and our past, now embodied, practices. By tracing emotions through the disparate fields that this book covers, we can see nurses, sports fans, social media users, and political actors in more complex, holistic ways. Nurses need more support than the pedestal of heroism can provide. Sports fans are not simply "crazed" fanatics. Social media users can be appreciated as more than merely pawns or malicious trolls. The rhetoric of political actors in times of crisis can be more precisely critiqued for its failure to value the emotional resources needed to address collective problems. Homing in on the routine and generative practices of these groups helps us to reclaim their humanity and push us beyond stereotypes that link each to a limited set of discrete emotions and tendencies.

As a whole, this book brings the sociology of emotion into closer alignment with the complex practices that shape our everyday experiences of the social world. As practical resources, emotions in a practice approach bridge the nonconscious and strategic (or "spontaneous and managed," Hallett 2003), the objective and subjective—dualisms that, while roundly critiqued, continue to inflect social theorizing and lay understandings of emotion. Seeing emotions as practical engagements with the world does not discount their energizing and effortful dimensions. Rather, connecting the sociology of emotions to social practice theory can return us to the social aspects of emotion's "signal function," as emotions are embodied ways of sensing our relationship to others and the world around us. They convey importance and meaning beyond what simple facts can accomplish. Emotion "gets people where they want to go" (Hochschild 1983, 214). Or, as Nico Frijda argues, "emotions exist for the sake of action" (2004, 170). When it comes to crafting a safer, more just, and equitable world, we still have a lot of ground to cover. Given how the COVID-19 pandemic has unfolded, we need all resources—including emotional ones—to meet the present and impending challenges of our times.

1

Toward an Emotion Practice Approach

> It is only in everyday experience that we encounter the various facets
> of life and the world as a unity, be it more or less messy or attractive.
> Once we start to reflect on any of these aspects and conceptualize
> them, we unavoidably abstract away from some other aspects.
> —Räsänen and Kauppinen (2020, 3)

Scholars in a variety of disciplines use a practice approach to understand
how the social world works. This chapter draws on this literature to consider
how emotions are *used* and *useful* for making the social world what it is. As
the opening quote suggests, this process of thinking about the world, rather
than living in it, inherently abstracts us away from the very thing we hope
to understand. But these abstractions, these conceptual developments, are
needed before we can fully apply this approach to the empirical contexts of
work, leisure, and digital and political spaces that I take up in the empirical
chapters that follow. As I will argue, a practice approach promises to help
us overcome limitations in prior approaches to emotion while also helping
us see how emotions are relevant in the context of nursing, sports fandom,
social media use, and the politics of epidemics. Abstractions, like emotions,
have their use.

The emotion practice approach I put forward here is grounded in both
the sociology of emotion and a theory of social practice. Before turning to
that specialized literature, though, it is useful to take a step back and consider more broadly what I mean when I talk of emotions as practical and
why this is distinct from approaches that frame emotion and practicality as
mutually exclusive. Thus, the first part of this chapter will take up in detail
the dualisms that remain entrenched in theorizing and lay understandings
of emotion, before describing how a practice approach attempts to overcome
these lingering dualisms. I then turn to how prior sociological frameworks
have approached emotion as both *effort* and *energy*, followed by a description

Practical Feelings. Marci D. Cottingham, Oxford University Press. © Oxford University Press 2022.
DOI: 10.1093/oso/9780197613689.003.0002

of the conceptual tools offered by a social practice approach. While different strands of emotion scholarship within sociology have emerged over the last four decades, seeing emotion as effort, energy, and practice, I argue, shares a clear lineage with the social philosophy of pragmatism. Returning to this shared history, then, can help us integrate these separate strands to form a robust sociology of emotion practice. With this theoretical background established, we can then turn to the empirical cases in the chapters that follow to show how an emotion practice approach illuminates the contours of diverse social contexts.

Lingering Dualisms and Their Effects

To understand what it means to move beyond a binary of emotion versus reason (or practicality), we need to appreciate the roots of this demarcation. Much of our thinking about emotions is indebted to an Enlightenment worldview that consolidated a mechanistic view of how the universe, and by extension, how the social world works. Elemental parts could be delimited from each other, and mechanical, causal relationships could be posited, tested, and, if necessary, revised. This worldview emphasizes control and mastery over the environment, and in this line of thinking, emotions come to be seen as part of the natural order that needs to be tamed by its superior opposing force: reason.[1] Reframing a good versus evil cosmology,[2] scientific thinking of the Enlightenment era entrenched a number of dualisms: emotion as opposite (and mutually exclusive) to reason, nature opposite to culture, child opposite adult, woman opposite to man, non-Western peoples opposite to white, Western people (Lutz 1998).[3] Within these dualisms, the left side is often placed beneath its supposedly superior opposite. Reason and culture, in this framework, are needed to overcome the natural, volatile realm of emotions.

More contemporary instantiations of this type of thinking can be found in managerial and organizational studies where, using concepts of management, regulation, and "emotional intelligence," emotion is again framed as an unruly impulse that must be tamed and regulated by corporate managers and workers in order to improve their efficiency and productivity in paid labor. Ian Burkitt cogently challenges this limited view of emotion and instead argues that:

> Emotion is not just something that we reflect on in a disengaged way, it is central to the way people in social relations relate to one another: it is woven into the fabric of the interactions we are engaged in and it is therefore also central to the way we relate to ourselves as well as to others. (Burkitt 2012, 459)

This centrality of emotion to how we navigate our social interactions begins to get at the practical framing of emotion as a resource, not simply for improving the productivity and outputs of workers, but for sensing and making sense of the social world.

What philosophers and social theorists (and feminist scholars in particular, Sprague 1997) have made clear is that a dualistic conception of emotion and reason is not inevitable. We can think of the world in radical ways that differ from this dualistic approach. Indeed, at different historical moments, the conventional notion that reason is both oppositional and superior to emotion has been challenged, as it was during the Romantic period of the early to mid-1800s (Barbalet 1998). Building on the idea that we might develop a radical view of emotion and reason as overlapping continuities, Jack Barbalet points to the feeling of confidence as inherent to our use of reasoning:

> All action is ultimately founded on the actor's feeling of confidence in her capacities and their efficacy. (Barbalet 1993, 234)

Barbalet later highlights emotion as "a source of evaluation of circumstances that while not based on reason (as calculation) is not necessarily irrational" (238).

Emotions, then, need not be seen as the opposite of reason—emotion and reason are always folded into each other in thinking/feeling processes (Jasper 2014). We sense, gain information, react to that information, develop new sensations, label a sensation, and consider new information in complex and sometimes seemingly instantaneous ways. A practice approach is *one* way, though certainly not the only way, to break out of this dualistic thinking. As the empirical cases in this book will show, these processes can feel instantaneous and instinctual because we have practiced them so thoroughly, but that does not mean that they operate outside of social influences. The habits of nurses, sports fans, Twitter users, or politicians are learned over time to the point that they might become second nature. Despite feeling natural, they remain learned. For example, nurses who "close off" from the types of demanding patients who overdraw on their emotional resources, sports fans congregating at events hoping to make an emotional withdrawal, and Twitter users relying on laughing emojis to express themselves all represent acts that can straddle the intentional/unintentional and the rational/emotional divide.

If practices offer a way to help us think beyond a binary of either/or when it comes to emotion and reason, then why does this book focus on *emotion* practice? Refocusing our attention on emotion as practical helps us to push intellectually against the idea that emotion is opposite to and inferior to reasoning. Reasoning and rationality remain elevated in contemporary Western cultures—these modes are valued and seen as superior to acting with feeling and emotion. The dispassionate judge, the unbiased scientist, the cool and reasonable politician—all of these stereotypes of leadership continue to elevate reason over emotion (Blix and Wettergren 2018). By placing emotions front and center, we can tip the scales back toward valuing emotions in and of themselves and for their practical value. By tipping the scales to focus on emotion, we might also dislodge our favoring of the other "superior" binaries mentioned earlier, including a valuing of social groups that have, both historically and in contemporary contexts, been especially disadvantaged by Enlightenment dualisms: women, people of color, indigenous groups, and people and nations positioned outside of the West and in the Global South. In this way, seeing emotions as practical engagements with the world is a radical reframing that builds on the work of feminist, antiracist, and postcolonial scholars (hooks 2000; Mohanty 1988; Sprague 1997).[4]

Beyond overcoming the "remarkably durable" (Barbalet 1998, 54) dualism that pits emotion against reason, a move to a practice approach provides the tools needed to both overcome and *explain* the durable nature of the emotion/reason dualism. Why is it that emotion continues to be seen generally as opposite to reason and even a "pejorative evaluation" (Barbalet 2002, 1) at odds with practical action? As I will take up directly in Chapter 5, an emotion practice approach allows us to recognize the value (as emotional capital) of a stoic, emotionally-controlled disposition (habitus) that has historically been associated with white, middle/upper-class masculinity. Particularly in the context of politics, leaders enact a practice of stoicism and calmness while portraying the public at large, and political opponents, as overcome by problematic feelings of fear and panic. In seeing how political leaders convert their emotional capital into political capital, we gain a better appreciation for how and why emotion and reason remain locked in as diametric opposites. Maintaining these oppositions can be politically expedient, while simultaneously problematic.

Before getting to that argument, this current chapter details the general strengths of an emotion practice approach and theorizes how we might connect a sociology of emotion with practice theory. A practice approach promises to trace what happens *before*, *beneath*, and *beyond* individuals and their felt or managed emotions. Taking a practice approach allows us to conceptualize the sedimentation of past practices (in the body)—that is, how the past comes to bear on the present in terms of dispositions, expectations, and habitual engagements with the world. In this way, emotions do not simply emerge from the mixing of ritual ingredients; they also demand a vocabulary, a stock of cultural knowledge, and the inertia of biographical experiences that have shaped who we each are as members of social groups. Before any sensation can be labeled an emotion, an individual must build up a vocabulary of knowing and feeling that allows one to match certain sensations with certain labels and, even more fundamental, to recognize a given sensation as distinct and in need of a label. All of us have done this learning, but we are quick to forget that this learned knowledge represents the past, the *before*, exerting its influence on the present.

A practice approach also allows us to conceptualize emotional experiences, not as a parade of easily articulated, discrete emotions, but a flow of subtle and simultaneous sensations that drain and charge up our emotional reserves. These subtle sensations can include mundane emotions often overlooked in sociological analyses. The sociological study of emotion often favors more extreme emotions of fear, love, anger, hate, happiness, and grief (Glassner 1999; Hochschild 2016; Illouz 1997). Certainly, a practice approach can attend to these noisier, primary emotions, but it can also highlight the social role of more subtle ebbs and flows, ups and downs of everyday feelings, including feelings of comfort/discomfort, minute attractions and repulsions, and efforts at conserving and expending emotional resources that we will see in the contexts examined in later chapters. These subtler fluctuations in emotion are key to tapping into emotion's practical role in everyday contexts of work, leisure, and digital and political realms.

Seeing emotion as a form of practice also allows us to better appreciate the social forces that shape what happens deep within us, *beneath* the conscious strategic actions that are on the surface of our social lives. When we navigate the world on autopilot, we tap into the established, nonconscious ways of being that no longer require conscious interrogation. That does not mean that the nonconscious is impractical. In fact, it is highly practical. It is the highly useful and repetitive parts of living that become part of who we are in such a deep way that we no longer even need to think about using them. The fact that we need not explicitly think about such actions (as practices) saves us the time and energy otherwise needed for reflexive examination. In this way, the nonconscious aspects of habitus (which I will detail later) can be seen as highly practical, energy-saving technologies (albeit technologies of culture that become embodied). Such a framing of emotion overlaps with conceptualizations in evolutionary psychology that frame emotions as "calibrational adaptations" (Holbrook and Hahn-Holbrook 2021).

Finally, an emotion practice approach can help us see *beyond* individually felt emotions to the broader structure of the social hierarchies that shape our lives, whether we recognize them or not. Gender, as an axis of inequality, has received the vast majority of attention from emotion scholars because, going back to the long lineage of influential Western male thinkers, the canon of Western thought reflects the tendency to conflate women with emotionality. More recently, sociologists have highlighted the importance of race for understanding gradations of emotion norms across society (Evans 2013; Harlow 2003; Wingfield 2010), along with social class (Nixon 2009). What we are expected to feel and express varies depending on the groups to which we belong and with whom we interact.

As I argue in this book, tracing the structure of contemporary social hierarchies to differential emotion norms is only one way in which emotions and social inequalities are intertwined. Thinking of emotions in terms of resources can help us to see these resources as unequally distributed and drawn upon by individuals, depending on the racial and social class make-up of interactants. In turning to the political sphere, we will also see how political actors work to transform emotional capital into a type of political capital that shores up their legitimacy during moments of potential crisis—moments when their hold on power is most fragile.

The framing of emotions as problems is party dependent on *whose* emotions are under discussion. Women's emotions have historically been framed as more problematic than men's (Sweet 2019). People of color in white supremacist societies must conform to more exacting emotion norms or risk sanction (Staples 1998; Wingfield 2010), violence, or death (Evans and Feagin 2015). Political leaders use the real and mythic emotions of the public to hold onto their political power during challenging times. Constructions of "mob mentality," the "hysterical woman," and the "scary black man" have long histories that remain entrenched in present-day politics and social interactions.

Before getting into detail about the terms and conceptual relationships that constitute an emotion practice approach, I now want to provide an overview of two influential theories within the sociology of emotion that inform the integrative approach I aim to develop: emotion management theory and interaction ritual theory. Sociological treatments of emotion have proliferated over the last four decades and are too numerous to cover fully (Bericat 2016; Stets and Turner 2014). In this chapter, I focus in particular on sociological theories that conceptualize emotion as effort (Hochschild 1979; 2012) and as energy (R. Collins 1981; 2004). Not only have these two approaches been foundational to the sociology of emotion and been taken up outside of the discipline, but they offer key concepts that are useful for developing a robust practice approach to emotion. I next turn to emotion as *rule-based effort* and emotion as *ritual energy* as two influential approaches to emotion. Following this, I connect these views of emotion as effort and energy to the shared lineage of pragmatism. Linking to pragmatism allows us to integrate each with a practice approach to emotions.

Emotions as Rule-Based Effort

Emotion management theory and interaction ritual theory have each been developed by two "founders" of the subfield: Arlie Russell Hochschild and Randall Collins. While the subfield of the sociology of emotion is relatively new, the relationship between social issues and "personal troubles," as C. Wright Mills (1959) puts it, is a classic concern within sociology (Cottingham 2019). But beginning in the late 1970s and 1980s, Collins (1981), Hochschild (1979), and others (Kemper 1981; Scheff 1979; Shott 1979; Thoits 1989) began to develop a sociological approach in which emotions were not seen as epiphenomenon or secondary concerns, but were centered fully as social outcomes and catalysts worthy of explicit sociological examination.

Like much of the foundational research in the sociology of emotion, Hochschild sought to make visible the often-invisible social forces that shape not just how we express emotions (or "display" them) but what we actually feel and the effort we invest in managing those feelings/expressions.

In positioning emotion management theory in conversation with the work of Goffman and Freud, Hochschild offered a distinctly sociological take on explaining what people feel and how they come to feel it. Her approach:

> fosters attention to how people try to feel, not, as for Goffman, how people try to appear to feel. It leads us to attend to how people consciously feel and not, as for Freud, how people feel unconsciously. (1979, 560)

In attending to "how people try to feel" at the conscious level, emotion management theory offers a vocabulary of concepts to capture how people work to feel. This includes *emotion work*—the active management or modification of emotions based on different situations; *emotional labor*—management of emotions aimed at fulfilling the demands of formal employment; *surface acting*—modifying the expression of emotion through masking or faking; and *deep acting*—modifying one's true feelings to match social expectations. Hochschild refers to these societal expectations as *"feeling rules"*—established "guidelines that direct how we want to try to feel" (1979, 563).

Together these concepts explain the effort we invest in trying to feel and express the right emotion at the right time and place. For example, a funeral goer might need to work at feeling and expressing the right amount of sadness. Too little and she will look cold. Too much and she risks appearing unhinged. Or we can think of the example of the nervous groom who works to feel confident and at ease on the big day. In the context of paid employment, emotion management theory highlights the often tacit (though sometimes explicit) emotional demands that employers place on employees. The classic example from Hochschild's empirical research (1983), and updated recently with an eye toward systemic racism in the United States (Evans 2013), is the case of flight attendants. When combined, airline advertisers, upper management, supervisors, and flight attendants themselves "set up the sale of emotional labor" (Hochschild 2012, 90). The sustained profit-making ability of an airline company depends on the sale of not just tickets, but experiences. Passengers want more than an efficient flight; they want to feel at ease, taken care of, and even pampered. Companies that can deliver, or at least convince customers of this in their advertisements, can maintain a competitive advantage in the airline industry.

This advantage for the company comes at a price for workers. Emotional dissonance between how they really feel and how they are expected to feel means that flight attendants need to "fake it until they make it." The cost of this continual surface and/or deep acting can be feelings of burnout, exhaustion, and a sense of alienation from one's true self. Stress and burnout have each received considerable attention from emotion scholars, and Hochschild's connection of these private feelings with structural (commercial) interests has been groundbreaking for developing a sociological conception of these negative experiences in a variety of occupations (Erickson and Grove 2007; Erickson and Ritter 2001; Näring, Briët, and Brouwers 2006).

In her extension of Hochschild's ideas, Louwanda Evans (2013) further highlights the fact that not everyone must play by the same feeling rules. The case of Tim, an African American pilot in her study, is a telling illustration of how race shapes the emotional demands of the job of piloting for a commercial airline:

> As he [Tim] waited at the gate, an old white man got up from his seat by the gate and said, "That [n-word] better not be flying my plane . . ." Tim was shocked by the outburst, unsure of how to respond, he considered it and thought, "Well, I was going to a completely different city, so I just kind of sat there and stared . . . I mean, really?" (Evans and Moore 2015, 440)

One's race and gender shape the type and frequency of emotional outbursts from the public that professionals must cope with and how much emotional labor (related to the demands of customers and clients) one must perform on the job. Research in healthcare contexts studying physicians, nurses, and home health aides also note the emotional demands of this work (Stacey 2011; Theodosius 2008), the relevance of gender and race (Cottingham and Andringa 2020; Wingfield 2009), and the presence of both negative and positive emotional outcomes for workers (Erickson and Grove 2008; Lopez 2006).

An emotion management perspective has been highly influential beyond the sociology of emotion. Organizational psychology (Grandey and Gabriel 2015), management studies (Seery and Corrigall 2009), and empirical work on a staggering number of occupational contexts has accrued over the years since Hochschild's publication of *The Managed Heart*. But there have also been a number of critical reflections on emotional labor as a dominant approach. Catherine Theodosius, for example, argues that emotion management theory "inhibits understanding about how the physicality of emotion is experienced and managed, and in how it is connected to conscious and unconscious emotion memory" (2008, 87). In focusing on "secondary acts" of emotion management (Hochschild 1979) as the conscious, deliberate ways we use symbols and language to organize social life, seeing emotion only as conscious effort can eclipse the social roots of emotions as experiences that span conscious and nonconscious acts (Emirbayer and Goldberg 2005). Primary experiences are challenging to measure, and this, along with a theoretical lens that privileges symbols and language means that social scientists have in the past assumed that their main aim should be to tease out the social origins of secondary, deliberative acts. A turn to emotion practice can help to overcome this limitation while retaining emotion management theory's important contribution to seeing emotions as *the product of effort*.

Emotions as Ritual Energy

Rituals have been an enduring concept in sociological studies of religious and social life (Birrell 1981). We might think of rituals as sacred rites we do in unison with others, the stuff of secret cults and fraternal societies. But rituals can span the formal and the informal—Christmas celebrations contain distinct rituals such as putting up an evergreen tree, decorating with lights, and eating particular foods together at a candle-lit table with family. But our everyday world is also filled with more mundane rituals. Randall Collins has developed a theoretical framework for linking face-to-face interactions across settings and attending specifically to the emotional draws and outcomes of these interactions. Interaction ritual theory has been used in a variety of research contexts, including how social movements lose and retain adherents (Summers-Effler 2010), analysis of global media events (Ribes 2010), and how violence unfolds in real time (R. Collins 2009). Its aim is to provide an explanatory framework for how social actions become patterned—a micro-level explanation for macro-level phenomenon such as organizations and nation-states. "What we need," Collins (1981, 985) argued, "is a micromechanism that can explain the repetitive actions that make up social structure such that interactions and their accompanying cognitions rest upon noncognitive bases." Collins proposes the metaphor of interaction ritual chains as the micromechanism for the job.

Interaction ritual theory delineates ritual ingredients from their outcomes. If we can determine the presence or absence of different ritual ingredients, then we can, to a degree, predict whether successful rituals will take place. These ingredients include (1) bodily co-presence, (2) barriers to outsiders,

(3) shared focus of attention, and (4) a shared mood (R. Collins 2004, 47–49). Outcomes of successful interaction rituals are emotional energy, group solidarity, group symbols, and a sense of shared morality (R. Collins 2004, 49). The culmination of these four outcomes is "collective effervescence"— "a heightened awareness of group membership as well as a feeling that an outside powerful force has sacred significance" (Summers-Effler 2006, 135). Symbols are then critical to a group's ability to maintain coherence across situations, as symbols emerge from and become containers for the shared meanings and emotions that group members can use for repeating (hopefully) successful interaction rituals.

Interaction rituals permeate not just sacred life but also the mundane and the ordinary. A boardroom meeting, a trip to the grocery store, a parent–teacher conference—all share elements of ritualistic acts. That is, they share patterns of actions that involve interaction between two or more people. In imagining these different scenarios, we place two or more people together in a given setting. Usually there is a barrier to outsiders—a closed door of some kind—as well as a shared focus of attention. A boardroom meeting might center on the agenda, while a trip to the grocery store orients shoppers to the items on shelves and behind glass cases. But between the two scenes, there is variation. Most people can casually walk into a grocery store without difficulty. But few can interrupt a closed-door meeting. And certain conflicts can interfere with a "shared mood" in any of these settings. But in the opening and closing of a meeting, there is a shared sense of protocol—how the event is expected to unfold. Fulfilling those expectations puts the group at ease. In this way, rituals have their own emotional payoff—not only can they free up energy by allowing us to operate on auto-pilot, but they also provide a sense of comfort. Even if one's goals for a particular meeting are not met, the introductory and culminating head nods, eye contact, and/or handshakes reaffirm that relationships remain intact. With those relationships intact, future encounters and opportunities remain available.

These mundane interactions are each an encounter. In a way, each is a "minigovernment" (Hochschild 1979, 556 in describing Goffman) or a "marketplace" in Collins's (1981, 984) conceptualization of microsociology. Interaction ritual theory, like other theories of collective emotions (von Scheve 2012; von Scheve and Ismer 2013), is at its core predicated on the type of face-to-face interaction that becomes less tenable in digital spaces. And in focusing on the minutiae of social life, or radical microsociology as

Collins calls it, it can at times underappreciate how moments of interaction are inevitably embedded in broader social hierarchies and enduring personal biographies (Barbalet 2006)—biographies that are in essence the distillation of past successful or unsuccessful rituals. Structural patterns in who is likely to be welcomed in a board meeting, a grocery store, or a parent–teacher conference at a particular school are linked to generations of social class entrenchment, gender inequality, and racism. And these structures of hierarchy and inequality become embodied in individuals (Kang 2003; Wacquant 1995). Biographies of opportunity and/or exclusion are embodied and exemplified in the calm, confident handshake of some and the uncertain, shaky voice of others. In starker terms, these embodied hierarchies emerge in the lop-sided legitimation of "white fear" over "black lives" in the case of interactions between black citizens and police officers (Evans and Feagin 2015)—interactions that far too often lead to violence and death at the hands of state actors.

While rituals can be seen in the mundane aspects of everyday life, and their ingredients and outcomes are useful to delineate, a focus on encounters alone risks overlooking how structural patterns such as social hierarchies shape both groups (Fine 2005) and the individual biographies that shape "taste, propriety, and other bases of evaluation that are independent of any given IR opportunity" (Barbalet 2006, 450). "Emotional energy"—a nebulous notion—also has clear methodological challenges (Erickson 2007). Collins's approach focuses on symbols and how they can be explicitly charged up and used to withdraw emotional energy. These claims can be integrated with concepts from practice theory in order to tap into the structural and biographical features that they inevitably entail. Thus, seeing emotion as *energy* remains relevant to developing an emotion practice approach. As I argue later, emotional energy can be integrated into an emotion practice approach as an aspect of *emotional capital*—as resources that individuals draw on to meet practical needs. In turning to Bourdieu's conception of *social practice*, including his concepts of habitus, capital, and social location, we can better theorize the structured patterns of groups and the individual biographies that shape emotional energy. Determining which interaction rituals will be repetitively encountered and how the energies of successful rituals are embedded in symbols remains an open empirical question. Using practice theory allows us to see symbols, in addition to their aesthetic qualities, as practically useful to individuals and communities.

Emotion as Effort, Ritual Energy, and Practice

Moving to an emotion practice approach, I aim to integrate the strengths of seeing emotion as simultaneously *effortful* in line with emotion management theory, *energy* through the lens of interaction ritual theory, and as *practical engagements* in line with a social practice approach. Emotion management theory provides a comprehensive view of emotion as something that is effortfully worked over—we work to feel what seems fitting to a given situation and to express the emotion that is appropriate to a given encounter. This can involve masking, repressing, faking, and cultivating authentic emotions to fit the feelings rules of a situation. Interaction ritual theory provides a comprehensive view of emotion as energy—in the individual form of emotional energy and the collective form of effervescence. Yet, as I noted earlier, there are limitations in how each of these approaches grapples with the role of social hierarchies in shaping emotion, the biographical elements that move with the individual across situations and interactions, and in how we empirically capture both primary, felt emotions and the work we do to feel in line with social expectations.

Rather than see these frameworks as at odds with each other or at odds with a practice approach, I believe we can see each as providing a complementary lens on emotions in social life. For example, Collins hints at areas of overlap in his interaction ritual theory and Bourdieu's social practice. But like others (R. Jenkins 1982), Collins sees Bourdieu's approach as too deterministic, providing little room for social change and dynamism (Collins 2004, 42–43). Yet this reading need not preclude the integration of concepts from interaction ritual theory with Bourdieu's own conceptual apparatus. A social practice approach tries to straddle the very tendencies that Collins identifies. This includes the tendency to reduce social life to "physics," with social forces pushing us around like billiard balls on a pool table, duped into thinking our varied colors make us unique. Or, if we swing too far toward agency, we risk seeing individual acts as fully free and unconstrained by precedent or external forces. Neither is sufficient.

Nor do I see a view of emotions as practical as one at odds with Hochschild's framework. As she herself emphasizes, in an extension of Freud's notion of "signal function," emotions are by definition a means of sensing the world and gaining valuable information about "where we stand vis-à-vis outer or inner events" (Hochschild 1983, 28). Both interaction ritual theory and emotion management theory build on the shared influence of pragmatism. While largely seen as a distinctly American tradition, pragmatism influenced European social thought, particularly through Durkheim's conceptualization of the emotionality of religious experience (Barbalet 2004). Within pragmatism, immediate experience is the foundation. Experience is:

> conceived, not as introspection, but as the intersection of the conscious self with the world. They [pragmatists] conceived of knowing subjects as embodiments of reason, emotion, and values, and they emphasized the inadequacy of philosophers' attempts to freeze, split apart, and compartmentalize the dynamic continuities and multiple dimensions of life as we live it. They conceived of individuals as always enmeshed in social conditions, yet selecting what to attend to from the multiplicity of conscious experience, and making history by making choices. (Kloppenberg 1996, 104)

This summary of the pragmatist worldview shows clear promise in working to overcome the dualisms discussed in the beginning of this chapter. Individuals cannot be carved up into rational and irrational parts, seen as mutually exclusive or with one part valued over the other. As Barbalet states, summarizing the work of William James, the "whole person is involved in the formation of philosophical opinions just as they are in practical affairs" (1998, 45). This conception of experience put forward by pragmatism also has clear overlap with Collins's aim to see the social world as dynamically created through chains of rituals as well as Hochschild's claim that emotions must always be seen in context and not abstracted from their social conditions.

Within pragmatism, individuals share experiences, and here again we see important parallels with sociological approaches to emotion. It is through the existence of signs or symbols that the sharing of meaning between individuals becomes possible. This overlaps with the relationships between energy, community, and symbols developed in Collins's work. As John Dewey states in *The Public and Its Problems*:

> A community thus presents *an order of energies* transmuted into one of meanings which are appreciated and mutually referred by each to every other on the part of those engaged in combined action. "Force" is not eliminated but is transformed in use and direction by ideas and *sentiments* made possible by *means of symbols*. (Dewey 1946, 153, emphasis added)

The sharing of experiences—of ideas and sentiments—through symbols is echoed in Collins's notion of symbols becoming charged up by ritual interactions and coming to serve as stand-ins for the group itself. Symbols are not merely cognitively perceived, but they evoke powerful feelings of belonging and energy from those who use them, including those who participate in charging them up with emotions in group settings. The group or community then provides order to our individual or shared "energies" so that they can be channeled into collective action.

In the development of pragmatism as a political and social philosophy, the term "experience" itself appeared to pose some difficulties for critics.

> Dewey toyed with exchanging the word "experience" for "culture" as late as 1951, but in the end he refused: "we need a cautionary and directive word, like experience, to remind us that the world which is lived, suffered and enjoyed as well as logically thought of, has the last word in all human inquiries and surmises." (Kloppenberg 1996, 106)

In sticking to the term "experience," pragmatism draws our attention to the "lived, suffered, and enjoyed" world rather than a narrow understanding of pragmatism as focused on strategic or instrumental action alone. Trying to capture this "lived, suffered, and enjoyed" world is at the center of an emotion practice approach.

In a pragmatist framing, similar to a practice approach, the expressive is folded into the instrumental. Human action is geared toward the "active projection of experience into the future" (Barbalet 2004, 337). Drawing on the full stock of past experiences, individuals seek to anticipate and meet future situational demands. Truth, then, or one's grounding in a sense of shared reality, is "essentially bound up with the way in which one moment in our experience may lead us towards other moments which it will be worth while to have been led to" (James 1907, 204–5). An individual conception of reality is affirmed when it takes the individual where they want to go. Shared reality (truth) is truth if it takes *us* collectively where we want to go. Emotions serve to guide us toward future moments of significance. Emotions, like bits of experience, "can warn us to get ready for another bit" (James 1907, 205).

We can see parallels in this aspect of pragmatism and Hochschild's approach. In highlighting problematic conceptions of emotions as opposite to rationality, she notes that there can be a mistaken conflation of "the inner state of emotion" as "always associated with outer action that is irrational"

(1983, 214). She instead emphasizes the value and *rationality* of fleeing from something fearful and nurturing someone out of love. Rather than see emotions as irrational, we can think of many scenarios in which they are actually critical catalysts for effective action:

> what a person does, under the influence of feeling, gets people where they want to go as much if not more than what a person would do if not under the influence of feeling. (Hochschild 1983, 214)

Feelings, like truth, can get us where we want to go. While she is here discussing emotions as "primary" experiences, working over our emotions also has a clear orientation to practical action. Within a capitalist system that demands certain expressions and feelings from workers, working on our emotions becomes instrumental to the practical aims of earning a wage and affording food and shelter. As she defines it, emotion is a sense, like hearing and seeing, and it is oriented to action (1983, 229).

While pragmatists like Dewey champion the term "experience" over alternatives like "culture," I believe *practice* as a term strikes a better balance of the passive and active. We often think of experiences as something we *have* rather than something we *do*. Practices are habits enacted over time that involve little conscious effort—established ways of being and doing that seem to *have us* as much as *we have them*. But they can at times involve effortful acts taken up deliberately—in this way they can span the deliberative and extra-deliberative demarcation (Summers-Effler et al. 2015). Emotion practices can involve the conscious working over of emotions that Hochschild's notion of emotion work calls to our attention—a process that anyone who has worked in the retail or the hospitality industry knows well. But it can also include the ritualistic entrainment of self with others that Collins's development of interaction ritual theory highlights—entrainment that seems to happen with little conscious intention when we are swept up into a group's shared activities.

An Emotion Practice Approach

Having traced the sociological approaches to emotion found in emotion management theory and interaction ritual theory and their roots in pragmatism, I now turn to the main assumptions, concepts, and relationships that constitute a social practice approach, its own overlap with pragmatism, and how we might fit these pieces together into a robust *theory of emotion practice*. Explaining social order and social coherence, on the one hand, and social conflict and disorder, on the other, are the main tasks of theorizing the social world. Social life, it is presumed, rests on an equilibrium between these two tendencies. Emotions help maintain order and can also signal disorder. But there also remains an emotional payoff to the establishment of this equilibrium. The "construction of order" is necessary precisely because it allows us "to cope with the challenge of chaos and absurdity" (Gieson, p. 327 in Alexander et al. 2006). This coping with chaos is fundamentally emotional—emotions do not simply play a part in the unfolding of social drama; they are the payoff and the signal that all is well or that something is off. Meaning, of the existential and everyday varieties, is by definition the banishment of absurdity. To make meaning—to have lives that are meaningful—is to have (or have had) a purpose, a point. Emotions orient us to purpose and effective action. They guide and fuel our actions toward particular ends. In reckoning with the human condition and the presence of profound suffering in the world, we want there to be a larger narrative into which we can fit personal and collective suffering. Suffering, without a point, is unbearable. To bear suffering—to bear conflict and chaos—as well as the miniscule indignities of life within hierarchies and norms not of our own choosing, we must cope with absurdity. This coping is a basic emotional process that underlies social life.

To understand both this underlying emotional payoff and how emotions orient us toward meaningful action, I turn to a framing of the social world as constituted by practices. Practices are "the building blocks" of social life (Feldman and Orlikowski 2011, 1241). As individuals, we carry with us "patterns of bodily behavior"—routines of knowing, being, and doing (Reckwitz 2002) that we inherit from others and pass on, in adapted form, to others. These patterns are qualities that we might think over and adopt intentionally, but they are also, and perhaps more often, patterned routines that we can absorb passively from others, outside of conscious awareness. Like a family resemblance between parents and children, we inherit noses, eyes, height, and gait from our parents as well as mannerisms, sayings, and patterned ways of interacting with others from those we are surrounded by as we develop. Our surroundings become absorbed by us while also leaking out of us onto the others we surround. This absorption and leakage is never a perfect transfer, or cloning of one individual to the next. Patterns become tweaked and changed, so that the practices my child absorbs from me will not be the same that he passes along to a child of his own.

The work of Pierre Bourdieu (Bourdieu 1986; 1990; Bourdieu and Wacquant 1992) does not explicitly focus on emotion, but it highlights the "systematic unity of practical social life" (R. Brubaker 1985, 748). Historian Monique Scheer (2012) takes up Bourdieu's work to argue that "practices not only generate emotions, but that emotions themselves can be viewed as a practical engagement with the world" (193)—engagements that are both embodied and socially shaped. A practice approach focuses on the action of everyday doings and sayings, but with special attention to the habitual acts and routines that span the spectrum of intentionality and whose implications move beyond the immediate situation. I follow Scheer (2012) and other scholars who adapt Bourdieu's framework for explicitly examining emotion (Emirbayer and Goldberg 2005; Erickson and Stacey 2013; Räsänen and Kauppinen 2020; Reay 2000; Threadgold 2020; Zemblyas 2007). This integration of concepts from practice theory with work in the sociology of emotion allows us to look before, beneath, and beyond the energy outcomes of rituals and individual acts of emotion management. In this way, the emotional complexities of everyday life can be examined more fully.

Habitus, capital, and *field* are terms from practice theory that can help us transcend the problematic dualisms that I discussed at the beginning of this chapter. These include the dualism between emotion and reason, as well as a number of other dualisms in sociological work, including a conception of the collective as opposite the individual, dynamism as opposite to stasis, and the mind as opposite to the body (Bourdieu 1986; 1990; Bourdieu and Wacquant 1992). Practice approaches decenter the individual actor to refocus on practices that one can "fall into" as much as (and at times more than) one consciously chooses to adopt. The seemingly lone individual enters a social world filled with established and ever-evolving habits of thought, feeling, and action. But the situations these accumulated habits confront, and the problems they have been fine-tuned to solve, are never static. These are continually being tweaked and changed in subtle ways, meaning that *habitus* (our internalized dispositions, tastes, and preferences) must also generate subtle adaptations in order to find (momentary) equilibrium.

The term *habitus* has a rich history (Räsänen and Kauppinen 2020), and we can see traces of this idea in Dewey's conception of "embodied intelligence" (1946, 210). In describing such intelligence, Dewey notes that "Capacities are limited by the objects and tools at hand" (210) and going further:

They [capacities/embodied intelligence] are still more dependent upon the prevailing habits of attention and interest which are set by traditions and institutional customs. Meanings run in the channels formed by instrumentalities of which, in the end, language, the vehicle of thought as well as of communication, is the most important. (Dewey 1946, 210)

We can see many parallels in what Dewey describes here and how Bourdieu and others have conceptualized habitus.[5] External channels of action become internalized into modes of being—and embodied knowing. Yet as external conditions are never static, we must change internally to adapt to new external demands. And these get into the body: "the body is not a static, timeless, universal foundation that produces ahistorical emotional arousal, but is itself socially situated, adaptive, trained, plastic, and thus historical" (Scheer 2012, 193). Emotions are "integral aspects of what he [Bourdieu] terms 'strategies,' or modes of response to and action within the world that are grounded in, and given shape and direction by, systems of enduring dispositions (cognitive but also affectual) which he terms 'habitus'" (Emirbayer and Goldberg 2005, 482).[6]

In her own refashioning of Bourdieu for analyzing emotion, Deborah Gould develops the term "emotional habitus" as a way to zoom in on the emotion-specific aspects of these enduring dispositions. She defines emotional habitus as "the socially constituted, prevailing ways of feeling and emoting, as well as the embodied, axiomatic understanding and norms about feelings and their expression" (Gould 2009, 10). As I noted earlier, there is a tension in trying to revalue emotion—to emphasize the value of those parts of the Enlightenment duality that have been deemed inferior—while also recognizing that feeling and thinking are overlapping processes that are only *analytically* distinct from each other. In practice, in everyday life, they interweave in nearly indiscernible ways. As the beginning quote from this chapter notes, "Once we start to reflect on any of these aspects and conceptualize them, we unavoidably abstract away from some other aspects" (Räsänen and Kauppinen 2020, 3). Whether it is in emphasizing *emotional* habitus or *emotional* capital (as I do later), the overarching point is to recognize that while Bourdieu sought to transcend rational choice assumptions in developing these terms (Bourdieu and Wacquant 1992), we likely need to go even further in emphasizing emotion so as to overcome the lingering dominance of Enlightenment thinking that privileges reason above emotions. I do this by building on the concept of emotional capital, but I largely agree with Scheer

(2012, 194) that the term "emotional habitus" seems redundant, since habitus itself as a concept is meant to straddle the external and internal, intentional and unintentional, rational and emotional. Habitus encompasses the affective dimensions of an individual's disposition: "disposition can include a propensity to fatalism, ambivalence, resilience, resentment, certainty, entitlement or even rage, just as much as a tendency to either theatre-going or watching soap operas" (Reay 2015, 10).

Capital is another key term alongside *habitus* that Bourdieu (1986) develops to highlight the types of valued resources and adaptations that exist in a particular *field*, or arena of social action. These resources include (as emotional capital) the emotional energy, capacities, knowledge, and skills needed to identify and manage sensations, moods, feelings, and emotions (Cottingham 2016).[7] Habitus is calibrated to distinct objective conditions; this calibration includes different amounts and forms of capital, including economic, bodily (Wacquant 1995), social and cultural (Lareau and Weininger 2003), as well as emotional capital (Nowotny 1981). In incorporating insights from interaction ritual theory, we can extend emotional capital to include the levels of emotional energy that one stores in the body and may be able to readily draw on from relevant symbols in one's environment. Emotional capital involves the knowledge of situated emotion norms (or *feeling rules* in Hochschild's approach), as well as the energy build-up and expense that interactions foster (in interaction ritual chains in Collins's approach).

While it may seem strange to talk of one needing *skills* to identify emotions, the emotion literature details a large body of empirical research on how even this seemingly natural act of feeling and labeling our feelings is dependent on our knowledge of our culture's emotional vocabulary, read of social context, and ability to identify salient physiological sensations (Barrett 2017; Gordon 1989; Russell 1991; Schachter and Singer 1962). In this way, discerning discrete emotions from a sea of inchoate sensations is a learned process—albeit one we learn so well that we forget having learned it. Affect studies is a burgeoning interdisciplinary field (Slaby and von Scheve 2019) that draws attention to the differences between the sensations and feelings we experience, on the one hand, from our labeling and demarcation of those feelings into discrete emotions, on the other (Threadgold 2020). Acknowledging affect is especially relevant here because it highlights the fact that our ability to transform sensations into discrete emotions (by labeling them with emotion words) is both imperfect (some aspects of our sensations will "escape" easy classification) and socially learned over time. Emotional labeling as an imperfect and learned process relies on a shared emotional vocabulary or discourse. In practice we experience affect and emotions simultaneously (Gould 2009), since we can readily recognize that *ineffability* is often tacked onto even our most valiant attempts to describe what we feel (we will see this especially in nurse diaries). Many sensations escape being readily described and there are fascinating cultural variations in emotional vocabulary whereby some cultures give names to sensations that other cultures discursively ignore (Lutz 1998; Russell 1991; Scherer, Wallbott, and Summerfield 1986). Even when cultures share similar emotion words, that does not necessary imply that these are experienced in the same manner (Mesquita, Boiger, and De Leersnyder 2017).

Part of one's emotional capital, then, includes knowledge of the emotion terms used within a given culture and the learned ability to appropriately apply an emotion word to the "correct" sensation. Identifying what bodily sensations mean is of course key even in basic physiological development. A child might point to their abdomen and state that they feel pain, but actually be experiencing hunger pangs and not yet have the skill needed to identify the sensation of hunger as such. Similarly, as the example of nurses will show, multiple emotions can be experienced simultaneously in addition to an element of affect or some lingering sensations that evade easy description. Throughout this book, I use the word *emotion* as a general term that encompasses specific discrete emotions and the "range" (similar to Threadgold 2020, 4) of nondiscrete sensations of discomfort/comfort or energy/exhaustion that might be applied to different states of being that other scholars might term *affect*.

The emotional capital—as emotion-based skills, knowledge, capacities, and energy—each individual carries with them in the world can be valued, accrued, and drained at differential rates depending on one's social location (and occupation, as we will see in Chapter 2) and the social field(s) they occupy. Members who share a similar social location (or group identity) develop similar forms of capital (and with it a similar habitus) while members of different groups differ in the forms of capital that make up habitus. As members of a shared group confront shared problems, they invariably come to embody similar modes of engaging and reacting to those shared problems. *Social location*, then, is another relevant concept in a practice approach. This refers to one's position within social hierarchies—in one's standing in terms of social class, gender, and race (though there are many other hierarchies of interest). But it can also refer to one's literal geographic position in a given community, city, nation, or geographic region. In this way, social location can be integrated into our understanding of even the most personal feelings of emotional energy and exhaustion. The charging up and draining of emotional reserves is not a straightforward debit and credit system. Rather, this process happens in conscious and nonconscious ways, getting into the body and hearts of individuals, and transcending time and space through symbols that become charged up with group emotions (as we will see most clearly in the case of sports fans in Chapter 3).

Bourdieu focused primarily on the social location of social class—examining how class dynamics are internalized into cultural tastes and dispositions and how these are used to maintain systems of exclusion (Bourdieu 1996). Bucking the trend of focusing only on "the distribution of economic resources and positions in the production process" (Heilbron and Steinmetz 2018, 40), Bourdieu's work attempts to account for the myriad ways in which class hierarches are maintained through insidious practices of power that serve the status quo. For example, Fielding-Singh (2017) examines how socioeconomic status (SES) shapes not simply what parents feed their children but also *why*—linking food's emotional and symbolic meaning to the differing habitus of middle-class and working-class parents. Low-SES parents use food to compensate for other forms of material deprivation and the context of uncertainty that they confront, while high-SES parents have the luxury of using food to emphasize values of self-restraint that imbue a middle-class habitus (Fielding-Singh 2017). Despite the prolific use of Bourdieu's concepts to make sense of social class, his work focuses less attention on gender and race/ethnicity and thus we need to turn to other conceptual developments in sociology to better theorize how multiple social locations intersect to shape social practices.

Patricia Hill Collins (1986; 2000) developed the notion of intersecting forms of social inequality and its epistemological implications for sociology as a discipline. Her foundational work emphasized the links between social position in matrices of power and how such positions shape the types of knowledge that are deemed legitimate. In doing so, she and other critical race scholars (Brah and Phoenix 2004; Crenshaw 1991) would develop the notion of intersectionality to highlight the way that social categories like gender and race are never lived one at a time but are simultaneously interlocking, shaping one's life chances and experiences. More recently, she has turned to the linkages between intersectionality and pragmatism, seeing them as fruitful complements rather than contradictory theoretical frameworks:

Pragmatism presents a provocative analysis of community that provides a useful framework for understanding the processes by which social structures are constructed, yet its neglect of power relations limits its own arguments. Intersectionality provides a distinctive analysis of social inequality, power, and politics, yet the relative newness of this field in the academy has produced provisional analyses of these themes. (P. H. Collins 2012, 444)

In assessing both pragmatism and intersectionality, Collins argues that pragmatism tends to focus on universalism in contrast to the particularism of intersectionality. Pragmatism's emphasis on the utility of experience, and the dynamic nature of action are clear strengths and she highlights the useful role of emotions in pragmatic thought—for it is through "strong, deep feelings" that communities "move people to action"—and it is through the flexible use of community symbols that these feelings are evoked (447).

Yet Collins also notes that pragmatism can underplay the bedrock of social inequalities that permeate experiences and dynamic action.

Social structures such as neighborhoods, schools, jobs, religious institutions, recreational facilities, and physical and cyberspace marketplaces are the institutional expressions of social inequalities of race, class, gender, age, ethnicity, religion, sexuality, and ability [. . .] social institutions use the symbols and organizational principles of community to organize social inequalities. Communities thus become major vehicles that link individuals to social institutions. (P. H. Collins 2012, 446)

In developing a sociology of emotion practice, we cannot ignore the social inequalities that shape individual practices and the groups and communities with whom we share not only symbols but patterned ways of seeing and being in the world. This becomes especially clear in Chapters 2 and 3, where we will see how social differences in terms of social class and race shape the generation, conservation, and expenditure of both bodily and emotional capital. Thus, in turning to the arguments provided by intersectionality, we can deepen our appreciation for how social location comes to shape communities, practices, and the internalized dispositions (habitus) of community members.

As Bourdieu notes, habitus is attuned to and tweaked by both consistent and novel interactions with the social world. This social world is one in which certain groups are all too often disadvantaged, dehumanized, and exploited. Thus, not only does an individual habitus align to an unequal world in terms of a given individual being positioned in advantaged and disadvantaged ways, but habitus plays a role in maintaining broader structures of inequality. Our alignments are aimed at practically navigating a world built up through and on the past and ongoing exploitation of ourselves and/or others. In integrating a conception of emotion as effort, energy, and practical engagement, we must keep in mind that the practical aims to which habitus is calibrated are by necessity formed in a social world permeated with social inequality. The practical aims of one group may differ drastically from, and even be in conflict with, the practical aims of other groups. An emotion practice approach does not deny the relevance of conflict here, but in trying to tease apart the social roots of conflict and how conflicts unfold, the use of emotions for varied practical aims remains key.

One difficulty (and perhaps the main difficulty) with merging a practice approach with interaction ritual and emotion management theories is the role of individual agency. The dynamic nature of the social environment means that our authentic emotions will never perfectly match the external demands we confront—this is why "effort" or working over our emotions becomes necessary. The need to manage emotions means that there remains an undeniable element of individual agency in our everyday lives. If the social world were fully determined—if objective conditions could perfectly structure internalized dispositions—then there would be no need for or sense of *effort* related to feelings and emotions. In fact, in such a world, there would be no need for emotions—as guides for calibrating the self to the environment—at all.

The sense of feeling slightly out of sync with or even uncertain about what the social norms *are* pinpoints where prior practices have not been wholly predictive of a current situational demand. In this way, even subtle feelings of discomfort, uncertainty, and ambiguity point to practices that are in flux. The fruitfulness of emotion *work* and emotional *labor* as concepts in emotion scholarship points to the ubiquity of these shared sensations of invisible effort in personal and occupational settings. These terms point to the present but constrained role that agency plays in shaping social life. I take up these subtle sensations most directly in the following chapter in examining nurses as emotional jugglers responding to ambiguity and complexity in the demands of the job. But we also see the navigation of uncertainty in the context of evolving public health threats that I cover in Chapters 4 and 5—threats that lay bare the uncertainty of shared norms and expectations in digital spaces where social media users and political leaders react to crises as they unfold.

Conclusion

In this chapter I have argued for conceptualizing emotion in line with a practice approach. I began by highlighting some of the problems with dualistic thinking that we have inherited from the tradition of Western Enlightenment—thinking that remains dominant, as I will show, in scholarly and lay understandings of emotion. This thinking has been robustly critiqued in the past (Barbalet 1993; Damasio 1994; Williams and Bendelow 1998), but overcoming its inertia remains an ongoing task for emotion scholars. We need to recognize both the practical value of emotions *and* the political value that powerful actors try to capitalize on when they reinforce a reason/emotion dualism, as I aim to show in Chapter 5. In taking a practice approach to emotions, we can more fully understand why this dualistic thinking remains and work to overturn its problematic framing of social life. I then summarized the main claims and conceptual vocabularies provided by two influential sociologies of emotion—emotion management theory and interaction ritual theory. We can trace both back to a shared appreciation of pragmatism and its focus on experience. While pragmatism is often seen as exclusively American, we see a number of similarities in the view of social practice put forth by Pierre Bourdieu and pragmatist thinkers like John Dewey. With this shared heritage, I argue that we can work to integrate the theories of Hochschild and Collins with conceptions of social practice developed by Bourdieu.

By framing experiences as practices, we can include the energy payoff of successful rituals and the concerted effort to work over our feelings in line with dominant feeling rules. Each of these approaches is part of a tradition in which emotions are seen as socially *emergent*. Social forces do not simply shape the release of built-up physiological tensions. Emotions themselves are the product of past practices now embodied and oriented to future action— they help us get to where we want to go. As such, emotions are thoroughly steeped in social forces and social goals. Concepts like habitus, capital, and field are helpful for explaining how social practices are transmitted and the values they have depending on the particular context in which an individual is embedded. Individual feelers attune themselves in conscious and nonconscious ways to shifting situations and environments.[8] These attunements (as habitus) conserve and maximize energy while orienting the individual to effective action. Such action is, in being oriented to the current social arrangements of a given field, inevitably shaped by social location and past and ongoing practices of exclusion and exploitation.

To say that emotions are practical is to challenge long-standing conceptions of reason as the primary and favored mode for engaging in practical action. As I will show in the empirical chapters that follow, emotion orients us to practical outcomes. We find ourselves in a social world filled with encounters that can drain or charge up our emotional resources; situations that require adaptable skills and knowledge in identifying and managing our own and the emotions of others; and moments of crisis that require us to both make suffering meaningful and work to act quickly to solve collective problems. Nurses who conserve emotional resources in what they feel and who they feel with, sports fans drawing on team symbols for emotional energy, social media users reacting to public health threats, and elites and leaders tackling a collective challenge like COVID-19 can together show the promise of an emotion practice approach across the domains of work, leisure, digital spaces, and political challenges. To say that emotions are practical does not discount the way they connect us to shared aesthetic or existential human desires. But rather, this framing aims to turn on its head the very notion that such desires are superfluous to everyday living or superfluous to the broader ambition of improving the human condition.

2

Nurses

Juggling and Embodying Complex Emotions*

> [. . .] the nature of nursing should really be about being able to sym-
> pathize and empathize with your patient and [even] if your patient is
> angry and lashing out . . . To add to that though, her—this patient['s]
> particular situation—brought me back to another one of my patients
> that I had taken care of about three or four months ago that had
> passed away that had similar symptoms. So it was more like déjà vu
> and a—and a fear that this would also happen to her [. . .]
> —Lianna, registered nurse at a Midwestern hospital

After a much-needed day off, Marla[1] returns to her job as a nurse manager at
the mid-sized urban hospital where she has worked for over fourteen years.
Upon arrival, she describes being "bombarded" with people, problems, and,
inevitably, emotions. A nursing assistant on the unit is afraid of losing her
job. Another is trying to get her job back even though Marla finds her "toxic"
to the unit at large. Marla tries to remain calm and neutral—to mask her true
feelings about each of her coworkers—but she finds it challenging. After
describing the variety of events and encounters that make up her day, she
makes the following summary statement:

> So you do have such a high range of emotion and I do tend to be a bit of an
> emotional person, and so I *try to maintain a calm demeanor* when I'm at
> work and not let anything affect me. But then you do really feel that it is all
> bottled up inside and with so many different conflicting things going on
> with the upper management, *you just don't know what the right answer IS.*
> So it can be a rewarding job but it can also be a very *deflating* job.

* Portions of this chapter are adapted from Cottingham and Erickson (2020b).

Practical Feelings. Marci D. Cottingham, Oxford University Press. © Oxford University Press 2022.
DOI: 10.1093/oso/9780197613689.003.0003

If sports fans, as we will see in Chapter 3, are able to draw on rituals and symbols for emotional energy, then nurses are often at the opposite end of the energy–exhaustion continuum. Nurses like Marla juggle their own and others' emotions throughout their shifts. They manage what they feel and how they express those feelings as a routine part of being a professional nurse. Yet at times they might not even know what to feel or what the feeling rules are for a situation, given the ambiguities and contradictions inherent to the job. At the end of a long shift, nurses often feel deflated and worn out. This exhaustion is not just something they know cognitively; it is felt deep in their bodies—in aching feet, heads, and backs.

In this chapter I look at the case of nurses—characterized as emotional "jugglers" (Bolton 2001)—to show the complexity of emotions that nurses experience and how an emotion practice approach can help us see and understand this complexity more fully. When emotion scholars focus primarily on the effort that workers put into masking, faking, or cultivating specific emotions to match job expectations (Wharton 2009), much of the messiness of nursing is swept into simple analytic classifications—emotional labor, surface acting, and deep acting. Emotion management theory provides few concepts to theorize when nurses choose not to (or feel unsure about how to) manage emotions in line with feeling rules. In contrast to the image of a lone emotion manager who strategically masks or cultivates emotions to match clear social norms, the case of nurses highlights a dynamic process that emerges from the interface of embodied sensations, certain and ambiguous professional expectations, and evocative environments. Using concepts from a practice approach, we can understand the nurse habitus as constantly being attuned to new demands and situations, working to conserve precious emotional resources, intentionally and unintentionally, as a form of valued capital. In the context of US healthcare, these practices are structured by the social location of workers and the clientele they interact with in terms of social class and race (Feagin and Bennefield 2014; Porter and Barbee 2004). In integrating the sociology of emotion with practice theory, an emotion practice approach provides a more holistic understanding of the emotional dimensions of nursing and, as a result, of how emotions come to infuse mundane work experiences.

In beginning with nursing and nurse diaries, this empirical chapter focuses on emotion practices at an intimate level. Nurses made their diary recordings on their way to work, whispering confessions into their handheld recorders while in janitor closets and stairways, and they processed their emotions as they transitioned from work to home life during the commute home and at the kitchen table. Thus, while later empirical chapters examine emotion practices in leisure, digital spaces, and the political sphere of public health threats, this chapter starts with the intimate work experiences of one of the most emotionally demanding jobs. Through the audio diaries of nurses, we can trace how emotions serve as resources for navigating a complex job like nursing, how multiple emotions are felt simultaneously, and how emotions are embodied in nurses and embedded in work contexts.

Healthcare and Nurse Emotions

For many patients, nurses are the face of healthcare, constituting the largest profession in the healthcare industry (World Health Organization 2020b). The World Health Organization designated 2020 as "International Year of the Nurse," and the COVID-19 pandemic has made clear how critical their contribution is to society. Nurses encounter life and death and the full range of human emotions on a regular basis. Despite their indisputable status as "essential" (Scales and Lepore 2020), shortages of nurses can be found throughout the world (World Health Organization 2020b). One reason for this shortage is the level of burnout that nurses experience. Studies estimate between 30 and 50 percent of nurses experience burnout symptoms (Bakhamis et al. 2019; Shah et al. 2021)—feelings of exhaustion, overwhelm, and/or cynicism. Among nurses who have left the profession, more than a third point to burnout as the primary reason (Shah et al. 2021).

Nurses must often work long, irregular hours and face complex demands for their technical, intellectual, and emotional skills. To understand how work experiences translate into the problematic symptoms of burnout, audio diaries provide a window into their daily experiences and emotions. In nurse diaries, we see that even nurses who are young and fresh in the field are concerned that they might one day experience burnout. As Megan, a nurse in her mid-thirties, describes it:

> I just hope and pray that my attitude never changes . . . I couldn't imagine not caring and I just, I notice a lot of that and it's just pretty sad. And I hope

the day that I stop caring, that's the day that I just quit cause you can't *not* care in this field.

In interacting with the public, nursing requires a range of soft as well as technical skills. This includes skills, knowledge, and energy needed to manage one's own emotions as well as the emotions of others (Erickson and Grove 2008). As I discussed in Chapter 1, we can think of this cache of trans-situational resources as "emotional capital" (Cottingham 2016; Erickson and Stacey 2013) that workers (nurses in this case) take with them as they clock into the job and as they clock out. One explanation for nurse burnout is the fact that they are expected to manage their emotions on the job, cutting them off from their authentic emotions. An emotion management perspective has become widespread in organization studies, psychology, and management studies (Diefendorff, Croyle, and Gosserand 2005; Grandey and Gabriel 2015; Lopez 2006; Scott and Barnes 2011). Yet this approach can come up short in illuminating the uncertainty and emotional whiplash that hospital nurses experience as they move from bedside to bedside, and interactions with colleagues, patients, patient family members, and physicians.

Taking an emotion practice approach gives us three distinct advantages. In seeing emotions as "practices," we can see *before* each act of emotion management in terms of the shifting stores of emotional capital that nurses have in connection with habitus (Bourdieu 1990). We can also begin to see what lies *beneath* each act of emotion management—that is, how feelings seep into the body and how practices operate at conscious and nonconscious levels. An emotion practice approach can help us to see *beyond* individual acts of emotion management and toward the social hierarchies and collectives that structure who nurses feel with and who they feel against. Finally, these elements mix together in nurse diaries, as the before, beneath, and beyond of any encounter are realized in multiple overlapping emotions that constitute the messiness of everyday life. While documenting the "high range" of emotions that Marla mentions in her quote at the beginning of this chapter, nurse diaries reveal the day-to-day embodiment of these emotions in aching feet, heads, joints, and recurring exhaustion and rumination (Theodosius 2008). In the application of an emotion practice approach to nursing, emotions are shown to be mindfully embodied (Scheper-Hughes and Lock 1987)—simultaneously embodied and consciously identified—as well as dynamically structured in the variety of emotions that nurses confront on a daily basis.

Sources of Deflation and Drain

Returning to Marla's case, she notes in the quote at the beginning of this chapter that masking, or covering up her true feelings, is a key aspect of her job and one that she identifies as causing her difficulty. As she puts it, "I try to maintain a calm demeanor." This process is well-established in the literature on emotional labor—it is an example of what Hochschild (1979) would call "surface acting"—modifying her demeanor and expression of emotions to match the expectations of her role as a nurse and as a manager. Established expectations are part of the professional norms that any novice nurse must learn (Smith and Lorentzon 2008). These are the norms that both Marla and Lianna (first quote of the chapter) point to when discussing what nursing *should* be. These are part of the fixed structure of emotion practices in nursing. An emotion management perspective highlights these established norms (as feeling rules) and the effort that Marla and other nurses must expend in order to meet those norms (maintaining a calm demeanor and bottling up felt emotions). In the context of paid employment, this work to match feelings with expectations is emotional labor (Hochschild 1983).

Yet we also see a more complex tale of emotion in nurse diaries. Part of why Marla finds her job so deflating is not simply because of the need to remain calm. It is the added *ambiguity* that takes a toll: "with so many different conflicting things going on with the upper management, you just don't know what the right answer IS." As defined in Chapter 1, feeling rules refer to established "guidelines that direct how we want to try to feel" (Hochschild 1979, 563). But what if we don't know how we want or should feel? Uncertainty and ambiguity in large-scale organizations, like the acute care hospital systems in which many nurses work, seem to coalesce in the frontline workers they employ.

Marla's sense of uncertainty and its impact on her feeling deflated are echoed in the stories of other nurses. Joyce, for example, highlights the "mishmashed" lack of clarity and a lack of connection with management as a catalyst for burnout:

So, you know, after a while I can see why somebody gets burnt out. And it's not burnt out because you're working with patients that are dying. They have a diagnosis where a majority are going to die. [. . .] but the thing that's the burnout with this job is the management right now. Management used to really be strong and supportive, and now our management is so mishmashed, you know, it's like the bare minimum. Like I said, you get your evaluation and you don't even get to talk to your manager. (Joyce, nurse in her late forties)

Lacking clarity and support from management translates into uncertainty in nurses' day-to-day jobs. Managing this uncertainty, perhaps as much as the overt feelings of grief that working with dying patients might elicit, depletes their emotional capital—including the emotional energy needed to meet each new patient with enthusiasm and confidence.

A second limitation of an emotion management perspective in the context of nursing is how it fails to account for instances when nurses know the feeling rules but seem to flout them. An emotion practice approach can focus our attention on how emotions—as practices—bleed over from different contexts. For nurses in our sample, one of the spaces in which they would often make recordings and process their emotions was in the car ride to and from work. This literal movement between the spheres of home and work was also a place for emotions to move and be worked over. In the following quote from Leah, we find she uses the time during her drive to work to work over the feeling of anger that she has because she has been called in to work on a day that was supposed to be her day off:

[. . .] I am mildly pissed off because of the schedule being screwed up. This was supposed to be a day off and it's a nice day. But, um, what I am going to do is shift gears and by the time I get to work *concentrate on just taking care of my patients* and taking care of what's going on there and not getting into all that. *I just need to retain enough righteous indignation so that when I am talking to my manager or whoever is going to be dealing with this schedule* [. . .] [emphasis added]

She says she wants to "shift gears and concentrate on just taking care of my patients." But note how she does not want to suppress her anger completely—she wants to also *use* that anger to have the energy and resolve to confront her manager later in the day. In this way, Leah shows how nurses might manage some but not all of their anger, recognizing it is a valuable resource to her—a form of emotional capital—that she can use to accomplish the practical aim of confronting her manager about the schedule. Only by recognizing emotion as a practical resource can we make sense of why Leah would choose to hold onto her "righteous indignation" when it seems to violate the feeling rules of nursing.

While these examples from Marla, Joyce, and Leah all point to their managers as a key cause of their negative emotions, patients can of course also be a source of frustration, deflation, and drain. Andrea, a nurse in her late forties, talks about a patient whose continuous demands during a shift lead her to feel mentally drained:

> You go in there and try to do everything she [the patient] wants you to do. Then as soon as you walk out of the room she's calling again. [. . .] That patient is—is certainly someone who has to be rotated. When I say rotated, like today I'm her nurse and tomorrow somebody else need[s] to be her nurse and then somebody else need[s] to be her nurse because she is just mentally draining.

Unfortunately, Andrea's draining patient was not rotated. In the next two shifts, she stifles her frustration at her manager for not making sure to assign this demanding patient to another nurse. Later that same week her feelings of being drained compound and, at the end of her third shift, she records the following:

> So with the help of my team, I took care of this lady and my other patients. And then we were—how many patients did I have? I think I had four patients—so it's, you see, it's just be like "wow." It goes so fast and it's just, you just feel like [sigh] like I can't even collect my thoughts. I'm like "wow."

Andrea's mental drain is made clear in this meandering quote from her diary recording—she's discombobulated from juggling so much. Call lights, paperwork, this task, and that task—these all add to the drip, drip, drain on Andrea's emotional reserves. If sports fans, as we will see in Chapter 3, illustrate how symbols become charged up with the emotional highs of spectatorship, then understanding nursing demands a different approach, one that explains the slow drain on the nurse—herself a symbol of unending care and nurturance.

Emotional capital is a term that, in the examples earlier from Marla, Joyce, Leah, and Andrea, can help us see the charging up and expending of emotional resources. This includes emotional energy, the concept that is well-developed in theorizing interaction rituals (R. Collins 2004) but also the emotional knowledge base that many of us carry around between work and home life without even realizing its relevance to our lives. Hochschild's feeling rules—knowledge about what to feel, express, or suppress in a given context is thus also part of this capital. Merging emotional energy with emotion-based knowledge and skills allows us to connect these more nebulous constructs to the occupational demands of nursing and the social hierarchies in which nurses and their patients are embedded. In folding energy and knowledge into the concept of "capital," we can also emphasize the *value* of this energy for meeting the practical demands of social life (and paid labor).

Emotional capital is needed at nearly every moment—making pleasantries at the cash register when we buy groceries, checking on a colleague who seems anxious, trying to calm down an agitated toddler. All of these interactions draw out skills, knowledge, and energy that are often so routine that we don't realize we are using them. That is, until things do not go as planned. If the cashier is strangely chatty, for example, we feel the discomfort of trying to end the conversation before our ice cream melts. If our colleague is distrustful of our motives, he might snap back that nothing is wrong. And toddlers, well, they can drain a well-rested parent before breakfast.

Nurses, because of the sheer volume and variety of people they interact with, illustrate the use of this emotional capital, how it is depleted, conserved, and how it shapes the body in unique ways. In this section, we have seen some of the causes of depletion—demanding patients as well as uncertainty in management directives. This depletion has important effects on nurses' well-being, which I'll discuss soon, but suffice it to say that emotional capital, by definition, is a valued resource that nurses are keen to preserve as much as possible (Hobfoll 1989). In the next section, we see how nurses try to conserve their emotional capital by not wasting it on the "wrong" patients.

Conserving and Expending Emotional Capital

To avoid the deflation and drain that Marla and other nurses describe so clearly, nurses consciously, but often nonconsciously, try to conserve their emotional energy as a valuable resource that they need to make it through the day. Throughout their diaries, they speak of reaching their emotional "limits"—often communicated as their limit in terms of empathy, sympathy, and compassion—and the need to be judicious in how they expend their energy, their emotional capital. Some patients, like the one described earlier by Andrea, are seen as extra demanding, and the way that nurses try to cope with demanding patients is to rely on colleague support as well as management policies that rotate these patients to other nurses during the week.

Nurses also detail other strategies for handling these types of patients. Certain patients and their families can become "known" within a given unit, and their return can spark a set of collective practices for conserving the emotional capital of nurses on the unit who work with them. Regina, a nurse in her mid-sixties, notes that there are patients who have a known history on the unit for being "users of the system" who "take advantage of being there, um sometimes will take more of the resources and leave nothing for other patients." The resources she refers to here are things like instant coffee, tea bags, and sugar packets—trivial items that seem to have an outsized impact on how nurses come to see these families as "users." Regina goes on to explain that in taking these simple, seemingly freely available items, families can unintentionally undercut their relationships with nurses on the unit:

> We do have families who just take all those things and bag them and take them home. If it's a known family that's done this in the past, we do have staff who are very negative about those patients. And while they take care of them, they *don't form an emotional relationship* and at times are pretty curt with that family. [emphasis added]

An emotion management perspective comes up short in explaining this seemingly established practice. The feeling rules of nursing dictate that nurses should be compassionate and nurturing to all patients, not just some (Erickson and Grove 2008). Being curt with a patient or their family flies in the face of nurse training as well as broader societal assumptions that women (the majority of nurses) are innately nurturing and caring (Ridgeway 2011). Certainly, Hochschild allows for agency in her conception of emotional labor. Rules can be broken. But the theory itself does not explain how or why professional norms would be violated in this particular instance.

Broadening to an emotion practice perspective, however, we can begin to explain this norm violation. Avoiding an emotional relationship with patients and family members who take resources is a strategy for conserving valued and limited emotional capital for those deemed worthy. While I frame this as a strategy, it need not be done in a conscious or purely strategic way. Prior encounters with known patients and their family members leave traces of their depletion in the nurses and units that they visited. As a result of these past encounters, nurses develop reflexive habits in order to avoid expending precious emotional resources on those seen as less worthy of them. Worth here is undercut by a patient or their family member's decision to take what the nurse sees as resources to be shared by all patients who come to the unit.

These assessments of worth are never purely rational calculations. Such assessments are simultaneously felt and thought, while also being linked to social hierarchies—in this case, the hierarchy of social class. Who takes amenities like coffee and tea from a hospital? What patients or families would see these types of items—items found in waiting areas, hotel lobbies, or readily available to buy for just a few dollars—as coveted commodities worth bagging to take home? Those who see such amenities as rare resources are likely to be the poor and working-class. In taking these items, they end up, probably unwittingly, foreclosing possible emotional bonds with nursing staff. Nurses themselves are likely habituated to a middle-class lifestyle where such items are seen as plentiful and taking them is seen as petty. When nurses conserve emotional capital by closing themselves off to certain families and patients, they simultaneously make judgments about deservingness that are invariably linked to their own class-based habitus. Social class is a defining location for Bourdieu (1990), so it is fitting to see it emerge as a mechanism for conserving emotional resources and determining worth.

While I have discussed the relevance of emotional capital here, habitus is also a relevant concept. As described in Chapter 1, habitus refers to the internalized dispositions, preferences, tastes, and habits that individuals (always as part of groups like social classes) develop over the course of their lives and the interactions that make up social life. With this concept, Bourdieu (1990) tries to elide the division between objective and subjective. The objective is folded into the subjective and vice versa—agents internalize the conditions of the world "out there" and through this internalization, they develop distinct habits and preferences (i.e., habitus) that are shared with others who share a similar social location. In this way, we feel at ease with those most like us, a process captured in the concept of "homophily" (McPherson, Smith-Lovin, and Cook 2001). An affinity to those who are like ourselves is an inevitable feature of developing a habitus attuned to shared objective conditions. Our habits and preferences, more often than not, match the demands of the objective world and link us affectively to those who encounter similar class-based, racial, and gendered worlds. In this way, emotions are active practices that "align individuals with communities," in Sara Ahmed's (2002, 119) framing. When our habitus is well-formed to the situations we encounter, we feel a sense of ease and comfort and many of our interactions run on autopilot. But when habitus is out of sync with the environment, this can lead to pervasive feelings of discomfort (Cottingham, Johnson, and Erickson 2018) or stronger feelings of frustration and anger.

While Regina, in talking about other nurses withholding emotional bonds with families who take home amenities, is able to explicitly identify this practice, that does not mean that all nurses do this or do it intentionally. Judgments and stereotypes of others can be made quickly and without much reflection. That does not make them any less socially conditioned. The emotion of disgust can be felt as nothing more than a subtle repulsion from those you find "off-putting" or "not my kind." It need not be accompanied by particularly strong feelings of anger toward others. A feeling of disgust is a key emotion in pathologies and healthcare (Davey 2011). In an example of disgust, Lianna, a nurse in her mid-twenties, sees a patient who is homeless request pain medication and footies [short socks] from the hospital secretary. Lianna assumes that this patient is "using the hospital as more of a hotel" and is demanding that the nursing staff "dispense these medication[s] for her whenever she feels like coming in." This causes Lianna to feel "pretty disgusted." We later learn that this homeless patient also has a brother with sickle cell anemia, suggesting that race as well as class likely plays a role in who receives compassion and who receives disgust.

Related to Lianna's reflections is another example from Ashley, a white nurse in her mid-twenties. Ashley, it seems, has already internalized a method for determining worth and, with it, a method for conserving emotional resources. Ashley describes in detail at several points in her diary her disdain for a patient with whom she finds it difficult to sympathize. At one point, she relistens to her own recordings and has a "looking glass" (Cooley 1922) moment—a moment where she perceives herself through what she believes would be the perspective of those listening:

> So I was going back and I was like listening [to a previous recording], and I was like "geez, I kind of sounded really, really mean" um and, you know, not—not very sympathetic for this woman who apparently like got slipped

a date rape drug. But she didn't and you know—going back to that, she was just a more difficult patient to handle.

And, you know, long story short, just kind of like immature and for a nineteen-year-old, and you know it's kind of—when you have those patients *it's kind of hard you know sometimes to sympathize with them.* And you know, you kind of see like, oh they get themselves in these situations and you feel bad, but at the same time, you're just like, "If you would just make some better decisions maybe, maybe you wouldn't end up in some of these situations."

Ashley feels "bad, but" this patient's situation does not immediately arouse sympathy in her.

This example is in contrast to the raw emotions of grief that she has earlier in the week when reflecting on the loss of another patient, a twenty-eight-year-old suffering from pulmonary fibrosis. Ashley highlights the fact that the fibrosis patient "basically did nothing to cause this pulmonary fibrosis and she wasn't born with it. She never smoked and basically like just developed in the last several years." The patient ends up not being able to receive a needed lung transplant and dies on December 26.

As a result of her patient's passing, Ashley is devastated. She can be heard crying and choking up while she makes the following recording:

Um, and I'd never—I never had a chance to cry [starting to cry, but then stops]. Like I, um, the only time I had a chance to cry was when I transferred her and went to my floor, and I literally got [there] like five minutes before I admitted another patient. And just like processing the whole thing, um, you know I'd know I've been really depressed this week just because of that, because she ended up passing away, um, on the 26th, and, um, my heart just goes out to that family and to her and, um, you know I just—I wish that she got—could've gotten those lungs sooner. You know, she definitely deserved them and you know [sniffle] no one deserves to die at twenty-eight years old. And this is—you know it—basically it felt like I was losing a friend [cries].

Her entry here is open and raw. She is quick to sympathize. Why do the two patients—the nineteen-year-old and the twenty-eight-year-old—evoke such different responses from Ashley?

Using the concepts of emotional capital and habitus, we can see why Ashley might cautiously reserve her compassion for those she sees as worthy. In the case of the second patient—the twenty-eight-year-old—Ashley sees herself. She is quick to identify with the patient who is closer to her in age (Ashley is twenty-five). In assessing the twenty-eight-year-old's condition, Ashley also emphasizes the patient's lack of culpability. Here is a patient who didn't engage in any of the bad health practices that would have caused the illness (such as smoking). Who Ashley connects and identifies with, who she sees as worthy, is part of what shapes her easy release of empathy in some instances and its stifling in others, though of course she likely does not see this directly. Through shared demographics she is able to identify and feel with some patients and less so with others. In comparing the two cases, the deservingness of the patient plays a key role and stems from her assessment of whether or not a patient had a hand in their own sickness.

In looking through Ashley's diary recordings, we gain a further clue about how the calibrated conservation of emotions might work for nurses, and not just Ashley. Ashley identifies as white and says earlier in the shift that, since another local hospital has closed, her unit has seen an increase in certain types of patients—"we're getting a lot of more—lot—more like *inner-city patients* who do have like a lot of mental issues." She later says that "the demands, the politics, you know, the populace—some populations of patients (pause) is—you know? It wears on you . . ." The types of patients that Ashley has trouble activating compassion for appear to be racially dissimilar to her. As Ashley describes them, they are from the "inner city"—coded language for poor and working-class racial minorities (White 2007). Social location (race and class) shapes Ashley's habitus—the habitual modes of feeling easily with some and against others. And with her habitus comes a patterned and well-practiced giving of emotional resources to some and a withholding of emotional resources from others. She is not explicitly calibrating this based on race or social class, but it seems implicit given that the influx of patients with more mental health issues means that she has to conserve emotional resources somehow.

Marshaling the concepts of habitus and emotional capital, we can see how the conservation of emotion (sometimes intentional, but largely nonconscious[2]) plays out in relation to broader social hierarchies. This helps us to see both *before* and *beyond* each of the individual emotional encounters that nurses relay. Before a single patient arrives in the unit, nurses carry with them embodied memories of repeat patients and visitors, demographic patterns in the types of patients that might come through the door, and habitual practices in conserving or expending emotional resources to others. Looking beyond each individual encounter that a nurse has on the job, the location and class and race dynamics of the country, city, and hospital where nurses work will shape how nurses feel across racial and class-based demarcations. But an emotion practice approach also helps in capturing what happens to the stress and sense of deflation that nurses experience—that is, what happens *beneath* each of these encounters. In this case, we must look beneath the explicit emotions they name and look to the embodied sensations and physical symptoms that coexist with what it feels like to be a nurse.

Beneath Emotional Encounters: Where Do Stress and Deflation End Up in the Body?

The aforementioned reflections from nurses seem to contradict the image of a selfless, always-nurturing nurse. Such heroic imagery is often used to avoid talking about the messy, darker sides of care work (Einboden 2020). Nurses are not mythical heroes; they are people—often with difficult and even impossible choices to make—choices that can weigh on the body. Despite their efforts to conserve valued emotional capital, it can be depleted, as we have seen. In Andrea's case, this led to a feeling of being mentally drained at the end of her third shift when she even forgot the number of patients she had that day. But the depletion of emotional capital does not simply leave cognitive traces. Just as frontline workers like nurses are most likely to feel the pinch of uncertain or vague organizational policies (Lipsky 1980), specific parts of the body come to feel the pinch of stress and ambiguous demands more than others. Feeling is a visceral sensation with physical implications: but unlike sports fans feeling elated and lively when their team does well or experiencing a sense of relaxation as they gather with friends before watching a game, nurses more often chronicle the physical aches and pains—the suffering—that comes with the job.

From headaches, to back and foot pain, insomnia and sleepiness, slurred speech, worries about high blood pressure, depression, dehydration, and a lack of time to urinate or eat, the frustrations of the job are somatically realized in the physical bodies of nurses young and old. Rather than bracket out these embodied experiences as somehow beyond the reach of social forces, an emotion practice approach integrates them into our understanding of nurses' well-being. Here we look *below* emotional experience and management to see what the implications are for the physical body. This aligns with work in anthropology that sees body, mind, and society as fundamentally interwoven: "the body [. . .] consists not only of the sedimentations of evolutionary time, but also the history of the society in which the organism is embedded, and its own history of constantly being molded by the practices it executes" (Scheer 2012, 201).

The molding of the body by the practices it executes is challenging to document, but nurse diaries include interwoven reflections on the emotional demands as well as the physical toll of their work. Clara is in her mid-fifties and has been working as a nurse for over twenty years. During those years, she has worked closely with a number of neurosurgeons. In her diary, she makes a passing reference to physical illness as she contemplates losing a beloved neurosurgeon who is relocating for another job:

> It makes me just *sick* to think about who I'm going to have to deal with next. And I guess it's the unknown because neurosurgeons are like cardiothoracic surgeons. . . [a] pretty high-strung bunch. And we were very fortunate to have two very laid-back people.

Like Marla and Joyce, Clara identifies the unknown or uncertainty of a given situation as being the source of her trepidation. Losing a neurosurgeon with whom she has worked for twenty years is a source of stress. In referencing sickness ("It makes me just *sick*"), she seems to be using it as a figure of speech, yet she later says, "The Motrin [pain medication] is needed."

There is little that Clara can do to exert any control over the type of neurosurgeon the hospital hires as a replacement and she is keenly aware of this:

> I am very concerned about what my day is going to look like after they're gone. They're leaving on October 21st and I will be working with surgeons from the adult side who do not like to look on children. A different one every week until we get a replacement. And the tentative feeling is that the replacement could take up to a year. So there's a lot of chaos. And they don't want to be there, and we don't want them there.

As Clara reflects on the upcoming changes and chaos that are likely to occur when her neurosurgeon leaves, she describes not only her need for Motrin to help with foot pain but also her experience of stomach issues:

So I was running from room to room . . . had not gone to the bathroom . . . it is now 4 pm. . . . I got the opportunity finally to go to the bathroom and I'm going to finally have a cup of coffee and get something to eat. Needless to say, I'm hungry. I'm *tired*. My tummy's a little messed up from having not been able to go to the bathroom when I needed to for eight hours.

A focus on managing emotions would examine only Clara's reactions to these sensations, without attending to the social forces that precede their embodiment. Embodied feelings of stress emerge from the continual dialogue between nurses' habitus and situational demands. This dialogue is both intentional—intentionally conserving emotional capital as we saw hinted at in the stories from Regina and Ashley in which they noted intentionally not forming emotional bonds and finding it difficult to sympathize with certain patients. Stress is also embodied, as it plays out in aching, anxious, and exhausted bodies. Clara's pain and discomfort appear to compound an already uncertain and chaotic work environment.

In a more direct example of embodied stress, Marge, a nurse in her early fifties, notes the link between her bodily well-being and the demands of job. While she started her nursing career in an Intensive Care Unit (ICU), she found that environment led to her feeling burnout to the point that she ultimately "didn't want to feel that way."

I didn't want to, I didn't want to not care, you know, about my patients. I just, I didn't, you know, when you're *that* tired, and I mean one thing after another, and kids are coding on you right and left. There's only so much of that you can take.

Moving to a pediatric surgical recovery unit led to its own challenges. For one, the first and second shift structure used on her unit means that there are times when she must start work at 6:30 am on some days and on other days she stays until 10:00 pm. She describes herself as a terrible sleeper, and the fluctuations in start time, along with being on call once a month, can wreak "havoc with my sleep patterns." By the end of the workweek, she is almost always tired.

Additionally, Marge has recurring headaches that she connects directly to working in a pediatric surgical recovery room:

Some days it's great or quiet—or fairly quiet. Some days every—every child is screaming at the top of their lung—top of their lungs, and they just don't quiet down. They have this emergence delirium or they're just behavioral type problems . . . and they just don't understand, and you can have a head-ache by the end of the day sometimes.

Sleep issues and screaming children combine to create recurring feelings of exhaustion and pain for Marge.

Joyce, who earlier described the "mishmash" confusion of managerial ex-pectations, also provides an illustration of how stress and complex emotions come to affect her physically. Like Clara, she first talks about sickness in a metaphorical sense:

I get so *sick* of hearing, "Oh well, she's [a new nurse] not out of orientation yet." SO WHAT, SO WHAT [angrily]. I've been one of your veteran nurses, so you gonna drag me in the ground? [. . .] What—I mean, what about me? *I'm drowning.*

In addition to the mishmash of management that Joyce identified earlier as a source of burnout, we see in this quote the feelings of being overwhelmed (drowning) and the anger that she feels toward a manager who insists on giving her more duties rather than pass them along to a new nurse who is still in orientation. At the end of her fifth diary entry, we learn that she experiences headaches "all the time" and tries a number of different strate-gies for coping with them:

So that's pretty much the day. I'm going to go to yoga class now, and hope-fully that'll take my *headache* away. I am gonna maybe just start, try to—last Saturday I went to a Reiki training where—where you get attuned, and so you can begin starting to practice on yourself and others. Maybe I'll do that cause I really don't enjoy having headaches all the time. Last two days I've had headaches and I don't know if it's something I ate, or medication, or what it was, but it's probably stress.

In her next shift, she describes it as "another horrible Monday," and she reaches for pain medication to cope with an oncoming headache:

I've taken my three Motrins, cause I feel this headache coming on. Drink a lot of water. And then in the afternoon I just really—I just feel my blood pressure going up. I just feel it, you know, that pressure in your head, um your eyes get blurred. [laughter] I just felt it all.

Management and coworkers are a large source of Joyce's stress. Earlier in her diary, she relays the experiences she has had with coworkers whose motives she doubts:

I know doggone well that she would not say this to one of my white coworkers that's a nurse that works with another doctor, I *know* she wouldn't. It just makes me mad.

Stressful interactions, and even racist microaggressions (Cottingham, Johnson, and Erickson 2018), get under the skin and into the body of nurses. This example from Joyce suggests that the difficult interactions with physicians and coworkers that she attributes to her race can lead to anger and feeling overwhelmed—experiences that might ultimately end up manifesting as a number of physical ailments. This includes headaches, as well as blurred vision, and feeling like her blood pressure is rising. More than simply the effort needed to mask emotions, her initial feelings, as "primary acts" (Hochschild 1979), lead to stress and added suffering. Simultaneously, these initial feelings are not asocial but linked to hierarchies of racial inequality (Evans 2013).

Tapping into the Multiplicity of Overlapping Emotions

Thus far we have looked at nurses' emotion practice in terms of the range and sources of what they feel, their conservation of emotional resources, and how these feelings manifest in the body. A practice approach, in addition to highlighting these aspects of nurses' experiences, can further highlight how nurses experience multiple emotions simultaneously. Thinking and feeling are often erroneously conceptualized as separate acts. But nurses think *and* feel their way through competing demands. Audio diaries allow us to tap into the ongoing flow of multiple emotions that can be experienced simultaneously. A single emotion does not necessarily dominate each nurse. Practices involve sensing and addressing a mix of emotions that bleed together.

Returning to the case of Marla illustrates the dynamic, overlapping feeling and thinking that characterizes nurses' emotion practice.

In the entry that follows, Marla is reacting to a recent discovery that her colleague, "C," violated protocol and instructed a younger nurse, "D," to administer medication without a physician's order on a unit where she was a "float" (a temporary substitute on another floor). Reacting to this news, Marla notes:

And then, I was *angry* because she did this. She's a float, floated to us, and did this on [unit name]. And so now is this going to give [unit name] a bad rap? "Oh, don't send your patients *there*, they overmedicate, or they put their own orders in"—you know, all the rumors that fly. And then I just feel so *sad* for C [deviant nurse]. You know *you kinda wax and wane, back and forth*, and then you kinda get angrier because you wanna say, "Why did you do that to D [complicit nurse]? It was *so* wrong of you to do that!" [details of investigation] . . . it makes you question yourself, you know, [C has] been a nurse for a long time, this is the first time maybe she's getting *caught*. How many other patients has she done other things on and things have just been pushed under the rug? But, then, why do we have to be the ones to deal with this, you know? So there's just a lot of *anger, frustration, sadness, don't understand why somebody would do this.*

The back and forth, "waxing and waning," that Marla describes is part of the situated flow between considering nursing norms ("is this going to give [unit name] a bad rap?") and new information. Emotions and their consequences (anger at her friend C) can shift through consideration of other emotions (sympathy as she feels sad for D) and through new information as she considers C's long tenure as a nurse which leads to feeling self-doubt ("It makes you question yourself"). Marla's reflections mix emotions with information in a stream of "thinking/feeling" about a past event.

If asked to classify her emotion on a survey, how would Marla respond? It might depend on the precise moment at which she is asked, as her narration suggests that she feels multiple emotions simultaneously. Nurses report feelings that are "widely scattered," you can feel the "full gamut of emotions," or "a variety of emotions" in a single day. This multiplicity of emotions can lead to feeling "overwhelmed" or like "your head is spinning" and suggests the relevance of both emotional ambivalence (Rothman et al. 2017) and the fact that "feelings can be ambivalent, conflicted, or divided" (Burkitt 2012,

470). Marla's reflection illustrates the dynamic multiplicity of emotions: "we do not experience isolated emotions, one at a time" (Bericat 2016, 495).

Using audio diaries in conjunction with an emotion practice approach allows us to capture the flow of Marla's emotions as they dynamically unfold rather than artificially limiting her emotion to a "final product" reached after reflection and deliberation. Studies of healthcare workers document the shared feelings of those working in the healthcare field (Erickson and Grove 2008). An emphasis on the dynamics of emotion does not discount these patterns. Yet each instance of a pattern remains a novel iteration that opens up subtle possibilities for deviation. Feelings of stress, exhaustion, and being overwhelmed were certainly highlighted among nurses in the sample, along with feelings of pride, fun, and a sense of purpose. Rather than measuring these emotions as static outcomes, an emotion practice approach draws attention to the ongoing flow of embodied emotions across settings and time and illustrates the interplay of cognitions with emotions.

Another example of this complex multiplicity of emotion comes from a diary excerpt from Lianna. At age twenty-four, Lianna is one of the youngest nurses in the sample. Throughout her diary recordings, she talks about feeling anxious and unsure. She uses the phrases "I don't know" and "I guess" throughout her reflections (over fifty times). In the scenario discussed next, Lianna is faced with a difficult patient and turns to other nurses on her floor for advice. Some try to be helpful, but one seems to exacerbate Lianna's anxiety by saying, "Oh, she's [the patient] weird and she's so mean. I'm glad I haven't taken care of her." Reacting to this, Lianna states:

> And granted, not all patients do act like her, but I just felt *disheartened* the way that this particular nurse kind of perceived the situation with that particular patient, because I think that the nature of nursing should really be about being able to *sympathize* and *empathize* with your patient and [even] if your patient is *angry* and lashing out . . . To add to that though, her—this patient['s] particular situation brought me back to another one of my patients that I had taken care of about three or four months ago that had passed away that had similar symptoms. So it was more like déjà vu and a—and a *fear* that this would also happen to her [. . .]

Lianna moves from disheartened by her fellow nurse to fear and sadness about her difficult patient as she calls up the emotion norms (static, structural elements) of the field ("the nature of nursing"). But in the moment that she is reflecting on the structured norms of what it means to be a good nurse, she is seemingly interrupted—haunted even—by the memory of a patient with similar symptoms. In recalling that memory, she feels fear. This "déjà vu" moment" appears unbidden, as the "situation brought" her "back to another" patient.

In this rich excerpt, we see Lianna's *intentional* efforts to align with the static occupational emotion norms of nursing (what she "should" feel) combined with the emergence of fear brought about dynamically and *unintentionally* by the situation. If we focus only on the management of discrete emotions (e.g., deep acting in order to feel authentic empathy for one's patient), the social relevance of a feeling of déjà vu would be lost and the dynamic and varied nature of emotion practice would be truncated to fit the manager–managed dyad. For Lianna, the past—a past patient who has passed away—haunts this encounter and links spontaneous feelings of fear to prior social encounters that are now a part of her habitus—a part of her evolving sense of being a nurse.

While Lianna's diary reflections are often filled with frustrations, annoyance, and fears of being judged by her colleagues, she notes two particular bright spots. In the first instance, her patient asks her to come and sit with her. Rather than discuss the details of the patient's diagnosis or health, or even converse about personal matters, this patient wants Lianna to, of all things, come watch the Super Bowl with her. Lianna only stays for a moment, but she reflects in her diary about how nice it felt to be invited. In another lighter moment, Lianna relays a small moment of joking around with her colleagues and how this made her happy. After a colleague asks another for pain medication, the first declines the offer of 600 mg dosage saying, "I don't need that much." The group of nurses around them then joke about what would happen if this colleague took too much Motrin, a relatively mild medication:

> Then we kind of went through the motions of laughing about how we would call a rapid response team on our coworker because we gave her too much Motrin, which obviously is not a particular[ly] [likely] situation, but I thought that was a good start to kind of breaking up that tension that I feel when I'm at work because I think about all the things that I have to do.

Lianna's diary reflections bring together many of the themes of this book—the relevance of sports spectatorship for connecting people, even a nurse and patient for just a moment in a hospital room, the complexity of emotions in nursing that include both working to feel the right thing, and being overcome by the unexpected haunting of past practices. And finally, the importance of humor in connecting groups even when it takes on morbid themes, as I explore in greater depth in Chapter 4's focus on social media responses to the 2013–2016 Ebola outbreak.

Positive feelings were certainly present in other nurse diaries, and these play a critical role in explaining how nurses, despite the uncertainty, frustration, and aches and pains, continue to return to their shift week after week and year after year. Muriel, a seasoned nurse in her mid-fifties, relays a particularly memorable interaction between herself, a colleague, and a loopy, medicated patient. She describes her colleague as *"someone I've known for years* and it was just one of those funny moments where we didn't even have to say anything."* She continues:

> This poor patient, he was just so cute, um trying really hard to be cooperative. And when we would ask him to move over to the bed, he starts moving his legs like he was riding a bicycle. [laughing] And, uh, I mean just *wildly up in the air.* And I said, "What are you doing?" and he says, "You told me to move my legs." And I said, "Well, no." And I couldn't even hardly respond to him I was laughing so hard. It was just one of those uh silly little moments that just strikes you as funny and the, um, T, the other nurse with me, was laughing just as hard. Neither one of us could talk to the poor guy.

She goes on to explain that the patient was "out of it," likely the result of his medications, and that this little moment was especially humorous because she could share it with a colleague whom she knows quite well.

> He [the patient] was trying so hard to try to do what we needed him to do but was just out of it because of medications he had received and didn't understand what we had asked him to do. Those kind of things, you know, where *you can share that kind of moment with someone you've known for [a] number of years does release some stress.*

Muriel acknowledges repeatedly that her colleague is someone she has developed a relationship with over the years. This means that she can share "little moments" where nothing needs to be said. Their established relationship gives them a shared outlook, allowing them to operate at the level of intuition and authentic simpatico. Such seemingly authentic moments are the product of past practices—the established relationship between her and her colleague translates into comfort and laughter in sharing an absurd moment.

Rather than interrogate her habitus—assumptions and reasons for acting, as experienced nurses must do when teaching younger nurses (Cottingham and Dill 2019)—these two seasoned nurses can avoid such exhausting reflexivity and instead be in the moment together. This is comfortable, easy, and, in the case of Muriel, fun and relaxing. It feels good. Here we see a built-in reward for working with those who share both a "feel for the game" (Bourdieu 1998, 80) and a shared social position. Given the complexities of orchestrating collective work, familiarity is a welcome respite. Applying an emotion practice approach to the audio diaries of nurses allows us to see these experiences of fun and comfort as the product of past social practices now embodied. Seemingly "authentic" emotional experiences are not disconnected from social context but shaped by them in equal measure compared to inauthentic or contrived experiences.

Emotions beyond Individuals and Interactions

The visceral, embodied nature of emotions emerges always from a body in relation to other bodies, objects, and environments. In the earlier sections, we have seen how an emotion practice approach allows us to address what comes before, lies beyond and beneath individual emotional encounters, as well as the overlapping of multiple emotions and cognitions. We can think of what lies beyond emotions not simply in terms of the social hierarchies in which nurses and their patients are located but also the professional health-care teams, physical hospital units, and environments that surround nurses. Taking an emotion practice approach can pull the lens back from the lone manager–managed dyad and onto the situation to show how emotions are evoked and shaped by collective environments and practices.

Nurses talk about their own feelings, of course, but they also talk about emotions and feelings at multiple levels. In looking at emotions beyond individuals, a practice approach can help us trace emotions as they reverberate from individuals and interactions to hospital floors and to units as a whole. Nurses ascribe emotions to a variety of nonpersonal entities, including rooms ("black cloud rooms," Andrea), situations (as "chaotic," Marge), the shift or night (as "high-energy," Regina), or their particular specialization ("maternity is 99 percent sheer boredom and 1 percent sheer terror," Regina). Marla, in another example, discusses how she senses the collective mood of the unit upon her initial arrival: "So, when I got there, you can always tell when you're walking on the floor, kinda the *mood*, whether call lights are going off or alarms are going off, or just the loud factor." Before interacting with even a single patient, nurses confront memories of past patients they have lost, noisy alarms, moods, and chaos that can permeate rooms, units and floors, nights and years. They might absorb these signals as soon as they enter the unit and try to process them in visceral and cognitive ways.

Hochschild's notion of emotional labor usefully draws our attention to the individual perceptions and strategies of managing emotion on the job as well as the increasingly restrictive emotional expectations of the commercial sector. But in shifting our perspective to a more collective level, we can see physical spaces themselves—as products of past practices—shaping emotions in individuals and groups. Collective moods emerge from intentional and unintentional social practices—from the beeping and call lights that Marla describes, as well as from the concerted efforts of nurses to intentionally calm themselves and others. In one example of this, Regina describes the use of whiteboards—public and readily viewable places for relevant information about a given patient—and how they are used in patients' rooms as a tool for communicating key information and managing emotions:

> On the children's boards we put the child's name, their weight, uh, the parents' names, and who the physician is who's going to be taking care of them while they are there. The reason we do that on the children's boards is that we have a lot of residents who come and *get very anxious* when there's a potential emergency or an emergency and *they may panic.*

Her unit uses whiteboards to preempt feelings of panic from incoming residents:

> They [residents] can look at the board and I—I'll have on the board what the mom's name is, what the dad's name is, what the child's name or nickname is, so that *there is this hope that there can be an almost instant relationship that forms,* and then also the child's weight so that they can immediately calculate any rescue medications that the child needs.

Regina uses the whiteboard to create an "instant relationship," but not between herself and the children, rather between residents and patients. We can see this as a form of collective, interpersonal emotion management (Francis 1997; Lively 2000) related but distinct from the intrapersonal processes that are often the focus of emotional labor scholarship. Whiteboards are part of the physical environment, fighting against the chaotic mood that tangled tubing and beeping machines creates for residents, nurses, and patients. This strategy is clearly intentional (a single individual must write names and information), but this individual practice becomes embedded in the environment. Regina could leave, but the whiteboard now remains as a part of the environment and as a resource that new nurses and residents can use to navigate the uncertainty of an emergency situation involving a child. Taking a practice approach directs our focus to the traces of past practices that exist beyond a lone individual nurse disconnected from space and time. Regina's practice becomes part of the fixed environment and plays a role in steering the future practices of her colleagues.

Thus far, I've discussed a number of emotions that emerge in nurses' day-to-day lives. These include feeling uncertain, sad, drained, deflated, angry, and afraid. We do see sympathy discussed briefly in Ashley and Lianna's cases. Sympathy and empathy are key defining emotions for nurses. They are built into the expectations we have about what makes a good nurse, and thus these emotions are part of the feeling rules of nursing (Erickson and Grove 2008). Yet we can see different paths to empathy—some paths involve real effort and some forms of empathy require little to no effort, as nurses feel alongside the patients they serve. This latter type can be a form of emotional contagion (Sinclair et al. 2017)—the nonconscious and unintended spread of emotions between individuals or to a larger group. Thinking of emotions as contagious immediately shifts our perspective to the group or collective rather than to isolated cases.

We can see an example of effortless empathy exemplified in the case of Jackie, a nurse in her late twenties who works on a surgical oncology unit. While other nurses work at empathy by, for example, viewing patient anger as a sign of fear, imagining the particular details of a patient's situation, or by role-taking with the patient's parents, Jackie doesn't need these strategies to feel for her patients. In her diary entries, she chronicles her own feelings right alongside the suffering of her patients without any apparent need to work at evoking compassion. We can see this play out in her diary. At various points, Jackie can be heard crying, her voice quivering, and the release of sighs and exhales as she talks into the recorder. Again, the body is implicated in how she processes the particular details of each of her patients. Concerning one patient, a forty-year-old father diagnosed with cancer, she relays her feelings alongside the details of his life and diagnosis without any intermediary strategies to link his situation to her emotions:

> And you know the *sad* part is today he turned forty, and he was in the hospital and he's dealing with these crazy cancers and he's got these three great boys and just great amazing life and he's *stuck* in this hospital and just *angry* at the world and you know h—, how did cancer pick him and this kind of cancer that they can't somehow get under control?

During another shift, her voice can be heard to falter as sadness overwhelms her:

> and it's just *sad* [voice quivering]. It's sad to see young age [patient] and just this horrible cancer and just the effect it takes on people and [sigh]. I just hope he makes it to see the birth of that baby.

Here we see feeling spread almost instantly from the patient's situation to Jackie. Using audio diaries, we can capture her sighs, quivering voice, and emphasis on "stuck" and "angry" as she records while feeling these emotions rather than relaying them to us dispassionately after the fact. Notably, at one point in her diary she describes her *unit* (not herself) as "emotional and very draining" because of the "life-changing" nature of the diagnoses and treatments administered there. Absorbing the emotions of her patients, her reflections point to a blurring between self, other, and what she sees as the qualities of the unit as a collective. It is clear that Jackie views this particular patient as an innocent victim, someone who is worthy of the emotional investments she nonconsciously makes by feeling the raw emotions of anger and sadness of his situation directly.

Conclusion

Emotion research on nursing and other frontline health workers has been primarily dominated by the theory of emotional labor. This focus has been fruitful for highlighting the real, though often invisible, work that goes into making social interactions run smoothly and the importance of emotions in making patients feel better (Theodosius 2008). But, as with any single frame, there are parts of nursing that are illuminated while others are dimmed. An emphasis on strategic masking, faking, and working to feel has, perhaps despite Hochschild's original intentions, bracketed out much of the raw emotions of nurses (Theodosius 2006), as well as their complexity, feelings of uncertainty, embodiment of stress, and the ways these feelings reverberate onto units, groups, and environments beyond individual patients.

Marla's and Joyce's lament about managerial uncertainty, Andrea's and Ashley's attempts to conserve precious emotional capital, and the way that deflation and drain are felt in aching backs and feet are brought into better focus using the conceptual tools of an emotion practice approach. The management of emotion, to be sure, remains a relevant feature of nurses' daily lives, but by taking a practice approach, we can more directly address the drain and conservation of emotional resources and the traces that past practices leave on the body and in the work environment. Similarly, in taking a practice approach to Lianna's and Muriel's experiences, we see the way in which multiple emotions can connect in a string of thinking/feeling, working to feel, and unbidden memories of past patients that can emerge while on duty. What we feel individually can reverberate into our environments, where units, floors, and specializations themselves come to be seen as marked by distinct moods. The haunting of past practices and the marking of units and floors become a way of making sense of how emotions seem to be both something we have but something that takes hold of us. They direct our attention, like the call lights and alarms that Marla emphasizes on her floor, to moments that require our vigilance and shine a spotlight on the importance of (certain) others with whom we share a connection.

Using the method of audio diaries allows us to see how these practices unfold over the course of the six shifts during which nurses in our study made their recordings. By collecting their reflections using audio recorders, we can capture the deep sighs and inhales, sobs, laughter, and pauses that communicate the texture and richness of their emotional lives. Their stories illustrate the importance of emotional capital in how social interactions unfold and the effects its loss has on the body. The aches and pains of the body seem to call out, like the feelings of stress, for relief and rest. But acting on this practical knowledge is not always possible, and nurses turn to pain medication, Reiki, and a variety of other coping mechanisms to allow them to continue to work and push the body despite its attempt to communicate this practical information.

Nursing and healthcare generally can be seen as a distinct field comprised of unique demands and uniquely valued resources compared to other occupations and social domains. Yet these findings reveal much about the complexity of confronting ambiguous and demanding work—something likely shared by many workers in a variety of occupations. In the following chapter, I turn from the distinct emotion practices of nurses described here to a radically different set of actors and social circumstances. In contrast to nurses, sports fans experience a different configuration of emotions and practices that include the peak emotional highs of watching an exciting game and feelings of solidarity with other fans that are forged over time. Here, too, I argue that an emotion practice approach can help us see complex emotions more clearly as practical engagements with the social world.

3

Sports Fans

The Feel of Fandom in and beyond Peak Emotions[*]

> She can choose her religion, but she can't choose what [football] team she likes.
>
> —Justin Eitel, of Pittsburgh, speaking of his newborn daughter (2011)

> The only time white people watch black people is if we're singing, dancing, or running a football.
>
> —D. L. Hughley, *The Daily Show* (2018)

When I moved back to western Pennsylvania after being away for five years, I was immediately struck by the influence of the local sports teams on the city of Pittsburgh. The Pittsburgh Steelers franchise, founded in 1933, is one of the oldest teams in the National Football League (NFL). And Steelers' merchandise was everywhere I looked. In 2008, I found that even my local grocery store, the regional chain Giant Eagle, devoted an entire section to each of the city's baseball, hockey, and football teams. Over the course of the football season, Terrible Towels—the defining symbol of the Steelers, striking in its black and yellow contrasts—were individually tucked into the handles of each sliding glass door in the frozen food aisles. Steelers mania would intensify during the weeks leading up to the 2009 Super Bowl—the NFL championship game. Terrible Towels multiplied across the city, decorating the doorways and counters of post offices, banks, and stores. An oversized Terrible Towel was even placed in the clutches of the Tyrannosaurus Rex skeleton replica that greets travelers at the Pittsburgh international airport.

---

[*] Portions of this chapter are adapted from Cottingham (2012).

Practical Feelings. Marci D. Cottingham, Oxford University Press. © Oxford University Press 2022.
DOI: 10.1093/oso/9780197613689.003.0004

Sports fans are common fodder for thinking about the sociological dynamics of popular culture and collective emotions (R. Collins 2004; Elias and Dunning 1986; Frey and Eitzen 1991; McCarthy 2017). Much of the empirical work on sports fans tends to emphasize their proclivity toward hooliganism and frenzy (Poulton 2008; K. Young 2002), framing fans as overly emotional and too easily swept up into the spirit of the game. This chapter turns to the case of sports fans to illustrate how an emotion practice approach can trace emotions in and outside the peak emotional highs that take place in public gatherings in arenas and stadiums. Fans certainly experience moments of collective effervescence and emotional energy—peak feelings of elation, cohesion, and individual confidence (R. Collins 2004) when watching games together. But their experiences also include emotions of belonging and connection that fandom fosters between family, friends, and neighbors long after the winning touchdown, goal, or shot.

In looking at these emotional experiences through a practice lens, we can better trace the investment and withdrawal of emotional capital into the salient symbols of sports fandom. Fandom is more than mere frivolity, but a leisure pursuit that can cement relationships between family, friends, neighbors, a city, and even a nation. In cementing these relationships, fandom has practical value—providing the emotional energy (as part of emotional capital) that can carry fans through the mundane aspects of everyday life, major life events, and personal and collective challenges. In fact, the loss of fan activities as energizing social opportunities during the COVID-19 pandemic has been covered from a number of angles by journalists, with fan emotions taking center stage (Kilgore 2020).[1] Symbols, and the emotional capital they encapsulate, become useful for navigating new spaces and relationships, for adding a sense of cohesion to city life and fostering a shared identity. Their value is evident in stores like the grocery store discussed earlier and in the corporate campaigns and public spaces that use these objects to entice customers.

Certainly, the feelings generated while attending a game and cheering on the home team are intense. But by following sports symbols as they circulate/operate outside of these peak moments, we can learn something unique about how sports have become a conduit for channeling familial and civic emotions. Everyone from nurses dressing newborns in sport-themed blankets, to brides-to-be planning themed weddings and civil servants planning events around the season schedule suggests that sports are a unique social field for connecting disparate groups through emotional bonds. These bonds rely on symbols infused with both the emotions of fans and the physical labor (created through bodily capital, Wacquant 1995) of players. With American football players taking on increasingly known health risks for the sake of the sport and with a disproportionate representation of racial minorities among these players, the costs and benefits of maintaining the sport's emotional eco-system are not shared equally. Sports symbols are sources of emotional capital charged up by the bodily capital of a few so that many, including corporations and businesses, can draw on their practical value.

In this chapter, I first begin with a descriptive account of my time observing and participating with local fans in Pittsburgh, Pennsylvania, during the 2008–2009 season. I look at the emotions and practices that build up to the game, the euphoria that crescendos in the stadium, and the lingering charge that dissipates as the game ends and fans return to cars and homes. I then trace Steelers symbols outside of their typical contexts of stadiums and sports bars to understand the practical value that these containers of emotion have for the people, institutions, and city that use them. In light of the contro-versy surrounding the former quarterback and activist Colin Kaepernick (Maher 2019) and the racial disparities in players, coaches, and health risks (Baron et al. 2012; Belson 2019; Roberts et al. 2020), I then take a critical eye, using the concepts of habitus, capital, and field, to understand how practical emotions rely on the expenditure of bodily capital from a predominantly African American labor force. This labor force takes on considerable risks to their physical well-being. This chapter, like the preceding one where I fo-cused on nursing, looks at the social aspects that exist before, beyond, and beneath emotional experiences to better understand the emotional appeal and the emotional economy of sports fandom.

Sports and Fan Emotions

Early in the 2008–2009 football season, I met Kevin[2] through a mutual friend who had learned of my interest in studying sports fans. Kevin was quick to emphasize his extensive knowledge of the Steelers franchise—its history and current roster—as well as his deep commitment to the team. He boasted that even during his time serving in the military in Iraq, he managed to miss only a single game via radio broadcast. Though I knew several Steelers fans already, I hoped that breaking out of my known network would offer a fresher per-spective on fan experiences. With Kevin informed about my research aims, I could also interrogate him more than most of my family or friends would tolerate. We started out by planning to attend some tailgating gatherings and then planned to travel to local Pittsburgh sports bars during the games, as neither of us had access to tickets to the games themselves.

Throughout the research, I asked myself: What draws people, most of whom are unknown to one another, to congregate to watch grown adults participate in fierce and aggressive competition? And not simply competition, competitions that ultimately have little at stake. Throwing a touchdown, scoring at the buzzer, or making a goal with a well-coordinated pass and head-shot—none of these are of any practical consequence to our lives. Yet to watch such feats garners untold crowds, in person and virtually. What emotions are generated in these crowds and how is it that they continue to draw so many people back again and again? Classic theories on sports include the work of Norbert Elias and Eric Dunning (1986) who, building on a catharsis theory of emotion indebted to Freud (1961), believed that sports and sports spectatorship allowed people to vicariously emit pent-up emotions that civilized society would no longer allow them to express in formal interactions and in their work. According to Elias and Dunning, the excitement drawn from participating in and watching friendly competitions stands in stark contrast with the "almost unshakeable habit of restraint" that permeates our everyday lives (1986, 71). Sports, then, allow people to satisfy a "need to experience the upsurge of strong emotions in public" and release built-up tensions (1986, 168). This conceptualization of emotions—as something pent up in daily living but in need of an occasional release valve—fits with the conception in Western Enlightenment that emotions are marked by volatility and chaos (Lutz 1998), and to be mostly suppressed as we go about the practical business of living.

But other approaches to sports focus less on its cathartic release and more on its ritualistic emergence (Birrell 1981; R. Collins 2004). Following Emile Durkheim (1915), this scholarship frames sports and spectatorship as more *generative* rather than *cathartic*. Emotions are not demarcated between the bottled up and the released, as the cathartic view would argue. Rather, emotions are the emergent outcomes of social gatherings and interactions. Certainly, some gatherings draw out stoicism or somberness, while others draw out elation and excitement. A number of important ritual elements (or ingredients, according to Collins [2004]) determine whether or not a given interaction will successfully foster emotional energy. Pent-up emotions are not simply released. Rather, newly emergent emotions, including individual emotional energy and collective effervescence, are generated in these contexts. As I noted in Chapter 1, rituals can provide participants with the emotional high that comes from active engagement with the group. It is a new, emergent experience, not simply the release of otherwise restrained chaos. It is this socially generative understanding of sport emotions that I adopt here and see as compatible with developing an emotion practice approach.

As described in Chapter 1, interaction ritual theory breaks down the elements needed for a successful ritual (R. Collins 2004). If a ritual is to successfully generate group solidarity, feelings of energy among individuals, and collective emotions, there are certain key elements that must be combined. These ingredients include a gathering of two or more people in one place, barriers to outsiders, a common focus of attention, and a common mood or emotional experience. This broad outline could apply to almost any social setting—as was Collins's intention—from watching a movie in a theater, a politician giving a speech, to gathering in school classrooms, workplace meetings, and at the family dinner table. Some interactions generate or tax our emotional energy based on the quality of these ingredients and the social expectations we have for how a particular interaction will unfold.

In applying this understanding of ritual to sports fandom, we can see that these ingredients are readily present in spaces where fans gather before games and matches to engage in "tailgating"—a time to gather before events, usually in parking lots and public spaces at the back end of a truck or car to drink, eat, talk, and energize themselves for the upcoming event. To an extent, these ingredients are also present in sports bars where fans gather to casually watch events televised on the screens that now permeate most bars and pubs dedicated to sports. I was ultimately able to attend a Steelers home game at Heinz Field and there the ritual ingredients and outcomes were easy to identify in the actions and faces of the crowd all around me.

These rituals, as Collins (2004) argues, are what build up emotional energy in individuals and these feelings of energy become encapsulated in important group *symbols*. Building on this, we can see that affiliation with a given team is not a matter of simply showing up at events. Fandom is worn on and around the body using symbols invested with emotional capital. Symbols are "simply, things which stand for other abstractions. They are vehicles encoded with meanings, which serve as the basic units of meaning in rituals" (Birrell 1981, 357). Tattooing as ritual act and meaningful symbol (Fisher 2002) is a more extreme example of "wearing" fandom. An online search for "Steelers tattoos" brings up nearly two million results. Under images, the categories of "forearm," "tribal," "Pittsburgh," "women's," "simple," "small," and "sleeve" appear ("Steelers Tattoos" 2021). Tattooing practices within the context of shifting and ephemeral fashion trends of late capitalism have a rebellious quality because of their relatively permanent marking of the body (Fisher 2002). But fans also turn to other forms of body/self-modification by wearing sports jerseys and clothing marked with the team logo and colors, as well as face painting, hair dyes and styles, fingernail painting, and use of accessories like hair ties and jewelry. Automobiles—cars, trucks, motorcycles—are decorated with Steelers decals. And "man caves"—basements or separate home spaces decorated by men—display masculinity using a variety of sports symbols and memorabilia (Tiffany 2019).

It is in both the embodiment of fandom and the use of symbols for practical, social aims that an interactionist tradition can fall short. Erving Goffman's work in particular focuses on the body as a tool for giving off cues to others in interactions. Goffman's (1959) "presentation of self in everyday life" illustrated a dramaturgical approach to social life—each individual could be seen as an actor playing at roles relevant to a given context. The role of parent, of child, of worker, of citizen could be taken on and taken off as the context demands. But, as most parents know deeply, such roles cannot always be easily put on or taken off at will. They seep into our bodies and can modify who we are in ways more profound than a dramaturgical approach would fully allow.

Similarly, sports fandom is not a role put on and taken off as easily as a lightweight jersey. If one were to engage with fan symbols sporadically or casually, one risks being deemed a fair-weather fan. If one need only put on a jersey, why have decals of the team etched on your nails? Why the painted face *and* headdress *and* Terrible Towel? The stacking up of symbols, particularly on game days, suggests that individuals and groups work to maximize the emotional value of each of these symbols. We saw how the body was implicated in the stress and deflation of nurses in Chapter 2. In the context of fandom, we see fan symbols being stacked upon each other to maximize the emotional capital drawn from their use, adorning the body in colorful and eccentric ways. In this way, fandom is not solely about cognitive knowledge or tacit affiliation with a team but involves tapping into the *emotional capital* of symbols through appearance, dress, attendance, and active participation in fan activities, as we will see later. In tapping into this capital, fans gain energy, forge emotional bonds, and confirm a shared mode of being (or habitus) that can become useful in a variety of other relationships and contexts.

Before turning to those other contexts, though, it is useful to first describe in greater detail the peak emotional experiences that are the hallmark of sports fandom.

Peak Emotions during Games

Modifying the body through appearance is one important pregame ritual that also corresponds with preparing for tailgating or planning gatherings of friends and family for game watching. Such preparation is a build-up to the actual game itself. To understand the peak emotions of fandom, I observed fans in parking lots while tailgating, in two sports bars in the city, and at Heinz Field, the Steelers's home stadium. In those settings I noticed variations in the presence of the ingredients that Collins (2004) identifies as necessary for successful rituals. For example, tailgating in open parking lots had few barriers to outsiders—anyone walking around the parking lot could in theory interact with other tailgaters. Sports bars usually required little more than a valid form of identification to prove that one is twenty-one or older and entrance comes with the assumption that attendees will purchase food or drink while watching the game. Depending on the popularity of the game and the importance of the game for the team's standing in the league, patrons might stand and congregate around the bar and televisions. When others are present and standing, this heightens the sense of a shared focus of attention, signaling to others the importance of the game and the need to pay close attention to the events on the field. Within sports bars, chairs tend to be positioned around the bar with multiple television screens visible. Where televisions are absent, decorations of posters with players, Steelers logo, and jerseys and pennants hang throughout the bar rooms.

During my time at sports bars with my informant, we noticed variation in the attentiveness of fans. When I commented to Kevin that some of the younger patrons in the bar did not seem to pay much attention to the game, he commented, "They weren't raised right." The day the Steelers were playing the Cowboys (the team based in Dallas, Texas), we went to a bar near the stadium after tailgating during the day. This was a game not only with a rival team that has a history of producing antagonism, but the weather had also been quite mild for mid-December and, as a result, the parking lot and stadium area were crowded with fans, including the intense early morning tailgaters as well as partners and children that joined tailgaters later in the day. Congregants participated in a variety of carnival-like events that had been set up outside the stadium. When not standing around to drink, eat, and converse, children could try out an inflated mini end zone bounce house. Merchants set up the usual stalls, but there were more offerings for children, including face painting.

At Heinz Field, the stadium in Pittsburgh named after the Heinz Ketchup company, the barrier to entry is stricter than with tailgating or at sports bars. Entrance to the stadium is dependent on having a valid ticket and submitting to the security check at the gate. Once inside, the design of the stadium funnels people to the array of seats that encircle the field. Large video screens are placed throughout the concession area and a display monitor above the field televises the events on the field in greater detail while also providing replays of critical moments. These screens and the design of the field channel the collective attention of attendants toward the events on the field, creating an increasingly shared focus of attention.

As the barrier to outsiders became stricter, the importance of the event is heightened, and attendees increase their attention to the events on the field. Even when purchasing food or drinks, or using the bathroom, attendees in the stadium can still watch events on the field because of strategically placed televisions that are displayed throughout nearly all parts of the stadium (with the exception of individual bathroom stalls). During one game, when the weather was below freezing, Kevin and I waited to purchase food at a stall just a few feet from the seating area in the stadium. We watched with the others in line as star quarterback Ben Roethlisberger made a seemingly unforced error and threw the ball away to the sidelines. Those congregated around the food stall groaned, and Kevin made a comment of disgust and chided the quarterback. At that point an older man in front of us in the line turned around and pressed Kevin, "Do you know how difficult it is to throw a football in freezing weather?" It seemed that Kevin's comment of disapproval had crossed a line. During these moments of heightened emotion within the context of increased barriers to outsiders (we were in the stadium), amplified co-presence, fixed attention, and shared mood, the Steelers' star quarterback became a symbol of the team itself. To the fan ahead of us, Kevin's critique of the play was problematic because it called into question Roethlisberger's status as the star player and symbol of the team.

One of the primary outcomes of successful rituals is the development of group symbols—objects that become charged up with the emotions of the group. Roethlisberger could be seen as one of these symbols and, in the moment that the other fan chastised Kevin for critiquing Roethlisberger, the fan seemed to suggest that as a sacred symbol, the quarterback should be above critique. Ironically, though, in making this claim, the man reiterated Roethlisberger's humanity—his fallibility to the elements, including the cold weather. In this way, Roethlisberger's weaknesses have to be seen in the context of the various challenges of the game and not as a sign of his inherent weakness as a player.

What explains this fan's desire to defend Roethlisberger's unforced error? Ritual theory suggests that one outcome of successful rituals is the development of symbols imbued with group meanings and feelings. Roethlisberger himself can become a symbol of the team, and in defending the player, this fan defends the group. Taking a practice approach to fan emotions can help us go even further in understanding fan behavior. Certainly, successful rituals, by definition, feel good—there is an element of hedonism in the elevation and electric energy that comes from witnessing an historic game or seeing in person the role models that, since childhood, fans have potentially held up as ideals of athleticism and success. But there is also a practicality to sports fandom, to loyalty to a particular team, often one that has been a part of childhood and family life.

Pierre Bourdieu's (1990) concept of *habitus* highlights the embodied traces of past social practices that we internalize through our membership in a variety of groups. The family and its role in imparting particular dispositions and preferences early in life is a key source for developing habitus. Habits are the patterns of being, feeling, and doing that we fall into without necessarily consciously choosing them. As a result, these are often tied to some of our earliest social experiences with caregivers and in family settings. Although habits can be disrupted and tweaked as well as reflected upon consciously, they retain a degree of rigidity— rigidity forged in the solidarity that shared social experiences provide. In this case, the emotional capital invested into and gained from a symbol overlaps with social capital—one's network of social relations. Successful rituals create a sense of collective oneness—solidarity—that drives us to engrain certain habits and ways of living that ultimately feel best to the individual. Thus, what feels good is not objective,[3] but the result of an ongoing string of shared subjective experiences—experiences shared with those with whom we identify most closely and from our earliest moments of self-awareness.

Kevin had remarked early on in our conversation that the Steelers team was a fixed part of his childhood. He grew up an hour or so outside the city and says he has been a fan for as long as he can remember, even going so far as to schedule his military leave time to coincide with a Steelers opening game. There were only two times in his recollection that he had missed watching or listening to a Steelers game: one was because he couldn't access a television or radio broadcast when he was stationed in Iraq. The only other time that he can recall missing a game was for the prefuneral viewing of his great grandfather. Reflecting on his childhood, he said that his father instilled in him the importance of watching the Steelers at an early age. His father would often state: "We are not fair-weather fans," and watching the team together formed one of their primary bonds. Growing up, he was not even allowed to get up and leave the room when the Steelers were playing, even if they were losing. Such an act, it seems, would be interpreted as disrespectful to the team. The lines of respect/disrespect for shared symbols appear to be important but also malleable. Fans negotiate with each other, as Roethlisberger's defensive fan did at the food stall, when to critique and when to sympathize with the team.

Having grown up steeped in Steelers fandom, it was not too surprising that Kevin seemed to easily connect with other fans around him. His habitus—the engraining of past practices—had already prepared him well for the moments he would encounter as a fan. Both at the sports bars and in the stadium, Kevin exchanged high-fives, grins, and even shrieks and screams with other fans after notable plays in which the team performed well. Kevin had no connection to them except in those moments, yet knew, seemingly instinctively, how and when to engage with others in those public settings. Using the concept of habitus in addition to interaction ritual ingredients and outcomes is useful because it allows us to look *before* a given ritual event and see the traces of the past that are called upon in those moments. Depending on the frequency of past practices, these can become sedimented in the body (Ahmed 2006) and need barely rise to the level of consciousness or strategic use. Yet even when nonconscious, they help to cement relationships, serve as ice breakers with strangers, and buoy otherwise depressed spirits.

Many fans seemed to engage in similar forms of active, collective participation while spectating—sharing smiles, hand-slaps, and hugs, even between strangers. From my field notes, a specific example demonstrated fans' level of emotional energy (i.e., levels of personal excitement, confidence, and initiative) following a successful play:

Late in the final quarter of the game the Steelers made a spectacular play, which resulted in much cheering, screaming, clapping, and waving. A man with a stern face in front of me, probably in his late twenties to early thirties, began to remove layers of clothing. Finally, he pulled his final shirt up over his head and stood cheering and screaming without a shirt in temperatures around 15 degrees Fahrenheit. After a second stellar play on behalf of the Steelers, the man beside him also took off his many layers of coats and shirts and the two clutched hands and screamed in earnest.

This moment—literally two men peeling off outside layers to connect, bare-chested, on a visceral level—seems to be the epitome of a cathartic view of emotion. What is practical or of use in this startling example?

The acts, gestures, and vocalizations that the two men made were not simply expressions of preexisting emotions pent-up inside; rather, it is through these acts that they create emotional energy for each of them individually and collective effervescence for those of us in the splash zone of their exuberance. As Collins notes, the level of individual emotional energy demonstrated in active participation affects the solidarity of a group: "[C]ollective solidarity and identity is stronger to just the extent that the crowd goes beyond being passive observers to actively taking part" (2004, 82). When these two men also turned to face my informant, to them a stranger who was also gesturing and yelling, and gestured for a high-five, this further suggested that fans will seek out "bodily contact with each other" as an outcome of the emotional energy and group solidarity felt during moments of heightened and active spectatorship. In participating and in observing the solidarity exhibited in this behavior, the two men and the spectators around them feel solidarity not just to each other but to the group of fans as a whole. In being present myself and seeing the two men exchange high-fives with my informant, I could not resist a smile if I wanted to.

These generative moments, like the many forms of team merchandise that fans use, stack up throughout the game day experience. But they do not stop when the game ends. Beyond the specific dynamics taking place on the field and in the stadium seating, feelings of group solidarity were palpable in the corridors and stairwells of the stadium as fans exchanged smiles, cheers, and collective chants on their way home. Gestures and verbal responses following the game's conclusion (a Steelers victory) were not as organized as they were during the game, but traces of these strong emotions reverberated among fans as they made their way to cars and homes. They took more than souvenirs with them; they took charged-up bodies and symbols that could be used to elicit new emotional capital in future encounters.

Going beyond Peak Emotions

To fully answer my earlier question about what makes fan emotions of practical use, we have to look beyond the stadium, tailgating in parking lots, and interactions in sports bars. In the field, I was overwhelmed with documenting the details of sports fan behavior. I watched fans react to events on the field, converse casually between plays, and manage the many items that displayed their loyalty—from hats, scarves, jackets, outlandish headgear, face paint, blankets, beer cozies, and, of course, Terrible Towels. Yet, going back to my first memorable observation of Steelers items in my local grocery store, I was struck by the places these symbols traveled. Not only did they find their way into public and commercial buildings, as well as on cars and in family homes, but they emerged during events that I did not expect. They emerged as blankets for newborns in labor and delivery units (Leahy 2011). They cropped up in wedding celebrations and in funerals for former players and ordinary fans. They were not simply used during game day, during football season, but could be found year-round, broadcasting a fan's loyalty while they dropped off the kids at school, traveled to work, and went about their everyday lives. These symbols appeared to be special and ordinary—both mundane and sacred (Birrell 1981; Remillard 2013). But they were not peripheral; they appeared to be imprinted, even if the black and gold colors were a bit faded, into the fabric of the city and loyal fans around the world, and beyond.[4]

Following my observations while tailgating, in sports bars, and at a game, I started to track the use of Steelers symbols in events far removed from the game and the stadium. Weddings and funerals seemed like the most extreme use of these symbols, but even at the hospitals, post offices, schools, banks, and at the airport, they were appeared to be both out of place yet right at home. Taking a practice approach to fan emotions, I believe, helps to explain the spread of sports symbols far beyond their origin in the stadium, arena, or field. Symbols, as containers of past practices, come to represent what are usually unarticulated feelings and sensations.

As containers of emotion, these symbols can be used to add meaning to special as well as everyday activities and events. In this way, these symbols hold emotional capital—allowing individuals to tap into and transfer the emotional resources they hold into contexts far-removed from their original setting. Charged up during game days and through the bodily capital of players, a variety of other actors can then use these symbols to add emotional meaning to non-sport activities. Brides picking out monogrammed Terrible Towels for their wedding, nurses adorning newborns in Terrible Towels at a birth center, and banks offering customers the option of personalized checks and debit/credit cards etched with the Steelers logo are all tapping into meaningful, positive emotions as they turn to readily available symbols of fandom.

Drawing from these symbols—as encapsulated emotions—fans can use symbols outside of sporting events because they are, in a way, pragmatic. These emotionally charged symbols are resource rich and adaptable—they require little explanation when used among fellow fans and can be easily understood by (nearly) anyone who is familiar with American football. Certainly, the symbols of one team can be used to taunt and disparage fans of another team and symbols of other franchises have been critiqued for their perpetuation of racist imagery (see Jacobs's [2014] in-depth analysis of the Indian mascot debate in Cleveland, Ohio). But in the case of the Steelers, the logo and Terrible Towel do not have the fraught and potentially alienating sentiments that other sources of meaningful symbols, such as political or religious affiliation, risk evoking. Hence they might be safer to use and more likely to generate positive feelings of belonging in increasingly multicultural, religiously pluralistic, and politically polarized societies.

During the 2008–2009 season, the Steelers would go on to play in and win the 2009 Super Bowl Championship game. During this time, I relied on journalistic accounts of weddings and funerals, as well as other events, in order to trace the movement of symbols outside of peak emotion events and into non-sports settings and events. Here I highlight examples from each of these settings to give a sense of how such symbols can be tapped for their practical and readily available emotional meaning. In this sense, "the elasticity of the symbol" is a "measure of its effectiveness" in cultivating deep feelings (P. H. Collins 2012, 448). Thus, while these examples are not representative of all fans, they can show us the range—the "elasticity" of sports symbols—in terms of travel beyond sports contexts and how they can be used to infuse life course events and city life. In looking beyond peak emotions, we can better appreciate the value that these symbols have, the *emotional capital* that is parlayed in their use by individuals, families, cities, and corporations.

Weddings

Certainly weddings are not ordinary, but unusual events that couples plan together to celebrate their relationship and, for some, to begin a life together. I turn to the use of Steelers symbols in this context to highlight their ubiquity in non-sports-related settings as well as the important meaning that their use seems to have for couples and their friends and family. In turning to Steelers symbols to add meaning to their events, couples seem to tap into the well of emotional reserves captured in these symbols. News articles described Steelers-themed weddings that incorporated the team's colors and the group ritual of twirling Terrible Towels (Axelrod 2017; *CBS Broadcasting. KDKA* 2009), a Steelers fight song (Lavis 2007), and couples competing for a sponsored, Steelers-themed wedding (A. Johnson 2006). One Pittsburgh couple had their wedding ceremony at a church but held the reception at Heinz Field (McMarlin n.d.). Reasons included:

> . . . besides being home to the couple's favorite football team—were the lounge's size and view, the opportunity to have wedding photos taken on the playing surface and a tour of the Steelers' locker room for the bridal party. Tina also wanted favors that people could keep and use, and Terrible Towels monogrammed with the couple's names and wedding date certainly fit the bill. (McMarlin, n.d.)

When she used monogrammed Terrible Towels as gifts for guests, the bride relied on a symbol of group membership that she likely believed would resonate with her friends and family and would also be useful to them (for later ritual use).

Understanding symbols and their use requires going beyond the conscious to the "unconscious component" (R. Collins 2004, 97) of social behavior. While the bride may not consciously infuse her blissful day with "borrowed" emotional energy, this seems a likely result. Tina's use of Terrible Towels and the placement of the reception at Heinz Field were certainly creative, but these acts were also instrumental. Perhaps without realizing it, Tina relied on the positive and intense emotions associated with these symbols to transfer the meaning and emotion associated with fandom to their special day. In this regard, Tina and her groom used these symbols as a form of currency—using the emotions of fandom embedded in the symbols to bolster the intensity and elation of their wedding. In other words, the feelings of elation and excitement that attendees will undoubtedly experience could be partially tied to the evocative Steelers symbols used rather than solely to the love shared between bride and groom. Seeing these symbols as containers of emotional *capital* helps us to zoom in on this currency-like transfer of peak emotional highs into spaces outside their traditional use.

In another example of a Steelers-themed wedding, a couple used the "Steelers Fight Song Polka" and a coordinated chant of "Here we go Steelers, here we go!" at their wedding reception. During the song and chant, the groom was encircled by his friends and had to break through their defense in order to retrieve and carry off his bride (Lavis 2007). For Nicole and Michael's wedding, "groomsmen waved Terrible Towels and the bridesmaids twirled black and gold boas" (*CBS Broadcasting. KDKA* 2009).

Searching for "Steelers wedding" in an online search produces over 12,000 results, including Pinterest and Etsy pages devoted to collecting various items needed for planning a wedding. These include Steelers-themed cake decorations, garters, invitations, floral and table decorations, wedding bands, shoes, dresses, and of course, personalized Terrible Towels that include the couple's names and wedding date. Tina and her groom's decision to use these symbols in the celebration of their wedding—a situation rarely associated with sports fandom—supports the notion that fans can have high levels of group solidarity and gain notable meaning from their identity as a fan. Emotional energy is drawn from group fandom in settings and situations far removed from their origin using these symbols as practical containers of emotion. Brides and grooms use these symbols to make the day more personally meaningful and transfer some of the stored-up emotional capital of fandom to their own special day.

Funerals

At the final request of her late husband, Kathleen Desrosiers brought his ashes to a Steelers game at Heinz Field in 2007. Her husband had never attended a game in his lifetime and was, therefore, unable to experience peak moments of heightened emotions that a game at the stadium would provide. Yet he had been a devoted fan from his home in New England—owning many Steelers clothing items and even deciding to name the family dog after the team. For the funeral, his stepsons dressed in Steelers jerseys and his body was covered with a Steelers blanket. After taking his ashes in an urn to the stadium in December 2007, Kathleen cheered on the team in her husband's place. She told reporters from the *Pittsburgh Post-Gazette* that it was

> an overwhelming experience. . . . It's sad to think that he got here in death. But this is where he wanted to be. It was what he asked me to do. I got to be with him one last time while he did something he wanted more than any-thing else in the whole wide world. (NH Woman 2007)

In following the wishes of her late husband and working to process her own grief, Kathleen takes up the symbols that he used to decorate his life.

More recently, we can find examples of Steelers fandom making its way into obituaries. In the case of Eleanor Miriam Gallagher of Nanticoke, Pennsylvania, we see that her death at the age of eighty-one on January 24, 2015, is connected by her family to the team's "poor performance" that season. While her obituary emphasizes her devotion to family, to the children she served at the school cafeteria, and her volunteer work, following this we see a strange claim:

> Eleanor was a devoted Pittsburgh Steelers fan, and the family firmly believes that the recent separation of Dick LeBeau [Steelers' defensive coordinator who resigned] and the Steelers' poor performance this season might have inadvertently contributed to her demise. (The Citizens' Voice 2015)

Another poignant example of fans incorporating Steelers references into end-of-life rituals was in the untimely death of Pittsburgh mayor Bob O'Connor in 2006. In this case, the mourning of the mayor and the use of Steelers symbols became a part of grieving the man as well as solidifying the bonds of Pittsburghers more broadly. During the funeral procession, the article notes that the mayor's son:

> will help escort his father's casket during the heavy-hearted procession from Mass to gravesite. Then, prior to the 8:30 p.m. kickoff at Heinz Field, he will

lead the official twirling of Terrible Towels, just as his father led the Steelers faithful in the incredible playoff run of last season. (Dvorchak 2006)

Mary Joyce Burger, a friend of the mayor and devoted fan, described the mayor and other fans as "all part of the Steeler *family* [. . .] a lot of our regulars work for the city and county and will be honor guards at the funeral, so we'll handle the occasion like a death in the *family*" (Dvorchak 2006, emphasis added). The notion of "family" used in conjunction with the fan group suggests levels of high solidarity and a blending of roles (both fan and kin).

This last example shows not only the incorporation of Steelers symbols and rituals into the grieving of a lost loved one and political figure, but the choice to describe other fans as family members communicates the significance of the Steelers community and their high level of group solidarity. Describing recent obstacles to tailgating in their customary space, Burger further reports that her

group has been moved several times during stadium and related construction, but they hope to occupy the same spot as last year. "They keep throwing obstacles our way. We'll find a way," she said. Which is the way the *Steeler Nation*, the *One Nation*, approaches life's challenges and season openers. (Dvorchak 2006, emphasis added)

The mayor's son leads the "official twirling of the Terrible Towels" and an interviewed friend describes Steelers fans as a "family" and "one nation," collectively engaging in family and nation activities such as dealing with grief and facing obstacles together. By comparing fans to family or a nation, the interviewee implies moral sentiments of devotion and loyalty to the group. Members rely on group symbols and rituals to grieve, comfort, honor, and persevere. Facing the obstacle of loss, they draw upon shared and well-known icons to help bring a sense of solidarity and shared feeling to the funeral ritual. In this way, they tap into the emotional resources embedded in these objects and practically use the energy gained from game day highs to serve as a salve for a city in mourning.

Steel(ers) City Life

The Steelers ultimately went on to play in the Super Bowl during the 2008–2009 season and ended up successfully winning the championship game, making them the first franchise in the NFL to boast six Super Bowl wins. This led to a fever pitch of Steelers interest around the city of Pittsburgh, including a victory parade downtown that caused one church to cancel confession (LaDow et al. 2009), public schools preemptively enacted a two-hour delay for classes scheduled for the Monday after the Super Bowl (Smydo 2009), and the mayor temporarily renamed the city of Pittsburgh to the "City of Sixburgh" (Lord 2009a). On a less convivial note, over one hundred fans in Pittsburgh were arrested the night of the Super Bowl for riotous behavior, with arson, drunk-driving, and "failure to disperse" as the most common explanations (McKinnon 2009; Schackner 2009). An estimated $500,000 was spent on policing the city the night of the Super Bowl (Lord 2009b).

Weddings, funerals, and even Super Bowl wins are relatively rare occasions. Yet my conversations with fans while tailgating suggested that family life can be imbued with Steelers fandom and the conception of family itself can be broadened to include fellow fans (as we saw earlier in the fan who describes the "Steelers Nation" as a family). Also indicative of the ways in which fandom shapes mundane life, the city of Pittsburgh itself has to continually reckon with the popularity and importance of the team. Anya Sostek (2008), reporter for the *Pittsburgh Post-Gazette*, writes about the impact of the Steelers' schedule on the lives of Pittsburghers and local business owners. Sostek summarizes:

> Scientists may argue whether a flap of a butterfly's wings in Brazil can set off a tornado in Texas, but there's no doubt that the release of the Steelers' schedule in April can determine not just the date of a design fair in Deutschtown, but also influence church concerts, high school alumni dinners, hotel rates, and even weddings.

Sostek goes on to describe the dismay experienced by a local couple that set their wedding date prior to the release of the schedule. The soon-to-be groom lamented after learning of a game scheduled in Philadelphia for the exact time of the wedding: "Most people who are going to come to our wedding are going to come to our wedding, but I could definitely see some people giving it a second thought." He later adds: "at least it's an away game" (Sostek 2008). Some friends and family advised the couple to include a television at the reception.

Realtors' scheduling house tours for the fall was another aspect of city life that was interrupted by Steelers fans. Real estate agents chose to delay planning of open houses until the Steelers schedule had been released. Jen Saffron, who organizes tours on the North Side, explained,

The number-one reason to have a house tour in our neighborhood is to promote the positive changes . . . it's really hard to do that when Steeler fans are drunk, screaming vulgarities, and urinating in our neighborhood. That's not our best foot forward.

While the schedule is a burden for some, it is a source of profit for local hotels that increase room rates for the nights before home games. "The phone calls started as soon as the schedule was released," said a hotelier. "They're all Steelers fans making multiple reservations for different games" (Sostek 2008).

In a more recent example, we can see how Steelers symbols became pervasive in the city of Pittsburgh in 2011 and in 2017 as the team played in the playoffs. Shown in Figure 3.1, nurses at a birth center dressed newborns in Terrible Towel blankets and Steelers beanies as their first outfits following birth. In coverage of the Steelers playoffs in 2011, *USA Today* reported on the unique practice:

In Pittsburgh, Terrible Towels are a birthright. A hospital in the Pittsburgh area is wrapping newborn babies this week in the yellow Terrible Towels favored by Steelers fans. It's in support of the team's run to Super Bowl XLV on Sunday. "They're born Steelers fans here in Pittsburgh," Sharon Johnson,

Figure 3.1 Steelers babies. Photograph by Haley Nelson.

clinical supervisor of the birth center at St. Clair Hospital told Patch.com. New father Justin Eitel was thrilled with the garb his daughter was given. "She can choose her religion, but she can't choose what team she likes," Eitel told Patch. com. (Leahy 2011)

In these examples, we see how life in the city is shaped in obvious and subtle ways by the importance of the team to fans. Police, realtors, wedding planners, and hoteliers must all work with and around this if they want to be effective in their jobs. Nurses who, as we saw in Chapter 2, are juggling so much (including their own emotional exhaustion) still found the time and energy to procure special outfits and to dress newborns in a festive way during the playoff season in 2011 and again in 2017. This, again, highlights the relevance of sports fandom beyond the moments of peak emotional energy generated at stadiums and shows the practical value of the emotional capital invested in sport symbols. Weddings, funerals, and births are all special events that some fans use not simply to display their devotion to the team, but during which they can draw on the useful and emotionally rich symbols of their team to make the event even more meaningful.

Of course, some might mock such uses of sports symbols as tasteless or crass. Such dismissals point to the fact that seeing such symbols as meaningful and useful for these types of events is the result of past practices developed with significant others over time. The fan habitus, like the nurse habitus described in Chapter 2, is learned and steeped in prior experiences that hone one's sense of taste in line with social location, including social class and family leisure pursuits. Though if the quote from Justin Eitel at the start of this chapter is any indication, this habitus starts at birth and becomes so ingrained in family life that "choosing a sports team" is almost out of the question. Practices of fandom, like the learned but eventually embodied practices of jobs and occupations, come to feel like second nature. These shape who we are—including our tastes and preferences in leisure and in celebrating important life events.

Fan Emotions across Geographic and Social Boundaries

In Pittsburgh and the larger region of western Pennsylvania, Steelers symbols (colors, logo, the Terrible Towel, etc.) are practical—they are ready at hand

and likely to be well-understood by others in the region. Yet part of what makes symbols useful is their ability to store and transport the emotional reserves of fandom across settings and across geographic boundaries. Part of their practicality is their elasticity in connecting diverse groups while remaining meaningful to fans. In his study of a Steelers bar in Fort Worth, Texas, Jon Kraszewski (2008) illustrates how far these meaningful symbols can travel while still finding a useful place among devoted fans. Despite living far from Pittsburgh and in an area with a rival team (the Dallas Cowboys are based in Texas), the fans that Kraszewski met petitioned a local bar to air Steelers games at their establishment and provide a space for an economically heterogeneous group to mingle, swap stories of their time living in or near Pittsburgh, and share familiar foods (pierogi) and drinks (Iron City beer). At a time when feelings of belonging and feeling at home appear unstable (Duyvendak 2011), sports fandom and the emotional capital contained in team symbols can be powerful resources for making and remaking a sense of belonging in new places.

Team symbols, it seems, can to an extent cut cross social class, gender, and racial ethnic lines—though men do seem to be the stereotypical fan base. During one experience tailgating, I arrived around 8 am at the Heinz Field parking lot. After about an hour, I decided to visit the Bettis Grille 36 (a bar and restaurant owned and named after a former Steelers player) so that I could use the restroom. I found a mixed group in terms of race and gender, but when I returned a bit later in the day to use the bathroom, the line for the men's room was notably longer than the women's line. While women were outnumbered in the early parts of the day when tailgating, more women and children arrived when the weather was warmer. From my field notes:

The home game against the Browns (December 28, 2008) took place on a particularly warm day, with temperatures in the mid- to high 50s. The warmer temperature seemed to draw more fans, especially children, which added a lighter, festive mood to the gathering. More vendors than before were set up outside the stadium and on the sidewalks. There were also games, much like carnival games, in which contestants attempt to maneuver through an inflated mini-football field without falling over or try to throw a football accurately into a target. Prizes included gift certificates or coupons to local business sponsors. Back with my band of tailgaters, we huddled less closely together and mingled more with the neighboring groups than we had on the prior, colder trip. We toasted a round of whiskey and, instead of taking it as though it were medicine against the cold—as we seemed to do prior to the Dallas game—this time there were smiles all around and even a small speech admonishing the Steelers to be victorious over the Browns.

Tailgating before games and watching games in sports bars are often activities steeped in alcohol. I saw fellow tailgaters arrive with kegs of beer, witnessed them doing beer bongs (using a funnel and tubing to quickly consume beer), and of course my own group shared a bottle of Crown Royal.

Certainly alcohol is an element that can contribute to the heightened emotions and loosening of inhibitions that we see among sports fans, including when they behave badly (Weiss 2013). But both the drinking and the excitement in anticipation of the game can break down barriers in the parking lot. When tailgating in parking lots, various social classes are more likely to intermingle. The beer choices (domestic macro-breweries) and vehicles (domestic vans, trucks, and SUVs) that were among most of the first arrivals to tailgate suggested a working- to middle-class demographic. This working-class ethos is further cultivated by the team's direct reference to steel workers; fans would embrace this element of working-class lore and imagery, with some choosing an outfit of beige-denim overalls with a black turtleneck and a proliferation among fans of Steelers-themed hardhats. In fact, the team's supposed representation of a working-class ethos is seen as one of the reasons for the success of the franchise in retaining such a devoted fan base (Luciew 2011). This might also explain the surprising reach of Steelers symbols into various aspects of fan and city life.

While sports fandom, and the emotional resources it provides, might cross gender and social class lines, sports are a sector of society that has always intersected directly with racial politics and social movements. We can see this with particular clarity in the recent protests and controversy surrounding Colin Kaepernick. Kaepernick was a quarterback for the San Francisco 49ers who used the singing of the national anthem before the start of a game as a time to draw public attention to the police shootings of black men and racial injustices in the criminal justice system. At first, he remained seated during the national anthem and then opted to kneel during the anthem (Maher 2019). His actions were seen as a form of public protest that to some disrespected the American flag and anthem (two other very potent symbols charged up with emotional capital), leading to booing from fans and accusations that Kaepernick was being unpatriotic. Later, it seems he was blackballed from the league and he successfully sued the league for conspiring to keep him from playing (Maher 2019).

The controversy surrounding Kaepernick can be further understood when we consider the practical role of emotions in fandom and the extent to which players are seen or not seen as sacred symbols by fans. The controversy surrounding Kaepernick's actions can be more fully appreciated when we consider that he is seen as disrupting the sacred symbols and sacred places held by fans (Remillard 2013), in addition to his supposed affront to the flag and national anthem. Despite taking a knee in the same seemingly respectful way that players kneel when in prayer or when another player is injured (Cook 2014), conservative commentators insisted on seeing his protest as disrespectful. Seen as contaminating sports with political activism—sports as a site where white-majority fans might hope to avoid political contention—seems to partly explain the vitriol and backlash his actions elicited. Thinking in terms of practice, we can see the community of NFL fans as largely defined by its ability to "move people to action, often by catalyzing strong, deep feelings" (P. H. Collins 2012, 447). While the symbol in question was the national anthem and American flag, the context of Kaepernick's protest (kneeling on the field) is also full of a different but potentially overlapping set of symbols that can catalyze strong feelings.

The case of Kaepernick highlights the important issue of race—a long-standing issue in American sports and athletics (Shropshire 1996). Symbolic interactionism and poststructuralist theories, including Bourdieu's approach to social practice, can come up short in providing a full explanation of the *racial* hierarchy that we see in the divisions within American football (Lapchick 2012). Patricia Hill Collins (2012) has recently worked to integrate pragmatism with an intersectional approach to social inequalities—an approach that sees the categories of gender, race, and social class as lived in complex, interwoven ways. Power and inequality are central to an intersectional approach to social life. As discussed in Chapter 1, Collins leans on the notion of a community of shared meaningful symbols that pragmatism offers while turning to intersectionality to highlight the role of power and inequality in how a community and its symbols might be used. The following is an extensive quote from her article, which I use to show how an emotion practice approach to symbols can illuminate the racial hierarchy in the NFL and the controversy surrounding Kaepernick:

[. . .] neighborhoods, schools, jobs, religious institutions, recreational facilities, and physical and cyberspace marketplaces are the institutional expressions of social inequalities of race, class, gender, age, ethnicity, religion, sexuality, and ability. Typically hierarchical, these structures offer *unequal opportunities and rewards*. Whether intentional or not, people use the construct of community to make sense of and organize all aspects of social structure, including their political responses to their situations. Similarly, social institutions *use the symbols and organizational principles of community to organize social inequalities*. Communities thus become major vehicles that link individuals to social institutions. (P. H. Collins 2012, 446, emphasis added)

We can think of Steelers fans as a mid-level community, similar to what Collins describes here, in that it provides emotional resources (via charged-up symbols) to its fans. As we saw in prior sections, nearly all of the settings that Collins identifies (neighborhoods, schools, marketplaces) became transformed during the playoff season with Steelers symbols. In this way, members of a community "use" these symbols as a "construct of community" in order to make sense of and organize the social world.

But *who* charges up these resources and *who* taps into their practical uses is not evenly distributed across demographics. In fact, the generation of emotional capital as a resource that imbues meaningful symbols is itself an outcome of unequal opportunities and rewards in the community and in the United States at large. African American men make up a large percentage of American football players and are statistically overrepresented in the sport when compared to the general population (Lapchick 2012). And it is through their expenditure of bodily capital (Wacquant 1995) as body labor (like Hochschild's "emotional labor") while training and playing that the entire ecosystem of energy (physical transformed into emotional) becomes possible. The presence of a racial hierarchy means that a largely black, minority class is tasked with providing the bodily capital needed to charge up team symbols with emotional capital. This minority class, in turn, takes on the health risks of concussions and injuries endemic to the game.[5] These symbols, then, move to weddings, funerals, special and mundane events in the lives of a racially heterogeneous (but majority white) fan base,[6] while also being used for a variety of commercial interests, as I detail next.

To be sure, players are paid hefty sums for the individual risks they take. Notably, though, star quarterbacks are paid some of the highest, most extreme salaries ("NFL Positional Payrolls" n.d.); have lower concussion rates than other positions like tight ends, running backs, and wide receivers (Nathanson et al. 2016); and are more likely to be white (Reid and McManus n.d.). Certainly, the large financial compensation packages provided to star players speak to the value of players' bodily capital, which is needed to cultivate the emotional capital that charges up sports fans and their symbols. But this does not change the fact that something of value to many is extracted from a minority few who bear the brunt of the sport's physical health costs. Even after the sport has exacted a health premium from players, the league's use of "race-norming" further disadvantages black players seeking payouts through the concussion settlement program (Madden, Park, and Smith 2021). The cost of a collective good, in this case, is borne predominantly by a minority group. It is in this reinscription of America's enduring racial hierarchy, where costs and benefits (and opportunities for livelihoods, Pager 2008; Wilson 2010) are so disproportionately distributed, that sports fandom and the sports economy appear at its ugliest, over and above instances of fan violence or hooliganism.

This returns us to one of the opening quotes from the beginning of this chapter. As comedian D. L. Hughley notes, "The only time white people watch black people is if we're singing, dancing, or running a football" (2018). While sports fandom and its symbols are part of an ecosystem of emotional meanings, at the root of the pleasure, excitement, and effervescence of fandom is the risky bodily capital expended by a racial minority denied many alternative economic opportunities. While an emotion practice approach draws our focus to the practical uses of emotional capital housed in transportable symbols, it is important to affirm that as with so many other social tools of contemporary life, practicality is not synonymous with justice or moral goodness. If we are to rethink the economy of bodily and emotional capital that circulates in sports fandom, we have to consider the sources of its emotional payoffs and who bears its costs.

With this unevenness of cost and benefits and investment and extraction in mind, we can return to the use of sports symbols in grocery stores that sparked my own personal interest in studying fandom as a sociologist. In this case, a particular grocery store chain presents sports merchandise not only as a commodity for purchase but also as an object of decoration aimed at transferring fans' good feelings associated with the team to their time spent in the store. We can see the red and white logo of this same store (a regional chain, Giant Eagle) affixed to the signs that decorated downtown Pittsburgh in the winter of 2010 pictured in Figure 3.2. Here both the city and the company

Figure 3.2 Street signs on Grant Street in Pittsburgh, Pennsylvania, supporting the Steelers before Super Bowl XLV. January 31, 2011. Text on the banners reads: "Congratulations 2010 AFC CHAMPIONS" with Steelers logo and Giant Eagle (grocery store chain) logo in the foreground banner and Heinz Ketchup logo in the far banner. The Pittsburgh city seal appears in the bottom left corner of each banner.

join forces to try to capitalize on fan emotions, to stoke feelings of connection to the city and an affinity for particular, seemingly local businesses.

Despite the fact that sports symbols are forged in a racial structure of uneven social opportunities and rewards, for fans these symbols can provide intense emotional payoff without risking the type of conflict that other symbols—such as religious or political symbols—might evoke. They are practical in the sense that they can transport emotional resources within families, neighborhoods, and cities. While charged up by the success of the team and the intensity with which fans engage as spectators, these symbols retain their practical use in crossing social divides and geographic space. Through players' investment of bodily capital, fans reap emotional rewards. Cities and corporations can tap into the energy-generating inertia of athlete and fan practices. And this can lead to an ever-expanding cache of objects for consumption, ready to be charged up by fans who take them to sports bars, tailgating in parking lots, spectating at the stadium, or by displaying them in living rooms where games are watched. In transferring this emotional capital into financial capital, we can see more clearly the practical value of these symbols. Without attending to this value, the dizzying array of sports memorabilia, objects, clothing, and use of logos is challenging to explain.

Conclusion

In this chapter, I zoomed in on one particular form of leisure—sports fandom—in order to better understand not only sports fans themselves but also the ways in which emotions can be seen from the lens of an emotion practice approach. Using the concepts of emotional capital and habitus can help us see what comes before and after peak emotions found in sports spectatorship. Fans of the Pittsburgh Steelers show their loyalty by taking on and embodying the symbols of their team—the colors, logo, and signature object of the Terrible Towel in this case. In doing so, they are turning to readily available resources for generating excitement and a sense of belonging, and even deep meaning for some. This connects them to family members, friends, neighbors, and local businesses, creating a sense of belonging. While weddings, funerals, births, and Super Bowls highlight the deep meanings fandom can have, these connections go beyond isolated events. This is not a frivolous identity, but one that is tied to the city of Pittsburgh, to family traditions, and to everyday connections with other fans. These feelings are not fleeting but carry over into mundane aspects of everyday life—scheduling events, planning family dinners, dressing children, and even in walking down streets lined with Steelers banners.

Since my primary data collection in 2008 and 2009, PennLive reporter John Luciew offers a more recent summary of the pervasiveness and importance of fandom to the city of Pittsburgh and its residents:

> Steelers faithful do not simply cheer on a football team. They see themselves and their city reflected in the team's mixture of blue-collar work ethic, family ownership and tough-as-nails mentality. So when Steelers fans want to show their black-and-gold allegiance, they don't just don jerseys and leave it at that. They make themselves part of the team, intertwining their own life experiences with those of the Steelers until the two are inseparable. (Luciew 2011, updated in 2019)

For many fans, their loyalty to the team is not compartmentalized to game days but pervades their lives every day of the week. Understanding the emotional payoff of fandom is key for understanding why sports have such a draw in contemporary American life and globally (Halldorsson 2021). Worldwide, the Olympics, international and local soccer matches, youth leagues, and the like are all part of the social rituals of families, communities, and nations. Understanding their appeal means taking the emotional capital that they provide seriously.

The portrait of fans that I have tried to present here helps us move beyond a dismissal of fans as frenzied and maniacal—notions that are part of the lineage of the word "fan" itself (from "fanatic"). Such framings can be dehumanizing and they miss the practical use of emotions that fans are engaged in, even when this is not an overt, conscious strategy. In line with Bourdieu's conception of habitus, feeling involves the practical knowledge that is now embedded in the body. These are the product of our past social practices, be they in family life, friendship circles, or in something as simple as a trip to the grocery store. And they are also futuristic—a force in pushing us toward the next moment that promises to restock our emotional energy. With a stock of objects (as symbols) connected to the emotions and meanings of fandom, we can shape future moments of connection with family friends, coworkers, and even strangers. In this way, past practices distilled in symbols become powerful resources for future social bonds.

Because of the power of fandom to solidify bonds through emotionally infused symbols, it is not too surprising to see fans like Justin Eitel, quoted in *USA Today* at the start of this chapter, say that his newborn daughter has free choice when it comes to her religion, but no choice when it comes to her favored football team. In this way, emotions serve as practical sedimentations of an individual's biographical experiences engrained over time through participation in family and community events, as well as the cementing glue that bonds individuals to groups larger than themselves. To allow his daughter to forego such a powerful tool for connection would be highly impractical. Thinking of the fan community itself as a family, a "country," and of more importance than religion points to the strength of the group solidarity created through the energizing rituals that transform the physical capital of players into emotional capital for fans.

Fandom helps us to see another facet of emotions as practical engagements with the social world, and in as much as this involves the use and drawing on of charged-up symbols, fandom can seem to be a relatively positive and energizing experience. Yet, when we look at the racial hierarchy within a sport like American football, we see that it is the physical capital (and risk) of primarily African American men that serves as the bedrock for the emotional, financial, and cultural resources that are generated in this particular field. In this way, concepts from practice theory help us to link emotional payoffs with bodily capital investments and the social inequalities that underlie and are maintained in the social field of sports. This adds to our understanding of how emotion practices reinforce existing social inequalities. Nurses, as we saw in Chapter 2, nonconsciously feel with certain patients and disengage from others to conserve precious emotional resources. Social class and race were implicated in their expense of emotional capital on some but not others. Sports fandom adds a different layer. The entire ecosystem of capital generated in the sport of American football rests on the bodily capital of a racial minority group that historically, and to this day, faces disproportionate exploitation and devaluation. In the next chapter, I turn to a different empirical context—the responses of social media users to the 2013–2016 Ebola outbreak—to further examine how emotions operate as practical modes in the context of digital as well as political spaces. Here we will again see the utility of using concepts like habitus and emotional capital to understand the practical use of emotion for forging social connections in the seemingly disembodied space of online communication.

4

#Ebola

Practical Feelings in Digital Spaces

If ebola smelled like pumpkin spice we would all be dead
—Tweet, September 2014

Scientists: Don't freak out about Ebola. Everyone: *Panic!*
Scientists: Freak out about climate change. Everyone: LOL!
—Tweet, October 2014

I am writing this chapter during a historic moment. In the spring of 2020, all nonessential shops in the Netherlands have closed, schools have closed, and universities have switched to offering all classes online. All public interaction must take place at a distance of 1.5 meters. In Amsterdam, a city known for its coziness and infrastructure for cyclists and pedestrians, this is no easy feat. "Shelter in place" and "stay at home" orders along with mask mandates have been implemented at different points in the pandemic's timeline throughout the United States and around the world. International news outlets are covering both the COVID-19 pandemic and the related economic disruptions it has caused around the clock. It is a surreal moment that raises many questions, both for the natural as well as the social sciences.

Even before COVID-19, though, social scientists noted the seeming ubiquity of disasters and health threats around the world. Sociologist Ulrich Beck identified such a trend as part of a new "risk society" (Beck 1992). According to Beck, risks—including health risks stemming from new zoonotic pathogens—are a primary product of modernization. The threat of crises and outbreaks can begin to feel more common, and as the global community confronts the COVID-19 pandemic, it seems as though life will never go back to a prepandemic conception of normal. The words we use to describe these events, words like "emergency" or "natural disaster" might even misrepresent what are, in reality, "*gradually developing, predictable, and enduring* clusters of events and interactions" that are "in fact products of human action" (Calhoun 2004, 376, emphasis added). The World Health Organization (WHO) and the US Centers for Disease Control (CDC) have each devoted considerable time and resources to anticipating and preparing for a global pandemic, suggesting, in line with activists and scholars, that there is no such thing as a "natural" disaster (Hartman et al. 2006). All disasters, including pandemics, unfold in ways shaped by human planning and intervention as well as their counterparts of neglect and indifference. Risk and its presumed antidote of resilience appear as countervailing forces in a worldview constrained by neoliberalism and cuts to the social safety net (Bracke 2016).

Media sociologist David Altheide further theorizes that increasing amounts of fear overlap with an increased perception of risk in modern society. According to Altheide, a risk-related "discourse of fear" includes "the pervasive communication, symbolic awareness, and expectation that danger and risk are a central feature of everyday life" (Altheide 2013, 230). Along with an increase in perceived and real threats, social media platforms are now established spaces where our everyday expression of thoughts and emotions are formed and broadcast. "[D]igital hyperconnectivity is a defining fact of our time" (R. Brubaker 2020, 771), and the digital is inherently interconnected with offline reality (Jurgenson 2011). We not only consume information about emerging risks through formal news channels, but we also consume the ongoing flow of personal and news information that streams through social media sites. Perhaps more important than the information gained through these platforms, we now turn to social media to express how we feel about emerging risks and connect with others during moments of uncertainty (Döveling, Harju, and Sommer 2018). No longer constrained to the face to face, our feelings about viral outbreaks can themselves "go viral" through the online mediums that many engage with on a daily basis.

In this chapter, I turn to the case of the Ebola outbreak and how Twitter users responded to its development. Predating the COVID-19 pandemic, the Ebola outbreak is not only useful for understanding how people respond to an emerging threat—threats that might begin to feel more common— but also how they use social media platforms to express as well as manage risk emotions collectively. With the Ebola outbreak now over, we can better trace the initial and peak reactions on social media and consider parallels to the COVID-19 pandemic as it has unfolded. Taking an emotion practice approach to this case highlights how various, overlapping emotions flow in these digital spaces during a time of uncertainty and risk. Despite the abstract nature of digital interactions, embodied feelings and the threat of real bodily harm remain relevant to how social media users respond to an evolving outbreak like Ebola.

As highlighted in the preceding chapters, an emotion practice approach attends to both intentional and unintentional practices as well as the spread of popular cultural symbols (including sports symbols detailed in Chapter 3) throughout social domains. In digital spaces, such symbols take on new meanings and sources of energy in memes, videos, and posts in which users respond to events and public debates. At its core, this *practical* approach to emotion assumes that even in the digital spaces of social media use, emotions are modes of orienting oneself and others toward emerging practical demands. The visually based modes of communication that we see exhibited on social media seem to partially compensate for the lack of physical co-presence that is typically needed to generate energy and effervescence (R. Collins 2004), but this move to the digital does not necessarily mean that embodied feelings are no longer relevant—only that they are now cast in new representations still linked to embodied practices. The popularity of the shorthand "lol" [laughing out loud] and the "face with tears of joy" emoji ("Emoji Statistics" n.d.) both point to the digital mediation of embodied emotions, and as we will see, these engrained digital practices remain entrenched even in the context of an evolving public health threat.

Social Media and Digital Emotions

Social media provides a platform where a large number of diverse members of the public can connect and respond to current news in an informal way. The estimated number of social network users worldwide was 2.95 billion in 2019 ("Number of Social Network Users Worldwide from 2017 to 2025" n.d.). In 2014, Twitter had roughly 288 million active monthly users and over 300 million monthly users in 2019 ("Number of Monthly Active Twitter Users Worldwide from 1st Quarter 2010 to 1st Quarter 2019" n.d.). Using these platforms often means understanding and adopting new norms of interaction and systems of communication and meaning. Various groups and subcultures form on these sites and can intermix. With changes in technology, digital infrastructure, and uptake of new digital habits, these changes offer researchers "a new way of knowing society" (Marres 2017, 2). Scholarship on our digital lives has looked at the "digital divide" in access to the Internet and online resources (van Dijk 2006) and how emotions are shared and shaped by new technologies and online cultures (Döveling, Harju, and Sommer 2018). Digital spaces are sites where both dominant emotion norms—what emotions are appropriate when and how these should be expressed—can be shared as well subverted and contested. As Döveling et al. argue, "social media offer a unique platform for such contestation" (2018, 2).

Social media platforms themselves shape the interactions that unfold. In the case of Twitter, a character limit per tweet, feeds of tweets in which each competes for the attention of other users, and an interface that fosters the use of images and videos to accompany commentary all combine to provide a particular experience to a user as well as particular constraints on its use. Yet media scholars recognize digital space (particularly social networking sites) as places where emotions can expand in their social, as well as temporal and spatial reach (J. R. Brubaker, Hayes, and Dourish 2013). While each social media platform has a distinct set of constraints and possibilities, in the case of Twitter, scholars find that this space is a "milieu of informality, conversation, and humor" (Holton and Lewis 2011, 1). This can create expectations within users about the types of content one is likely to encounter on this platform and the types of emotion norms governing the interactions that take place there. As a result, users who might not typically joke about topics like epidemics or the threat of death might find themselves engaging in these *engrained digital practices* in line with the norms of informality that they have habitually encountered and enacted on the popular site.

Scholars studying online interactions tend to emphasize the information flows that these new mediums allow, often overlooking emotions altogether or framing emotions as inherently problematic (McIntyre 2018). The limited research that applies a practice approach to digital spaces has focused on how digital networks inform an individual's social capital—that is, their connection to other people—and how this social capital fosters the transfer of *knowledge, ideas,* and *information* (Julien 2015). But this prior work does not directly attend to the sharing of emotions, often through energy-infused symbols in these settings. In the context of digital interactions, such symbols often take the form of memes. The power of memes—a combination of images with text—lies in their ability to succinctly encapsulate a shared knowledge base that can differentiate group insiders from outsiders. Specialized language, images of known celebrities or figures known only among the group, and shared sequences for developing jokes and humor all come together in a single meme (often connected to current events) that functions both to share information but to also, and most critically, foster feelings of belonging and camaraderie among members of a distinct subculture. Humor, like rumors, are an "affect-mobilizing part of the social realities lived by people" (Barrios 2017, 113) and thus should not be dismissed as irrelevant.

Thinking along the lines of an emotion practice approach, the practice of sharing memes in online interactions is simultaneously the sharing of information and cultivation of emotions within a shared, mediated environment. In fact, it is in drawing the boundaries of distinction around those who "get" or know the many layers of meaning within a meme and those that do not "get" it, that feelings of belonging and inclusion are fostered along with feelings of mirth and pleasure. This fits with Chris Julien's claim that in online interactions "knowledge is concealed from those who do not have the distinguishing capabilities necessary to perceive specific knowledge" (2015, 362). In taking an emotion practice approach we can better appreciate that this act of concealment is also a way to preserve and shore up the emotional capital embedded in meaningful symbols. These feelings, in a practical sense, confirm shared group membership generally, and in the context of an emerging outbreak, confirm connection at a time of threat from an external, real-world force. One defining feature of memes, as we will see in the examples that follow, is that they not only convey information, but through layers of meaning, they can generate humor and amusement, as well as feelings of belonging and solidarity among a group of insiders who have access to the knowledge needed to be in on the joke.

Humor in Digital Interactions

Sharing memes through digital spaces involves a bid for "a name, a place, a function, within a group or institution" through which we can "escape the contingency, finitude, and ultimate absurdity of existence" (Wacquant 2008, 264). Like the current event memes that Julien (2015) identifies, there are layers of humor within memes and online jokes that render them appealing to broad online publics. For the most part, a superficial level of meaning can be gleaned even by outsiders. Through the use of distinct language and symbols, layers of concealed meaning are added. This practice of layering meaning is similar to humor practices in other contexts, such as disaster humor (Kuipers

2005). To tease apart the meanings embedded in digital humor practices, a look at prior sociological considerations of humor is helpful.

Humor scholars highlight the inherently ambiguous nature of humor and the need to better integrate humor studies with the sociology of emotion (Kuipers 2008). Sociologist Gary Alan Fine focuses explicitly on the group as the main unit of analysis when it comes to understanding humor in context. Fine and DeSoucey argue that "joking is embedded; it occurs within the context of an on-going relationship. As a general rule, joking does not occur between strangers" (2005, 2). Yet, in online spaces, interactants are not likely well-known to each other, nor do they necessarily form part of a group beyond that of "Twitter user." This raises questions about how emotions generally, and humor specifically, are shared in ways that allow for broad appeal among users who might share little background knowledge of each other. As discussed earlier, one explanation for how groups are formed online is through the sharing of current event memes that are layered with meanings that include concealed knowledge of past popular memes and phrases.

Sociologist Linda Francis has explicitly traced the links between humor practices and emotion management theory. Humor can be a strategy for working over emotions and in this way can be conceptualized as a type of emotion work (Francis 1994) that goes beyond the individual making the joke to shape the "emotional tenor of the group" (1994, 154). Emotion management theory, as I argued previously, can close off consideration of the unintentional and offers a limited conceptualization of collective emotions. Following other media scholars, thinking of emotions in terms of practices can take us "beyond individualized feelings to instead explore the flows of emotion" in digital spaces (Döveling, Harju, and Sommer 2018, 3). Thinking along the lines of an emotion practice approach can also draw our attention to both the intentional and unintentional ways in which emotion (and humor) practices might be enacted. In these digital spaces, diverse and perhaps incongruous social media users might share little in common other than a mutual interest or common friend. Otherwise unknown to each other and hardly constituting the types of close-knit groups often studied by sociologists, what humor practices make up the interactions between loosely connected users online? While Francis suggests that interactions between strangers would be "circumscribed largely by etiquette" (1994, 155), violations of norms and crossing boundaries into the absurd are a key hallmark of humor. How do these humor practices unfold online and in the context of an evolving public health threat—a context that, on its face, seems to hardly be fodder for the types of humor practices endemic to social media platforms?

Turning to the case of Twitter responses during the Ebola outbreak, we can see this as a useful space for examining how diverse users only loosely connected to one another respond to an emerging health threat, including how humor and other emotion practices are enacted during such a threat. While prior research on Twitter has emphasized its health surveillance potential (Odlum and Yoon 2015) and note its role in spreading health information of varying degrees of veracity (Merchant, Elmer, and Lurie 2011; Vance, Howe, and Dellavalle 2009), little research has taken up Twitter data to understand the emotion practices that emerge in the context of a public health threat. Looking at emotion practices in the context of a public health threat is particularly appropriate, given that journalists and citizens "flock to social media when disruptive events take place" (Döveling, Harju, and Sommer 2018, 5). In the sections that follow, I first summarize the events related to the 2013–2016 Ebola outbreak, including turning points which shaped the global conversation about Ebola. Following that overview, I then turn to what I found when I analyzed Twitter responses to the Ebola outbreak and the emotion practices, including uses of humor, used on this popular social media platform.

The 2013–2016 Ebola Outbreak

While it has undoubtedly faded from collective memory in light of the COVID-19 pandemic, one recent disruptive event was the outbreak of the Ebola virus that began in 2013 and lasted until the spring of 2016. Spreading across multiple continents, the virus infected over 28,000 people and killed over 11,000 (World Health Organization 2016). The 2013–2016 outbreak was the worst in the disease's history, catalyzed by the increasingly urban and interconnected nature of contemporary societies, and infecting caregivers at unprecedented rates (World Health Organization 2014). Its highly contagious nature and devastating effects on the body make it a uniquely terror-inducing illness. The vast majority of cases were concentrated in the West African countries of Guinea, Liberia, and Sierra Leone. Yet the hint of cross-continental spread catalyzed concern far and wide. Ultimately, the virus would spread to seven other countries outside of West Africa: Italy, Mali, Nigeria, Senegal, Spain, the United Kingdom, and the United States.

While the WHO declared the Ebola outbreak a Public Health Emergency of International Concern (PHEIC) on August 8, 2014, it was not until the cases of Thomas Eric Duncan in Dallas, Texas, and Teresa Romero in Madrid, Spain, that international concern about the epidemic reached peak intensity (Ihekweazu 2017; Sastry and Lovari 2017). Both Romero and Duncan were diagnosed with Ebola roughly around September 30, 2014,[1] and we can see a large spike in Ebola-related discourse on Twitter around this time frame. Sifter, a Twitter archive service, estimated roughly 700,000 Ebola-related tweets the week before September 30 (September 23, 2014–September 29, 2014) and over 6 million the week after (September 30, 2014–October 6, 2014). This growth suggests that this date was an important turning point in the global Ebola conversation. Further attesting to the international public interest in the outbreak, the term "Ebola" itself was the third most searched-for word or phrase on the Internet in 2014 (Google.com 2015).

In order to look both before and during this peak interest, I sampled a selection of tweets the week before September 30 (September 23–29) and the week after the announcement of Duncan and Romero's diagnoses (September 30–October 6). This allows us to get a sense of how social media users were responding to the outbreak as it unfolded over the course of this two-week window as well as how responses might have changed with the diagnoses of Duncan and Romero—notable for being the first instances of diagnosis outside of West Africa. Using these data, we can gain a better understanding of the emotional contours of digital practices—specifically how emotions operate as practical resources during an outbreak, even in the relatively disembodied and seemingly superficial spaces of social media platforms where users interact.

#Ebola in Week 1: Twitter Reactions before the Case of Duncan

International interest and concern surrounding the Ebola epidemic grew over the course of the month of September 2014 and centered on its location in West Africa and the need to take quick action in order to save lives and stop the spread. Then President Obama spoke on September 16 of the threat that Ebola poses to national and global security and announced that the US government would be sending troops and medical supplies to West Africa to assist with treatment and containment. With Obama taking the stage at that point in the development of the epidemic, his speech and the various press releases from nonprofit and international aid organizations would come to dominate social media discussions of Ebola in the week of September 23.

As the threat remained "far away" to most Americans and Western Europeans during this period, Twitter users shared primarily abstract reports about the outbreak, as well as personal reflections of concern, suspicion, and some jokes. Press releases and posts from organizations like the WHO, United Nations (UN), UNICEF (United Nations Children's Fund), and Doctors Without Borders were common. Tweets from news outlets included primarily matter-of-fact reports on the outbreak in terms of the case count and death toll:

> Death toll from Ebola in West Africa has climbed to more than 2,800, the World Health Organization says
> Ebola toll passes 2,800: WHO
> RT @nytimes: Updated: What you need to know about the Ebola outbreak

The top, retweeted tweets during this time made the link to established media outlets and health organizations explicit by using the mention function on Twitter (the "@" allows a user to mention another user). Some of the top mentions were to CNN, NYT, BBC, UNICEF, and WHO. Thus, along with there being fewer overall tweets referencing Ebola during this week, qualitatively there is a focus on communicating specific information about the epidemic's development using established news outlets and international health organizations as sources. These tweets included information about how to modify behavior to avoid catching the virus as well as treatment options that could paint a more optimistic picture than the raw statistics on the outbreak's development would suggest.

> RT @WHO: #Ebola is very infectious even after death. Pay respect from at least 1 metre away, without touching
> RT @UNICEF: #Ebola is not a death sentence. Early treatment means a much better chance of survival.

While "hard facts" about the Ebola outbreak circulated primarily through established, mainstream sources, there were examples of users discussing fear openly. However, tweets during this week that do discuss panic or fear tended to refer to the panic of others—of "locals" in West Africa, for example, and not of the tweet author or other social media users themselves. For example, the following tweet communicates this in highlighting the fear of "locals" in an "African village":

RT @DailyMirror: Ebola victims in African village "rise from the dead" causing panic and fear among locals

In this way, the emotions of social media users are not frequently directly expressed, but the emotions of others closer to the outbreak are prioritized. While this Daily Mirror headline appears highly sensational, it highlights the emphasis of most tweets at the time on events happening "over there" and the need to turn to news sources (mainstream or otherwise) for information on events rather than respond personally to the outbreak.

Yet, even in this week of Twitter responses to Ebola, when the outbreak had not yet reached peak international interest, we see tensions in what the "appropriate" emotional response should be to this evolving outbreak. For example, concerns about overreaction are already discussed in week 1 of the dataset, before international media interest would reach its highest peak:

Media Attention on Ebola Can Be Alarmist

Criticism of the media for causing alarm was present even in the week before Duncan and Romero would be diagnosed. This practice highlights the role of social media (and social media users to an extent) as seeing themselves as operating outside of traditional media sources and a site for countering not only dominant news frames of an issue (Qin 2015) but the emotional framing of an issue.

Despite claims that the media was being alarmist or overreacting to the threat of Ebola, we also see the WHO jockeying for international attention and calling for a more aggressive response to the outbreak:

EBOLA ALARM WHO warns 20,000 could be infected by November

Thus, even in this week before cases emerged outside of West Africa, we see ambiguity in what constitutes an overreaction or underreaction to the outbreak. While news reports emphasized the growing threat, they simultaneously emphasized the fact that Ebola reaching US soil remained highly improbable. Mirroring this cognitive ambiguity was a visceral ambiguity about if and how one should feel in response to new developments. One user seemed to perfectly capture the mixed messages news consumers experience in the following tweet (edited lightly for anonymity):

> Hey—remember when that Ebola outbreak was no big deal? The UN just declared it an international public health risk

And in another heavily shared tweet from week 1, users called attention to both media sensationalism and the misplacement of panic when it comes to Ebola versus other threats to human well-being:

> Fox News panic over Ebola. 100% of scientists say not to. 99% of scientists panic over climate change. Fox News says not to.

If and *how* to feel fear remained an open question as users struggled to decide what emotions made sense in the current context. In another example of this ambiguity, one Twitter user cautiously combined fear and science:

> I don't like using "scary" to describe science, but @NEJM #ebola projection is

Thus, while information on the development of the epidemic, how Ebola is spread to others, and what organizations and governments are doing to combat the disease were circulated heavily during this week, such information was intermixed with critiques of news outlets and ambiguity in how to feel. This ambiguity suggests that emotion norms or feeling rules are not well-established in this context. When feeling rules are unclear, users must try to calibrate their emotions and expressions to fit an uncertain and novel event. As the habitus is both structured (by past practices) and structuring (in anticipation of future practices), novel moments mean that past practices can only provide limited guidance to individuals. Users can no longer rely upon the "pre-verbal taking-for-granted of the world that flows from practical sense" (Bourdieu 1990, 68) when facing novel scenarios infused with inherent uncertainty, and in this case, the threat of real bodily harm. This points to emerging public health threats as times or micro-moments of rupture with past embodied and digital practices.

Despite elements of disruption and uncertainty, even in week 1 we see some users return to the established well of humor practices that are common on social media, and particularly Twitter, where "humor is both expected and rewarded" (J. L. Davis, Love, and Killen 2018, 3899). Even in the context of discussing the Ebola outbreak, users made jokes and shared memes and vines (a video-sharing tool similar to TikTok) related to Ebola. Overall, jokes and humor were less pronounced in this week (compared to week 2), but one popular tweet—quoted at the start of this chapter—used humor to connect Ebola with the seasonal changes associated with autumn:

If ebola smelled like pumpkin spice we would all be dead

Interestingly, the joke does not center on fear directly, but rather on taking a self-deprecating stance that consumers (as "we") are obsessed with pumpkin spice flavors in September. Part of the humor here relates to the absurdity of placing something threatening next to something silly. As Francis describes this practice: "Reducing something threatening to something trivial can provide people with a welcome escape from discomfort, stress, or embarrassment. Humor, in other words, can be a form of dissipating threat" (1994, 151). With such humor practices already well-established as routine in digital spaces like Twitter, it is not surprising to see these practices continue even in reaction to an emerging public health threat—a threat that was classified by the WHO as a "public health emergency of international concern" on August 8, 2014 (World Health Organization 2015).

Another popular joke shared during week 1 was the following, sent in accompaniment with an image of Tom Ford soap:

This soap is $195, it better wash Ebola, wash HIV, wash Malaria, It better wash all my sins away

This joke also engages in a practice of self-deprecation that has no clear "out-group." Indeed, like the pumpkin spice joke, it invites the audience to try to stand outside of our own consumer culture in a way that can be inclusive to anyone willing to take such a stance (and willing to irreverently place Ebola, pumpkin spice, and fancy soap in the same category). In this way, soap and pumpkin spice jokes allow for wide acceptance by not denigrating a specific, excluded group, although the plight of Ebola sufferers is certainly sidelined in these jokes. This relative inclusivity might explain the popularity of these types of humorous tweets. Their timely connection to current events, self-deprecating stance, and attempt to "punch up" at consumer culture generally might make them especially appealing to a broad swath of Twitter users. In this way, feelings of amusement and connection can expand across diverse social collectives who are otherwise relative strangers, completely unknown to each other except through these types of digital exchanges on social media sites.

#Ebola in Week 2: Twitter Reactions after the Case of Duncan

Beginning October 1, 2014, after the diagnoses of Spanish nurse Teresa Romero and Thomas Eric Duncan in Texas, news outlets were covering Ebola developments around the clock (Ihekweazu 2017). As the Ebola timeline developed, we can see changes in how Twitter users responded to the threat. Fear and humor are present in both weeks, but in terms of the share of tweets referencing fear or humor, these would increase in October. Fear and humor were evident in 10 percent and 6 percent of tweets in week 1, respectively. In week 2, we identified fear in 16 percent of tweets and humor in 38 percent of tweets. The nature of how fear and humor were enacted also seemed to change. As noted earlier, the case of Thomas Eric Duncan, a Liberian man who flew to Dallas, Texas, and would be later diagnosed with and die from Ebola, was a clear turning point in the discussion of the evolving outbreak. His case significantly amplified interest in Ebola as well as a sense that a threat was now "closer." More individual users, in addition to news outlets and nonprofit organizations, reacted to the news of Ebola in the first week in October. In this sense, the "alarmist" practices of the media did not have the same influence as an actual change in the outbreak's development. Like Johnson's (1988) fire evacuees, it was not until actual flames and smoke became visible (an Ebola case on US soil) that Twitter came alive with interest (including expressions of fear and humor).

Qualitatively, we can see a change in tone, as Ebola was less an abstract event and increasingly seen as a personal threat. For example, statements like "HOLD UP WE MIGHT HAVE EBOLA" in all caps and the phrase "And so it begins," crowded out the generic news summaries that were most dominant on the platform in week 1. Several prominent tweets from week 2 capture this shift:

The Ebola virus is super scary, hopefully it can be contained!
Retweet this in 15 seconds or you're gonna get Ebola!

Ebola is the devils [sic] disease 😩 [tired face] but it will not touch me
I am covered by the blood of Jesus. In JESUS name we pray amen 🙏
[folded hands]

Instead of "scary" or "ebola scare" being used to describe science or the situation in West Africa, as it had been used in week 1, it now became more commonly used to describe one's *own* feelings and catalyzed retweeted prayers and chain-letter like calls for retweets. Instead of discussing the fear of "others," the fear of users became more prominent in this second week following the first Ebola case in the United States.

In week 2, there was also increased discussion of "Dallas" and "Texas," and we saw an increase in Twitter users discussing, facetiously, that they plan to "never leave the house," "flee to Alaska," and that Twitter users took the virus more seriously ("this Ebola shit serious," "oh shit ebola reached [U.S./European City]"). Many jokes and memes during week 2 connected with celebrities or popular culture, similar to the "pumpkin spice" joke discussed earlier. These included references to popular films like *Mean Girls*, *Monsters, Inc*, *Dory*, *I Am Legend*, and television shows like *Spongebob Squarepants*. Images of Akon, Will Smith, Lindsey Lohan, Kermit the Frog (an image in which he is seated with his head turned sideways and mouth slightly open to suggest surprise), and other celebrity figures were used to add levity and channel the uncertainty of the present moment into well-known tropes and humor devices.

Following humor scholarship, we can see this incorporation of popular culture figures as a blurring of the real and unreal. An emerging global pandemic seems to be the realm of fiction (for example, in movies like *Contagion* and Stephen King's novel *The Stand*). Unprecedented events can be experienced as if we ourselves are living in an apocalyptic movie, as we have little routine knowledge outside of Hollywood to make sense of these types of events (De Keere 2020). But this does not explain the use of cartoon figures and otherwise benign figures from children's media. In taking an emotion practice approach, we can go further in seeing the implications of this use of known symbols of entertainment. Not only do combinations of threatening topics with frivolous cartoons and celebrities serve to dissipate the threat, but in using these symbols, social media users are drawing on the familiarity associated with these images and the embedded emotional capital that these symbols carry with them. Fond memories of consuming different types of media can assuage the difficult emotions caused by the uncertainty of the outbreak. Use of such symbols can also disrupt or rebel against dominant media discourses on the outbreak as inherently scary or implicating feelings of sorrow for victims.[2] The established practice of making jokes online carries forward into even somber and serious topics as users turn to the known energy-enhancing practices of sharing humorous memes, jokes, and videos. The inertia of these practices carries them forward even when these seem to so clearly violate established emotion norms that would govern face-to-face interactions in the context of a matter as serious as an evolving epidemic.

In line with the elastic strength of sports symbols discussed in Chapter 3, sports symbols and references were also used to make light of the Ebola outbreak, including a reference to the Terrible Towel, the iconic symbol associated with the Pittsburgh Steelers franchise discussed previously. In one image, the Jaguar mascot of the Jacksonville, Florida, NFL team is seen holding a sign that reads "Towels Carry Ebola." This image, along with the text noting that the team apologized for carrying the sign, are both shared by the influential "NFL on ESPN" official Twitter profile, a profile with roughly 2.9 million followers.[3] In a second sports-related image, three supposed fans wearing full hazmat suits gather in the parking lot outside of the arena for tailgating. Overlaying the image is the text "DIE HARD FANS TAILGATING IN DALLAS DESPITE THE RECENT EBOLA THREAT." This meme gives a whole new meaning to the phrase "diehard fan."

As the many references to popular culture suggest, Twitter is a space for playfulness and creatively making connections between disparate topics in lighthearted ways, juxtaposing the trivial with the serious, as well as being a space for sharing information and news. In the aforementioned case of the Jaguar mascot, the NFL team would later apologize for the sign because it caused outrage for being insensitive to the seriousness of Ebola. In many cases, like the two football-related jokes from earlier, jokes and memes were clearly couched in the fear linked to Ebola.

One popular video shared during week 2 was of a cat, with the text "Just a cat giving a presidential speech on Ebola." In the short five-second video, a cat appears to be talking and a male voice attempting to mimic President Obama's cadence is dubbed over the video saying, "My fellow Americans, there is Ebola in America. Which means, we are screwed." Linked, undoubtedly, to Obama's press conferences during this time, this example illustrates a particular type of humor practice in which humanizing the non-human is a way to emphasize absurd contradictions and elicit amusement (Plessner 1970).

In another popular example, one of the single most popular tweets in the sample featured an image of singer Akon who appeared to be in a clear plastic bubble as he crowd-surfed at a concert. With the image came the text:

> Akon crowd surfed in a plastic bubble to avoid catching Ebola. I'm sorry but this got me weak as hell 😭 😭 😭 [tears of joy emoji and two crying emojis]

This tweet, like many others, introduces PPE (personal protective equipment) and discusses the changing health practices and behaviors that individuals might take up in light of Ebola. Emotion scholars note that humor is a way to cope with potentially threatening scenarios and manage difficult emotions (Francis, Monahan, and Berger 1999). Francis emphasizes that humor is practical—"there is a use for humor" (1994, 148). But humor does not simply suppress negative emotions, making it easier for individuals to trudge through life unfazed. It also generates positive feelings of joy, camaraderie, and connection (Kuipers 2008), even if this is only briefly felt and does not lead to lasting identification with a fixed group of online interactants.

Seeing humor only as a "coping device," just as seeing the emotions of sports fandom as cathartic release, overlooks the socially *generative* ability of these practices to create emotional energy in what might otherwise be a draining context. "Coping," like "repression" and "catharsis" in an early Freudian conception of emotion, positions emotions as innately physiological, with social forces only dampening, repressing, or providing a release valve.[4] Relatedly, seeing humor's utility in what it does for a group in terms of "smoothing interaction" (Fine and DeSoucey 2005, 8) or "creating and maintaining powerful social bonds" (Fine and DeSoucey 2005, 9) becomes less tenable in contexts such as Twitter where groups are not clearly demarcated and interactions with relatively unknown users are more commonplace.

In a practice framing, where energy as a form of emotional capital is centered in the analysis, humor becomes a mechanism for generating new emotional energy creatively from the stuff of mass media and popular culture—symbols which already house the energy of past successful rituals and can carry in them traces of prior bonds with significant others (as we saw in Chapter 3). Using popular celebrities, cartoons, and public figures, as well as local sports symbols loaded with emotional energy, jokesters draw on the energy contained in them to playfully and creativity generate fresh energy even in facing a sobering event like an outbreak. This can lead to multiple readings and varying emotional responses to the same joke or image. Using an emotion practice perspective might better explain the broad, even global appeal of humor in the context of disasters. As Giselinde Kuipers emphasizes: "Explaining the appreciation of such disaster jokes with one specific emotion, such as coping with grief, seems unhelpful for such global genres" (2005, 72).

Along with the increase in seemingly more personal expressions of fear and fear-based humor during week 2, themes of policing feelings of fear and humor also emerged. Using the hashtag #dontfreakout and pointing out the inconsistencies in public reactions to Ebola versus other collective problems were some of the ways that Twitter users tried to counter or critique the fear associated with the risks of Ebola. One of the most popular tweets in week 2 was the following:

> Scientists: Don't freak out about Ebola. Everyone: *Panic!* Scientists: Freak out about climate change. Everyone: LOL!

We can see that this tweet reuses themes from a prior tweet from week 1 that focused directly on Fox News. Here, though, "everyone" takes the place of Fox News and the joke centers less on criticizing the media and more on the supposed misplaced panic of the public when it comes to Ebola. Fear of Ebola is contrasted with a naïve, nonchalant attitude toward climate change.

Similar to the policing of fear that is done in the "don't freak out" tweet earlier, there were examples of policing humor. Overall, though, these were much more isolated. As the following example (all caps in original) suggests, the entrenched humor practices of online interactions were not shared by all, although it is challenging to interpret the level of sincerity in even these types of tweets:

> ACTUALLY THO WHY ARE PEOPLE MAKING JOKES ABOUT EBOLA THIS IS SERIOUS

Some Twitter users called for those making Ebola jokes to be punched in the face, while others emphasized that "EBOLA isn't a joke." These reactions highlight the fact that, even when jokes like the pumpkin spice one in week 1 do not seem to have a clear out-group that is being denigrated, the victims and those suffering from the outbreak are relegated to the position of "unintelligible other" (Döveling, Harju, and Sommer 2018, 4). This positioning means that they likely fail to garner active compassion in that moment. Feelings of resonance or attunement are generated when these jokes are successful and, in this way, implicit demarcations between "us" and "them" can be tacitly affirmed in even the more "harmless" jokes.

Taking an emotion practice approach, as I argued in Chapter 1, entails pushing against entrenched ideas in scholarly and commonsense thinking that frame emotions as inherently impractical or dangerous. Research on public emotions and disasters has worked to tease apart the various factors that can shape public sentiment and behavior, including news and social media coverage of said events. Scholars across a number of disciplines have attended to these issues, often with the assumption that fear is innately dangerous, that it catalyzes problematic behavior, or that it is simply overblown or misplaced (which I discuss in greater detail in Chapter 5). Rarely in studies of news media being sensationalistic or causing panic do scholars measure public emotions directly. For example, in their examination of Ebola news media and its likelihood of being reposted on the website Reddit, Kilgo and coauthors argue that "Reddit users were significantly more likely to share or be exposed to news articles that spread the panic" (Kilgo, Yoo, and Johnson 2019, 815). But the panic-inducing devices that they identify in the study have not been verified in focus group or survey methods that directly ask readers if they feel fear or panic in response to such devices. Ungar's (1998) influential article on this topic does not directly ask viewers, readers, or members of the public about how specific features of news coverage make them feel.

Media effects studies are not conclusive about the relationship between media consumption and individual feelings because it is challenging to tease apart whether consumption is an instigator or byproduct of personal feelings of fear or worry. Oh, Lee, and Han (2021) find in a cross-sectional study that use of social media is positively associated with feelings of fear and anger in the context of a MERS outbreak in Korea. Klemm, Hartmann, and Das (2019) conducted an online experiment in the Netherlands using news coverage of a fictitious outbreak and found that it was the objective risks of the hypothetical outbreak (its severity and geographic proximity to respondents) that influenced feelings of fear and not the level of sensationalism used in the news coverage. The authors found "no evidence supporting the common assumptions that such [epidemic] fears and the resultant behaviors can be attributed to emotional [news] coverage" (Klemm, Hartmann, and Das 2019, 81). This seems to match the findings here. It was not until an objective change in the epidemic's development (the case of Thomas Duncan in Texas) that social media users increasingly discussed the outbreak and in qualitatively distinct ways that suggested an increase in perceived personal risk.

In a different context, albeit one where health risks remain front and center, Jill Fisher and I looked at how Phase I clinical trial participants respond to fictional portrayals of biomedical risks. We found that participants respond to and use "panic-inducing" media in unexpected ways (Cottingham and Fisher 2017). Representation of extreme research side effects in movies and in television shows were referenced by participants as they discussed their preconceptions about clinical trials and the risks they entail. But, surprisingly, they used extreme media representations as a foil that made the real risks seem comparatively harmless. Compared to Hollywood examples of research subjects growing a tail or having their penises shrink, their own side effects of experiencing a headache or nausea during a clinical trial appeared tame and, thus, appeared to be less risky by comparison.

Similarly, then, the type of extreme examples of zombies or victims rising from the dead that were prolific in social media discussions of Ebola might be perceived by the public as sensationalist, leading them to discard these accounts (Klemm, Hartmann, and Das 2019) and perceive the actual symptoms of diseases like Ebola or even COVID-19 as less extreme and less fear inducing. In this way, sensationalistic news portrayals, rather than induce panic, might in fact do the opposite. When comparing the symptoms of a fever or cough to the images of zombies that proliferated in discussions of Ebola, it might be difficult to maintain a sense of alertness about the seriousness of a spreading pathogen. This fits with empirical data on the "surprise effect," in which "epidemiological outcomes that fall below expectations tend to generate a feeling of relief" (Sherlaw and Raude 2013, 166). Certainly, more empirical studies of how diverse populations respond to these metaphors and imagery in news and social media are needed to answer this question definitively, but these prior studies suggest that what people do with imagery and portrayals of disease might not involve a straightforward mimicry of fear or panic.

Disaster scholars have long noted (and as I discuss in greater depth in Chapter 5), that popular and scholarly discussions of disasters can reproduce the panicking public myth (Quarantelli 2001; Tierney, Bevc, and Kuligowski 2006). This myth entails the deeply held belief—one that is often portrayed in Hollywood films (Clarke 2002)—that the public will engage in wild, irrational behavior during a disaster. According to the myth, this panic behavior is, at best, unhelpful and, at worst, exacerbates harm during a disaster. In contrast to the stereotype of the panicking public, the analysis here points to the variability of responses to an outbreak. In a context of uncertainty that is endemic to emerging outbreaks, we can see that feelings of fear are present, but also take on different forms (abstract to personal) and connect with different actions, including retweeting, prayer, joking, and suggestions, perhaps facetiously during Ebola, of isolation. Humor practices on Twitter fit the established emotion practices of this platform, but they point to energy-generating efforts to forge connections across diverse users even during times of uncertainty. Taking a practice approach demands that we temper an overly agentic or deterministic view of these practices, while looking beyond crude emotion classifications and the tendency to see emotions like fear as universally impractical. In applying an emotion practice approach to the digital sphere, we can better appreciate the emotional payoff of digital interactions and see the energizing potential of sites like Twitter.

Conclusion

In March 2020, the Executive Director of the American Sociological Association, Nancy Kidd, shared a timely quote from C. S. Lewis's 1939 essay "Learning in War-Time." In that piece, Lewis argues that:

> Plausible reasons have never been lacking for putting off all merely cultural activities until some imminent danger has been averted or some crying injustice put right. But humanity long ago chose to neglect those plausible reasons. They wanted knowledge and beauty now, and would not wait for the suitable moment[s] that never come. [. . .]
>
> They propound mathematical theorems in beleaguered cities, conduct metaphysical arguments in condemned cells, make jokes on scaffold, discuss the last new poem while advancing to the walls of Quebec, and comb their hair at Thermopylae. This is not panache; it is our nature.

Making jokes during an emerging health threat, like telling jokes on a scaffold or soldiers combing their hair before battle, might seem frivolous and misguided. But these practices can serve as powerful energizing and comforting moments that, rather than dismiss fear, might even transform it into hope, solidarity, and the energy needed to face a collective threat. An emotion practice approach allows us to tap into the routine and creative practices online that can provide at times consistency and comfort as well as chart new routines for producing emotional energy in times of threat. As habitus involves the internalization of past practices, the comfort of these routines stems from the fact that they present us with symbols and remembered actions steeped in familiarity. This can convey comfort, ease, and relaxation even when an outbreak rages outside of our social media bubbles. In this way, even looking at an unusual situation like Ebola or COVID-19, albeit at a time when disasters can seem more common, allows us to tap into the practices that make up our everyday realities—for it is those practices that are most ingrained and difficult to disrupt.

An emotion practice approach also attempts to see emotions not as discrete, isolated states, but to conceptually capture the flows and overlaps between various sensations and emotional registers. Just as nurses report feeling multiple emotions simultaneously, even in the case of feeling fear and panic in the context of a public health threat, there is a kernel of hope that, through speedy action, an impending threat can be avoided (Quarantelli 2001). Similarly, in looking at the digital practices of Twitter users, humor, sarcasm, and wit allow for different interpretations among different users. In allowing for multiple resonant meanings, diverse publics can become "in on the joke" and gain a degree of emotional energy however momentary or fleeting. This degree of open interpretation and ambiguity stems from the fact that the platform "collapse[s] multiple contexts and bring[s] together commonly distinct audiences" (Marwick and boyd 2011, 115). Ambiguity itself can be seen as a resource (Polletta et al. 2011) in this case because it gives stories and symbols the elasticity needed to reach diverse populations.

As the COVID-19 outbreak has developed, we see discussion among scholars and the public about the role of misinformation on sites like Twitter, Facebook, and other social media sites. One study found that at one point in the pandemic, nearly half of all Twitter users posting in support of a policy to reopen the US economy were bots (V. A. Young 2020). This is important research and more needs to be done to determine the effects that these campaigns have on persuading social media users of particular policies or political arguments. Yet, because I take an emotion practice approach here, I argue that we must also recognize that thinking of social media sites solely as information sources misses the deeper emotional and social role that these sites play in the lives of users. Emphasizing the spread of false information can miss the larger goal of these digital social gatherings. Just as confronting one's uncle for telling an exaggerated story misses the emotional energy and social bonds that the act of storytelling is intended to cultivate (McCarthy 2017; Sarbin 1995), telling social media users that tweets or posts shared online are propaganda seems to miss the emotional meanings that are at the center of these virtual exchanges.

Social media posts, like the examples of Ebola humor detailed in this chapter, are efforts to share and gain emotional energy (as capital) and/or acts of rebellion against dominant media discourses. When scholars and policymakers try to tackle falsehoods on these sites, they often assume a rational choice model of decision-making based on the belief that by revealing misinformation for what it is, users will logically discount what they read and change their habits.[5] But habits, as part of habitus, are formed through repetitive practice, and only through environmental changes in the digital news landscape are new habits likely to emerge. We develop dispositions, including digital ones, in anticipating new external demands. To return to the example I used in the introductory chapter, no matter how rational a person is or how healthy cycling is cognitively understood to be, an established infrastructure (including paved roads and regulations) that makes cycling easy and painless is needed for large numbers of a population to develop the habit.

Taking a practice approach to the digital emotions conveyed during the Ebola outbreak reveals the practical, entrenched, *and* creative ways that publics can express and channel various emotions, including fear, through the digital affordances of social media. Memes, vines, gifs, TikTok videos, and laughing emojis abound in this space alongside fear, worry, empathy, and compassion. Seeing emotions as practices allows us to highlight this complexity. We can trace the presence of certain emotions but also what people *do* with them in digital spaces. Action—doing, being, and getting where we want to go—are, after all, the point of feeling. But to understand action without feeling is to ignore the complex social navigational tool that emotions, and the symbols that house them, provide. Emotion is the fuel that we need to put plans into action. I continue this line of thinking by turning from the social media responses during an emerging outbreak to the ways that politicians and health leaders frame emotions during epidemics. Both the 2013–2016 Ebola outbreak and the COVID-19 pandemic are useful cases for examining how political actors frame emotions during public health threats. In these contexts, we will see how the lingering dualisms that I outlined in Chapter 1—namely that emotions and practical action are diametrically opposed—continue to exert their influence over the political framing of crisis events and emotions.

5

Viral Fear

Emotion as Barrier or Resource in Facing Collective Challenges

> The sudden increase in new [COVID-19] cases is certainly very concerning. I have spoken consistently about the need for facts, not fear. Using the word pandemic now does not fit the facts, but it may certainly cause fear.
>
> —Dr. Tedros Adhanom Ghebreyesus, Director-General, February 24, 2020 (World Health Organization 2020c)

The World Health Organization (WHO) declared the COVID-19 outbreak a pandemic on March 11, 2020 (World Health Organization 2020a). As with the Ebola outbreak discussed in Chapter 4, emotions came to the fore. Fear and panic were routinely discussed among political leaders, journalists, cultural leaders, and the public as people tried to discern what constituted an underreaction or overreaction to this novel virus shrouded in uncertainty. Collective discussions of fear and panic framed both as problematic and counterproductive. Emblematic of this was the WHO Director-General Dr. Tedros Adhanom Ghebreyesus's emphasis on facts over fear in the opening quote.

While the WHO, following others, would eventually use the term "pandemic," their resistance to its use was based on an *emotional* calculation. Believing both that the term would cause fear and that this fear would be a barrier to effectively containing the outbreak, the WHO and other organizations and leaders made decisions over the course of the outbreak based on a clear belief that emotions are antithetical to practical action. Their conception of emotion matches the dualistic thinking of Western Enlightenment discussed in Chapter 1. In this line of thinking, reason and emotion are seen as mutually exclusive, with reason the dominant mode needed to solve

Practical Feelings. Marci D. Cottingham, Oxford University Press. © Oxford University Press 2022.
DOI: 10.1093/oso/9780197613689.003.0006

pressing problems. For reason to triumph, it must dominate and tame dangerous emotions like fear and panic.

Thinking with an emotion practice approach means challenging the assumption that reason and emotion are antithetical and using more refined concepts from the sociology of emotion and social practice theory. This integration, I have argued, allows us to see more clearly before, beneath, and beyond discrete emotions, individuals, and interactions. Having examined emotions in the intimate accounts of nurses caring at the bedside, in and beyond the peak emotions of sports fandom, and in the digital spaces where social media users react to threats, this final empirical chapter pulls our analytical lens out even wider in order to examine the role of emotions in how political actors confront collective challenges.

Wielding political power is often seen as a largely unemotional act. Emotions are framed as "a problem that power has to *deal with*, not something with which power is itself intimately involved" (Ost 2004, 229). As Jonathan Heaney notes, we are quick to see emotion as endemic to "social movements, or protestors, or populists, or demagogues, rather than the embodied men and women, formally attired and firmly ensconced in formal party politics" (2019, 226). Yet endless wars, global terrorism, and climate change are all enduring social problems that characterize American politics, none of which can be seen as untouched by or disconnected from human emotion. Emotions, as I will show, are just as relevant to these arenas and to established political actors as they are to nurses, sports fans, and the social media users examined in prior chapters.

In this chapter, I take an in-depth look at the political framing of both the Ebola outbreak and the evolving COVID-19 pandemic. Using a dataset of news media covering the 2013–2016 Ebola outbreak, I aim to understand how fear and other emotions were discussed by politicians and world leaders. Given the relevance of the COVID-19 pandemic, I also draw out connections to similar patterns in how emotions are understood and used during this now more widespread and lethal event. Taking a critical lens to the political rhetoric on epidemic emotions, I argue that political leaders try to project an image of cool rationality because this type of emotion practice fits with the Enlightenment image of leaderships while also providing a useful foil to a supposedly panicking public. Converting their emotional capital into political capital, political leaders must meet the new demands for personalized, mediatized, and "theatricalized form[s] of 'audience democracy'" (Heaney 2019, 234). But underneath these cool projections and panic myths, empirical data on how people actually respond to a crisis suggest that it is *under*reaction and indifference, not panic or fear, that should be our main concern when tackling large-scale collective challenges.

Public Threats and Crisis Emotions

In sections that follow, like the opening quote from Dr. Tedros Adhanom Ghebreyesus, we will see calls for calm and calls for action from across political divisions and governmental and transnational organizations. Part of the reason that fear and public panic become a critical concern to leaders during a crisis is based on the belief that the public, reacting to a disaster or threat, will feel panic and that this will lead to uncontrollable, chaotic behavior. This is known in disaster research as the "panic myth." It is a popular myth, but one that has been repeatedly debunked in disaster response research. People do not necessarily exhibit panic during a crisis or epidemic (Sherlaw and Raude 2013), and even if they feel fear, this does not automatically lead to irrational or dangerous behavior (Gantt and Gantt 2012; Tierney, Bevc, and Kuligowski 2006). Antisocial behavior can also be caused by denialism and "psychological reactance"—a set of negative attitudes and emotions, like anger and resistance to authority when told what to do during a pandemic (Taylor and Asmundson 2021). When we think people are acting "irrationally," often this means that they are acting in ways that an outside observer cannot understand. Facing inexplicable behavior, the panic myth turns to emotions of panic and fear as the presumed catalysts. Assigning blame to irrational emotions is one way to avoid direct discussion of structural problems (Graeber 2015, 161).

The set of assumptions that underlie the panic myth have a long history in the social sciences, shaping even their inception as a field of scientific inquiry. Going back to some of the first scientific accounts of social life, we see a fascination with crowds (Le Bon 1896/1996) and the suspicion that unbridled chaos lies just beneath the surface of a calm and orderly group. Enrico L. Quarantelli, an American sociologist, helped to pioneer the field of disaster research, and in summarizing the vast body of research on panic and disasters, he highlights a number of tensions and contradictions that remain in this field of study (Quarantelli 2001). In this section, I first detail these tensions to then show how an emotion practice approach can help us overcome them.

The first contradiction in scholarly work on panic, as noted in Quarantelli (2001), is that panic is irrational but also rational. The flight response to a threat (one of the primary behavioral responses that is used as a marker of panic) can indeed remove one from a threatening situation. But if this response leads to the trampling of others in a crowd, for example, it is seen as excessive and, thus, irrational. The classic example is that of yelling "Fire!" in a crowded room. Spooked by the threat of fire, the assumption goes, people will simultaneously stampede for the door, injuring or killing each other in the pandemonium. *Pandemonium* being a term that combines all (*pan*) with little demons (*demonium*)—a time when we let out all our demons. Note, though, that in cases where such panic is said to have existed and led to excessive suffering, researchers have found prosocial as well as antisocial behavior, and orderliness alongside a rush to act or flee (N. R. Johnson 1988). How we act during an outbreak or an emergency might not be terribly different from how we act normally (Kinateder et al. 2015). And falling back onto our well-worn habits can be both good and bad—we might be polite and prosocial in helping others reach safety, but we might also move too slowly or resist following instructions when quick action is needed.

Even in contexts in which emotions must be "managed" in order for practical help to be administered,[1] we can see that the initial feeling of "freezing up" or initially responding in an uncooperative way is a prelude to the development of trust and understanding with helpers. Take, for example, the case of Lorna discussed in Jennifer Lois's ethnographic account of search and rescue responders. Lorna has had a terrible accident while hiking and ended up being tossed around in a cold river before pulling herself up onto a small island in the middle of the water. After her husband gets help from a search and rescue team, they arrive and inform her about how they want to get Lorna back to shore:

> They were very clear with their directions on how they wanted me to achieve this. They had to put me back in the river and pass me from one [rescuer] to the other until they reached the shore. I was not exactly cooperative initially! The thought of being dunked in that cold water again was not what I had in mind. They held me tight and made me feel safe, I knew they would not let anything happen to me. (Lois 2001, 149)

In Lois's account, Lorna refuses at first to reenter the cold waters of a river that she had just barely survived. Her refusal does not ease until her rescuer takes the time to reassure her that he has her best interests at heart. This creation of trust then becomes a bond that allows the two to work together to get Lorna to safety.

While Lorna's initial hesitation could be seen as a barrier to practical action, we can also see it as a catalyst to forging closer bonds with her rescuer before putting her faith in his efforts. Her initial hesitation stems from her vulnerable state and requires that her rescuers prove their good intentions by convincing her that they have her safety in mind. After she is reassured of this, she cooperates fully. Thus, while a victim's feelings might be seen as impeding "the rescue efforts because they were too petrified or traumatized to cooperate physically" (Lois 2001, 148), it is only because we as the reader (and Lois, as a search and rescue volunteer herself) believe unequivocally that the rescue team is working in the interests of victims that we see this as impractical. From Lorna's vulnerable perspective, having some misgivings about following the instructions of relative strangers seems quite prudent.[2]

A second, but overlapping, division among disaster scholars who look at panic is "between those who argue that panic behavior is very contagious, and that human beings are easily swept up into the behavior, and those who strongly disagree with such a conception" (Quarantelli 2001). This tension is endemic to how we view emotions. In one classic investigation of panic and disasters, Johnson (1988) empirically examines first-person accounts of a fire at a Cincinnati dinner theater that killed 165 people. Using these accounts and organizing them according to the order in which people exited the building revealed the key moments when panic seemed to emerge. This was not through the contagious spreading of feelings of panic from person to person, even as some people screamed and pushed, but through directly witnessing smoke, flames, and then the loss of lights in the building. These latter observations were the key elements that seemed to send people into a "save your own life" mode (N. R. Johnson 1988, 17).

Johnson's (1988) findings align with more recent scholarship on crisis response and risk perceptions during fire evacuations. Risk analysts identify human behavioral responses during crises as an area in need of ongoing research. Emotional arousal and anxious states are connected to higher risk perceptions. But depending on how "risk perception" is measured, this higher perception of risk can lead to information-seeking behaviors that can delay evacuation or, in some studies, directly correlate with quicker evacuation. Emotions in evacuation research can be seen as barriers such as when "emotional attachment" leads residents to delay evacuating their homes

(Ronchi and Nilsson 2013). But feeling anxious can also prime someone to act and evacuate quickly. Research that focuses on risk as *feelings* tries to take emotions seriously as necessary elements for making risk meaningful to individual perceivers. Emotions though, can still be framed as a "bias" or antithetical to problem-solving (Kinateder et al. 2015). Emotions matter, but perhaps more clearly, the behaviors of those around us in the moment of a crisis can also shape how we act. This influence is not necessarily through the contagious spread of panic, but through the contagious spread of normalcy or a "business as usual" approach. In other words, "passive behavior of others may trigger the normalcy bias (i.e., that nothing is wrong) and reduce perceived risk" (Kinateder et al. 2015, 20). Responses to a crisis are thus shaped by norms enacted by specific others (and later internalized as the generalized other; Mead 1934).

One final insight from disaster scholars that relates to an emotion practice approach is the inherent complexity of emotions that individuals experience in crisis moments. Similar to the multiplicity of overlapping and even somewhat contradictory emotions that nurses relayed in their diaries in Chapter 2, disaster scholars highlight the interplay of multiple emotions as individuals and communities respond to a disaster. Quarantelli (2001) notes that there is an implicit element of hope in the types of panic discussed in the literature:

> Disaster researchers in particular have emphasized that hope of escape rather than hopelessness is what is involved. Persons who perceived themselves as totally trapped such as in sunken submarines or collapsed coal mines do not panic because they see no way of getting away from the threat. (Quarantelli 2001)

Thus, we see in the literature on disaster emotions the dichotomy between the rational and the irrational and between contagion and intention play out in these divisions, as well as a recognition of the multiplicity of emotions in times of crisis. While these findings can appear contradictory, this is only because of a continuation of dichotomous thinking that sees emotions as mutually exclusive of reason and emotions as discrete entities.

Each of these contradictions can be overcome with a turn toward seeing emotions as practical engagements with the world. Emotions, in everyday life and in the crisis moments, are modes of being and doing that straddle the rational/nonrational and the intentional/unintentional. Taking an emotion practice approach allows us to better capture the complexity of multiple emotions as they are experienced during crisis moments. While feelings of fear and panic can seem rational when facing an impending threat, attending to the complexity of multiple emotions and the contexts in which they are felt is critical for understanding the potential practical use of these feelings, including feelings of fear, panic, hope, and trust or distrust of others. Finally, an emotion practice approach can turn the analytic gaze onto politicians and cultural leaders to understand how they frame emotions during crises and what this framing might mean for the accrual and conversion of emotional capital into other types of capital (social, financial, political) during times of upheaval.

In the following sections of this chapter, I turn to two recent examples of disasters—the 2013–2016 Ebola outbreak and the COVID-19 pandemic. More specifically, I look at how fear and panic are discussed by news media and political and cultural leaders in relation to the public use of personal protective equipment (PPE) during Ebola as well as toilet paper hoarding and decisions about public use of masks during COVID-19. In thinking with a practice approach to emotion, we can look for areas where crisis emotions might be assumed rather than known, where these are assumed to be problematic, and how elites use their emotional capital to shore up political capital during times of crisis. It is in the link between emotional capital and political capital that we can address the question that Quarantelli and others (Clarke and Chess 2008) have continued to pose: Why does the myth of the panicking public persist?

When Fear Becomes the Problem

The conception of fear illustrated in the quote at the beginning of this chapter was underscored again and again in the official responses to the COVID-19 outbreak. Similar to calls for facts, not fear, political leaders throughout the international community emphasized repeatedly that the public should not panic but remain calm. In a press conference on March 10, then President Trump stated, "Just stay calm. It will go away" (The Associated Press 2020). News coverage at the time focused in particular on the act of hoarding toilet paper, framing this behavior as a hysterical overreaction to COVID-19.[3] And then, as efforts to gently suggest restrictions on travel and public gatherings became government mandates in the spring of 2020, it seemed that the risk of overreaction was not the real threat, but rather apathy and indifference were the real barriers to effectively containing the outbreak.

Scholars studying the media and crises have highlighted the risk of fear-mongering and moral panics (Altheide 2009; Cohen 2002; Furedi 2007b; 2018; Garland 2008; Glassner 1999). There is a rich and established body of scholarly research on these risks. Moral panic is one of the few sociological concepts to transition from scholarly to public use and has been hugely influential in how news producers frame social problems and public debates (Altheide 2009). The term itself is meant to highlight any issue that has come to be seen as posing an existential threat to a group's well-being or way of life and these types of panic usually center on classic forms of deviance specific to young people and related to drugs, sex, or other behaviors that pose a threat to the moral order. Fear-mongering is a concept that focuses on misplaced fear and efforts of politicians and elites to manipulate the public (Altheide 2013; Furedi 2007a; Glassner 1999).

But what about calm-mongering? What about the risk of extinguishing the emotional capital (fear as a catalyst for energetic alertness) we collectively need to solve big challenges? In that same March 10 press conference noted earlier, President Trump goes on to say that "everybody has to be vigilant and has to be careful" (The Associated Press 2020). Vigilance, watchfulness, and the need to act collectively and decisively were common refrains along with calls for calmness. Yet our shared adaptation for vigilance—for heightened watchfulness—is precisely the emotional response that many leaders, not just Trump, were and are quick to dampen.

Emotions, as I have argued throughout this book, get us where we want to go. Feelings orient us and move us to action. It is in this way that we can think of them as practical orientations to the world. Without emotions, our individual and collective responses are sluggish and incoherent. We need emotions and feelings. Certainly, there can be unintended consequences and at times they can seem like maladjustments that deplete bodily resources unnecessarily (in the case of panic attacks or heightened stress, for example). But emotions ultimately have a purpose, or a "signal function," in Freud's terminology.[4] They alert us to our values and heighten our ability to make urgent change. Like nurses working to get through a tough shift, we need emotions to guide us through our connections with others, to help us *sense* and *make sense* of the world around us. Emotions can alert us to a misuse of resources (causing anger), a helpful colleague or friend (causing solidarity), a lost loved one (causing sadness), or a looming threat (causing fear and vigilance). Taking this approach to the Ebola and COVID-19 outbreaks can help us see where emotions might lead to practical helpful action as well as where they might lead us down unfruitful paths.

In both the drumming up and dampening down of public fear, how leaders frame a collective problem is steeped in practices of power. The role of social hierarchies in shaping how we feel was apparent among the nurses in Chapter 2 who disparately feel with certain, similar others and also in the case of sports fans who draw on emotional capital through symbols charged up with the disproportionate bodily labor of, and risks taken by, African American players. The social distinctions are even greater when we look at elite leaders compared with ordinary citizens who possess relatively little political capital. Using the emotions of others to delegitimize their concerns, leaders can wield enormous influence by adopting a culturally dominant emotional habitus which emphasizes stoicism and the dominance of emotion through reason. In using the term *emotional habitus*, like Gould's (2009) use, I refer to a group's "embodied and axiomatic inclinations toward certain feelings and ways of emoting" (2009, 32).

In the case of elite leaders, their emotional habitus represents the most culturally dominant way of thinking about and expressing emotions within a given context. Similar to Hochschild's notion of emotion norms, but distinct in that it is embodied and inherently tied to social location, the emotional habitus of leadership seems to match the stereotype of the predominantly white, upper-class men who have historically occupied such positions. Part of this emotional habitus involves knowing how to harness the right emotions (through emotion discourse; Loseke 2009)[5] to elicit compliance and exert political power. Knowing how to do this forms their own base of emotional capital—the skills and knowledge that they marshal to shape collective feelings—and is a necessary precursor to transforming this emotional capital into political capital. The latter is "a form of power that both moves and mobilizes, while also adding to the symbolic power or prestige, reputation, and status of the politician, and thereby improving their standing or position within the political field" (Heaney 2019, 234). Thus, the power of political and cultural leaders as decision-makers contrasts with the relative powerlessness of ordinary citizens. The vulnerability of such citizens is even more glaring during a public health threat like a pandemic when those in power make decisions that can be of enormous consequence to the population at large, often relying on scientific knowledge and jargon that can be inaccessible to the broader population, creating further feelings of disconnection between the public and political leaders.

In what follows, I detail how fear is framed in the Ebola and COVID-19 outbreaks and what this says about the value of particular emotions and emotion practices. There are of course many notable distinctions between the COVID-19 pandemic and the 2013–2016 Ebola outbreak. One originated in China, the other in West Africa. The two diseases have different symptomatology, different rates of infection, and different means of spread. Ebola's symptomatology includes fever, vomiting, diarrhea, and in some cases unexplained bleeding. This contrasts with COVID-19's primary symptoms of fever and cough (though the whole range of symptoms, particularly among long-term sufferers [Callard and Perego 2021], is still being documented). Ebola, as experts reiterated again and again, is only contagious when the carrier is sick and experiencing symptoms. COVID-19 may well be spread even among asymptomatic carriers. The COVID-19 outbreak is ongoing even as I am writing, but we can already see that it has proven to be more lethal and widespread than the Ebola outbreak. The Ebola outbreak in 2013–2016 infected some 28,000 people and led to over 11,000 deaths. The numbers of COVID-19 are difficult to estimate and continue to grow, but they currently stand at over 300 million cases of infection and over 5 million dead.[6]

Yet, despite these differences, we see a similar rhetoric used in each of the two outbreaks when it comes to calls for calm and the banishment of fear. In October 2014, much like his successor, then President Obama urged Americans to put the case of Ebola in perspective: "What we're seeing now is not an 'outbreak' or an 'epidemic' of Ebola in America," he said. "This is a serious disease, but we can't give in to hysteria or fear" (Rampton 2014). And similar to the quote earlier from her successor, then Director-General of the WHO, Dr. Chan explained during the Ebola crisis that fear was a problematic response. Fear, she claimed, had spread through social media and had negatively impacted her organization's ability to effectively contain Ebola:

> Six months into the outbreak, fear is proving to be the most difficult barrier to overcome. (Chan 2014)

And later, in assessing the WHO's response to the outbreak, she again flagged fear and its connection with social media as especially problematic:

> In wealthy countries around the world, information technology, including social media, allowed fear to spread faster than the [Ebola] virus. (Chan 2015)

President Obama and Director-General Chan were not the only leaders to emphasize the problematic nature of fear in the context of the outbreak. During news coverage of Ebola, which we saw in Chapter 4 peaked in October 2014, the Ugandan Minister of Information, Rose Namayanja, accused Western nations of creating "mass panic" by basing policies such as travel bans on panic rather than sound scientific knowledge ("Uganda: West Creating Ebola 'Mass Panic'" 2014). Dr. Isabelle Nuttall, Director of WHO Global Response Unit, also turned to fear to explain the lack of volunteers early on in the outbreak: "Unlike a natural disaster, Ebola was striking fear in people's minds" ("W.H.O. to Review Ebola Response" 2014). This led, in her estimate, to fewer healthcare workers volunteering to travel to West Africa to help with the Ebola response. And the BBC's Neha Bhatnagar lamented in her report on Ebola that "Panic is spreading almost as quickly as the virus itself" ("Ebola Crisis: Fears Quarantine Could Deter Ebola Workers" 2014).

News outlets would later discuss whether or not they played a role in ramping up fear or if they were merely providing important information so that the public could decide how to feel. CNN's Dr. Sanjay Gupta argued that:

I think there is a lot of irrational fear and I think in part it's because there's been a lot of attention but there's also been a lot of confusing messages that have come from higher ups—you know people who say one thing and then a couple of weeks modify those statements. I think it leads to a challenging of your faith in some of the systems and that breeds some of this fear. (Gupta 2014a)[7]

Predating the WHO General-Director's statement in 2020, Brian Stelter, CNN host, ended a 2014 news cast with a call for "facts over fear."

Simultaneous to these concerns about fear and panic were calls for action. Even in his address to the UN in late September 2014, President Obama emphasized the need for swift action. One Tweet summarized Obama's message:

Obama at UN: More cash, faster response needed to contain Ebola crisis.

Scientists as well called not just for a response or for action, but *speed*:

"We need to act fast with Ebola" says lead Dr Peter Horby.

Organizations around the world called for more and faster action on the part of governments and the public. Paanu Saaristo of the Red Cross emphasized the need for action:

> We still need to find more people. We still need to mobilize more funding, more human resources. And we still need to scale up. ("Intense Training for Ebola Caregivers" 2014)

In this dominant framing of fear, there was a single instance in the October 2014 coverage of the epidemic in which fear was framed not as problematic, but as practical. Cuban physician Dr. Osmany Rodriguez was interviewed by CNN reporter Patrick Oppman during a segment on the Cuban training camp set up to prepare doctors from Cuba before they travel to West Africa. Because of the highly contagious nature of the disease, healthcare workers treating Ebola patients must be extremely cautious and vigilant in both putting on and removing each item of their PPE. In discussing training, Dr. Rodriguez did not argue for calm but instead focused on the *practicality* of fear:

> To be afraid is not a big problem. I think that being afraid will help us to protect even more against that viral disease [Ebola]. Because if we feel that we are so sure about everything that we are going to do everyday, it may be more dangerous than being afraid of the disease. ("Cuban Doctors Train, Then Fight Ebola in Africa" 2014)

Perhaps it is not surprising that this view of fear comes from a Cuban physician rather than from leaders from the United States or Western Europe— cultures steeped in Enlightenment assumptions that emotions are volatile signs of chaos and weakness antithetical to reason (Lutz 1998).

Here in Dr. Rodriguez's comments, we see that another view of emotion and fear is possible. Rather than being a source of chaos or a barrier to overcome, fear can be a practical tool—a means for creating the vigilance and everyday cautiousness that is necessary when working to protect oneself from this invisible danger. In this framing, the concerns of others need not be dismissed as irrational but can be channeled into the very types of action that can help safeguard a healthcare worker's well-being. Public health leaders like Saaristo of the Red Cross, Nuttall of the WHO, and expert epidemiologists like Dr. Roy Anderson (interviewed on CNN) all pointed to the need for quick collective action—for raising awareness and funds, recruiting volunteers, and "scaling up" efforts to address the challenges created by the Ebola outbreak. To initiate and carry forward these types of co-ordinated action, though, requires *energy*—cool rationality is not enough when it comes to instigating quick action among governments, leaders, and the public. In this way, harnessing emotions like fear could be a way to also harness time and put actions into motion more quickly, but the dominant framing of fear in this context is that it is inherently impractical. We see a similar theme in discussions of PPE among the public in the context of Ebola.

Public Use of Personal Protective Equipment during Ebola

Disaster scholars note that, not only do we tend to assume that the public will panic in times of crisis, but the panic myth can also gloss over the complex emotions that many feel during a crisis or disaster. In the context of the Ebola epidemic, one area of focus for news coverage was the use of PPE that health-care workers needed in order to treat Ebola patients and the use of such items by the public. News headlines throughout the outbreak made direct links between fear and PPE (see Figure 5.1):

Shares soar for US hazmat gear makers amid Ebola fears—Agence Press (France)

Afraid of Ebola? Local company selling protective suits—Northwest Florida News (USA)

Hazmat suit maker's stock up 50% on Ebola fears—CNN (USA)

Online mask-seller cashes in on Ebola fears—Taranaki Daily News (New Zealand)

News headlines like the ones here connected the purchase of PPE and the buying of stock in PPE manufacturing companies as both driven by direct and indirect feelings of fear. "Fears" here is used as a noun—a thing—that seems to exist separate from individual feelers. In this way "Ebola fears"

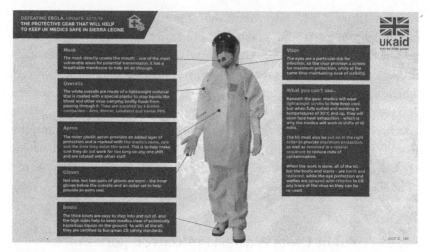

Figure 5.1 "Doctors, nurses and medics from across the UK's National Health Service are joining Britain's fight against Ebola in Sierra Leone [. . .] The safety suits they will wear—including overalls, visors, gloves and more—must be put on in the right order to provide maximum protection, as well as removed in a special sequence to reduce risks of contamination." January 22, 2015.

Ricci Coughlan/DFID. Creative Commons Attribution 2.0 Generic. https://commons.wikimedia. org/wiki/File:Protective_gear_that_will_help_keep_UK_medics_safe_in_Sierra_Leone_ (15663938629).jpg

become something separate from the disease but also seemingly more powerful in dictating unpredictable behavior. Such fears seemed to fuel consumer and stock market behavior while also being something that one could "cash in on."

News headlines also highlighted examples of journalists and laypersons wearing or trying on PPE and how this behavior connected to individuals' emotions:

"It scares the Jesus outta me": Outrage as Nigerian "Nollywood" star posts image of himself wearing Ebola mask in first class airport lounge as he flees Liberia—MailOnline (UK)

Plane passenger fearing Ebola outbreak wears full virus protective suit and mask at US airport—Irish Mirror (Ireland)

In the first headline, we see a direct quote from an individual who cites fear as the reason for wearing a mask in an airport lounge. But in the second, even a detailed reading of the article in its entirety does not indicate that fear was the precise motivation. Despite not talking directly to the plane passenger in question, the Irish Mirror goes on to state that "This panicked plane passenger was taking no risks as the Ebola scare sweeps the planet" and "The sight was sure to have shocked fellow travellers [sic] already rocked by the news on the same day that a second nurse was diagnosed with Ebola in Dallas." Yet the links between such behavior and emotions are not always an open and shut case.

In another example of the public use of PPE, Dr. Gilbert Mobley explicitly used the "Ebola" suit and its connection with the virus and fear. Dr. Mobley, an emergency trauma physician, wore a full suit, mask, and gloves at the airport in Atlanta, Georgia. Written on the back of his white suit were the words "CDC IS LYING." When interviewed on CNN about his actions, which others would call a "stunt" and a "performance," Dr. Mobley detailed a recommendation of what would essentially become a widespread policy of temperature screening at a number of US airports. Wearing the gear proved effective in getting news attention and an interview on CNN. His message was nearly identical to that of a number of commentators and politicians, including Representative Marsha Blackburn (Tennessee)[8] and Keith Vaz, British Labour Party politician.[9] Both political figures seemed to recognize that policies of temperature screening at airports work more as a form of security/hygiene theater aimed toward reassuring the public, rather than one that would single-handedly contain the spread of the disease and stop the outbreak altogether. Thus, while fear might remain connected to the use of PPE in the public, this was, in the case of Mobley a strategic way to push particular policy recommendations that were already in discussion by commentators.

While the use of PPE in public and by laypersons, as exemplified by Dr. Mobley, suggests that the suit can be used to heighten fear and/or be used strategically to influence policy, we can also see examples during the Ebola outbreak in which the *lack* of PPE seemed to also raise concerns. Nurses in California, Spain, and Texas all protested a *lack* of adequate PPE supplies. And the case of "clipboard man"—a man in plainclothes who is seen escorting a patient for a flight transfer—was discussed at length on CNN as causing "concern" (CNN 2014). According to a post on *Princeton Public Health Review*, the incident caused:

an uproar on sites like Twitter, with people wondering why safety protocols seemed to be breached, why the virus was being taken lightly, and whether or not the man was infected and now a risk to society. (Rao 2014)

The same review would frame this event as an indicator that "mass hysteria is easily spurred by the media. As such, a lot of speculation about the Ebola virus has been based in ignorance and the human tendency to sensationalize" (Rao 2014). "The media" is an easy target and certainly does have an interest in gaining the attention, clicks, and likes that the social media ecosystem prioritizes. But in redirecting attention to the media, social scientists can gloss over the complexity and ambiguity of emotional meanings connected with the outbreak and with the protective equipment that became a symbol of the Ebola outbreak itself.

The ambiguity of the suit's meanings—the suit being both a source of fear and comfort—points to the uncertainty of the moment and the fact that the most practical response in times of uncertain risks are often only clear-cut in retrospect. Looking in hindsight, concern over Ebola now seems overblown, particularly as we see the numbers of cases, suffering, and deaths pale in comparison to what COVID-19 has wrought. But in the moment, choices like whether to wear PPE on a plane or, as I discuss next, to stock up on toilet paper are choices always made with imperfect information. Emotions can be practical guides in such contexts for directing such behavior, but all behavior during a crisis need not be the result of only blind panic or cool reason. Such caricatures are the stuff of stereotypes, not reality.

Toilet Paper Hoarding during COVID-19

One of the most widely discussed panic-fueled behaviors at the beginning of the COVID-19 outbreak was the initial run on toilet paper supplies at stores in the United States and Europe. Pictures of barren store shelves and images of customers removing packages of toilet paper from pallets brought directly from a truck shipment suggested that consumers were "panic-buying"—excessively stockpiling nonperishable items rather than being measured and reasonable in their purchases. This provided fodder for many of the memes, viral videos, and jokes that emerged on social media in March 2020 (Tenbarge 2020). Social media and news content played up the absurdity of toilet paper as the one staple item that the public would seek out, with comedians roundly mocking both the shortage and members of the public who were seen as self-serving and irrational. NBC's *Late Night with Seth Myers*, ABC's *Jimmy Kimmel Live*, *The Daily Show with Trevor Noah*, and others incorporated the toilet paper shortage into their comedic routines as they transitioned to producing content during the US lockdown.

In one popular video shared on Twitter in March 2020, two violinists played in the empty toilet paper aisle of a grocery store while wearing life preservers (Rodd 2020). The artists likened it to a scene from the film *Titanic*, where musicians continued to play even as the famous ship sank (see Figure 5.2). TikTok was a popular outlet for posting related toilet

Figure 5.2 Bonnie von Duyke and Emer Kinsella perform "Ode to RMS Toilet Paper—"I'll never let go." A screenshot from their posted video, March 16, 2020.
Bonnie von Duyke and Emer Kinsella. Reprinted with permission

paper jokes and songs (Tenbarge 2020). But news outlets covered the trend by emphasizing the centrality of "panic." One headline in *The New York Times* read: "People Around the World Are Panic-Buying . . . Toilet Paper?" (Westbrook 2020). *BBC News* writes: "Coronavirus panic: Why are people stockpiling toilet paper?" (Mao 2020). In the Netherlands, the Dutch Prime Minister, Mark Rutte, emphasized in his address to the country that there was plenty of toilet paper. As *Reuters* summarized: "Dutch PM tells citizens to relax, saying there's enough toilet paper for 10 years" (Reuters Staff 2020).[10]

At its core, the public discussion of hoarding toilet paper turned our collective attention onto individual hoarders as antisocial and irrational. Yet, because this outbreak did not end quickly, investigative journalists looked further into the issue to discover that despite the assumption of mass panic, toilet paper purchasing was not a clear-cut case of irrational hoarders who were "panic-buying" and selfishly taking too much toilet paper. What we learned later in the outbreak is that, in fact, when families, including multiple children and adults, are now confined at home, they inevitably need more toilet paper.[11] And part of the reason for the empty shelves at grocery stores was as much, if not more so, an issue of supply. Manufacturers who serve commercial industries chose not to convert their production and shipping practices to serve the now increased needs of individual consumers purchasing toilet paper at supermarkets. Restaurants, offices, hotels, professional buildings, airports, and other commercial spaces no longer needed the supplies of toilet paper that they did before stay-at-home orders were in place. Rather than redirect this supply to consumers shopping in grocery stores, manufacturers hesitated to risk sunk costs involved in this transition should stay-at-home mandates be lifted soon after they were initiated (Oremus 2020).

What looks on the outside like irrational, panic-based behavior, starts to appear completely practical if one now has a family of four or five that now never leaves the house. This is why authors like Quarantelli (2001) and Tierney and colleagues (2006) note that labeling inexplicable behavior as a sign of panic is inherently problematic—such labels say more about the labeler's lack of contextual information than about the actual motivations behind such behavior. Despite the journalistic accounts that sought to debunk the irrational panic-buying myth, that didn't stop further discussion of the supposed presence of panic and the repeated claim that emotions are irrational and impractical (Chow 2020). The case of supposed panic-buying during the COVID-19 outbreak makes clear that the panic myth remains alive and well.

The emphasis on panic and overreaction was not limited to comedians and political leaders, but filtered down to how some members of the public (similar to the Ebola outbreak) emphasized the importance of avoiding over-reaction. *Panic*demic had already earned its way into the Urban Dictionary prior to COVID-19, but it became a term that could easily frame all discussion of coronavirus and COVID-19 as overreaction and media hype ("Panicdemic" 2009). In a photo taken in October 2020 in Amsterdam, the phrase "*panic*demic" is seen as graffiti in a local park (Figure 5.3). As with mockery of panic-buying, the term centers the conversation on the presumably irrational and impractical emotional responses of the public and perhaps political figures and the media. Certainly a sizable portion of the public feels fear, worry, and/or concern in the context of an uncertain threat. Indeed, Sloan and colleagues' research on COVID-19 finds that "a majority of respondents worried about various aspects of the virus, from being exposed to dying, and reported often worrying about others" (Sloan et al. 2021, 1). But the conflation of emotions with impractical and chaotic behavior remains a myth not borne out by the disaster or emotion scholarship. In perpetuating the panic myth, ordinary citizens, political leaders, and even health experts rearticulate dualistic conceptions of emotion and practical action at precise

Figure 5.3 "End the Panicdemic" graffiti in Erasmus Park, Amsterdam, the Netherlands. Photographed by the author on October 21, 2020.

moments of crisis when emotions are so critical to mobilizing urgent, coordinated efforts to safeguard the health of large segments of the population.

Face Masks during COVID-19

As the COVID-19 outbreak became widespread and efforts to contain it became more serious, the use of face masks received significant attention in Europe and North America. Some of these discussions centered on the scientific knowledge concerning if and how face masks limit the distribution of particles and thus their inherent effectiveness at preventing the spread of the virus. Underlying much of this debate, though, were unexamined assumptions about human behavior and emotion that directed leaders in how they approached the use of masks. Again, as in discussions of whether or not to use the term "pandemic," an emotional calculation appeared to underlie health debates at key junctures in the pandemic's development.

Early in the outbreak, some news outlets framed the wearing of masks as itself a sign of panic. In late February 2020, Professor Robert Dingwall, a researcher at Nottingham Trent University, argued against public use of face masks, claiming that wearing masks was not effective and that to do so would provoke fear:

> He (Dingwall) also warned the prevalence of face masks provokes "an epidemic of fear alongside the epidemic of the virus."

While the WHO held a consistent message that said face masks should not be compulsory, their reasoning was the exact opposite of Dingwall. Rather than believing masks would provoke fear and panic, the WHO emphasized the "false sense of security" that masks might create. Early in February 2020, WHO representative to the Philippines, Dr. Rabindra Abeyasinghe, spoke at a hearing and urged health experts to "be rational about the use of masks."

> Factually, it shows that [among] non-symptomatic people, using masks will give them a false sense of confidence and put them at more risk because they tend to wash hands less. ("WHO Warns: Masks May Give False Sense of Security, Lead to Neglect of Proper Hygiene" 2020)

Later, Dr. Rabindra Abeyasinghe and the WHO would relent that home-made masks can provide some protection, albeit not 100 percent protection from viral particles. And the argument *for* wearing masks, and the symbolic meanings conferred to the face mask as an object, have shifted over the course of the outbreak to a symbol of empathy and putting the needs of society and others above oneself (Business Insider US 2020). The face mask, like the Ebola suit, has come to be a defining symbol of the outbreak, with multiple meanings. With such varying meanings comes the potential for different groups to interpret and draw out different forms of emotional capital from that symbol. For some it might implicate government overreach and contain within it stores of emotional capital linked to anger and a sense of injustice. For others it might house strong feelings of protection and compassion. And for still others, such as nurses and doctors, its use might be so habitual that its energizing ability is only in the most mundane sense that routines and habits—through their bare repetition—provide us with comfort and consistency.

Underlying political decisions about how to respond to the outbreak—to close some shops and not others, to mandate masks by employees or the public, or decisions about opening schools—political leaders relied on assumptions about how people would *feel* and, in turn, how those feelings would influence behavior. Rarely do these emotional assumptions make use of context-specific, empirical data on how people's emotional responses align with particular health behaviors. It is painful to retrospectively examine how these emotional calculations played out, particularly among vulnerable groups. For example, as COVID-19 spread rapidly in overcrowded prisons in the United States, NPR reported on April 28, 2020, that decisions about masks were made based on an unsubstantiated emotional calculation:

> According to unions representing correctional officers in the state [Arizona], at least 20 officers have tested positive, though union leaders believe the number is much higher. They say hundreds of employees have shown up to work with COVID-19 symptoms and been sent home. [. . .] Compounding the problem, union leaders say, is that the *correctional officers were barred for a time from wearing masks for fear that would cause panic among the inmates.* (Jenkins and Katz 2020, emphasis added)

The state of our knowledge about crisis emotions does not allow us to fully answer the question of whether wearing masks causes panic or if panic is always problematic. We need further research on the complexity of these issues, but we know from the disaster and crisis literature that assuming panic where it is not, and assuming that panic will inevitably lead to problematic behavior, do not provide a sound foundation for effective leadership and public health policies during a crisis. Rather, these assumptions and the types of emotional calculations that they entail, be it from the WHO Director-General, prison wardens, or politicians, are part of the broader cultural assumption that emotions are problematic barriers to effective practical action, and that panic, above all other emotions, should be avoided no matter the cost. Despite the many technological advances made toward vaccine development, surveillance of the spread of viruses in populations, and testing for viral antibodies, political rhetoric and health policies remain fixed to antiquated notions of emotions and their presumed impracticality.

Empathy as Precursor to Practical Action

In addition to illustrating some of the contradictions and complexities in how we think about crisis emotions, news coverage of the Ebola outbreak also highlighted another key practice that illustrates the utility of emotion. The multimedia storytelling of digital news outlets now, more than ever, can serve to help or hinder how diverse audiences across the globe think and *feel with* particular suffering others (Bleiker et al. 2013; Höijer 2004). International news sources often synchronized their coverage of the Ebola outbreak, particularly when it came to portrayals of the suit and PPE. This was especially clear in the "How to wear a hazmat suit" segment that was first done by CNN (October 13, 2014) and a type of segment that would later be reimagined several times by a variety of outlets, including *The New York Times* (October 17, 2014) and the BBC (October 15, 2014). These reenactments of the same type of segment highlighted the layered symbolic meaning of PPE during the Ebola outbreak, as the same materials could be seen as a source of comfort and reassurance or, and especially if taken off too hastily or haphazardly, could be the very source of contagion.

In CNN's initial segment, the audience sees Dr. Sanjay Gupta standing in front of a white, draped sheet. One by one, he puts on each of the PPE items used by healthcare workers treating patients with Ebola. This includes the gown, two layers of gloves, face mask, and face shield. He then takes a bottle of chocolate syrup and squirts the dark brown liquid on his hands as a substance that can visually show where blood can end up, even after careful removal of each element of the suit. In its own version of this type of segment, *The New York Times* included a large time stamp with minute and second counter to emphasize the amount of time—down to the second—that it takes to effectively put on the suit. After gloves, gown, hood, apron, and even duct tape around the edges of the gloves, the total time reads thirteen minutes and nine seconds. In another CNN version of this segment, Rosie Tomkins dons the suit and highlights the thin nature of the material used to make the suits. Heat and stress both make spending much time in the suit difficult, especially when working in hot climates. Danny Savage, for BBC, details the difficulty in breathing and the speed with which the suit heats up causing him to perspire as he speaks through a double layer of mask and face shield.

In these segments, healthcare workers are key players with whom the audience is invited to role-take—taking on the role of and considering what it would be like to don and remove each item of the suit in perfect and speedy succession. Segments like this place the audience and the journalist in a distinct relationship to the Ebola epidemic. Healthcare workers are the main "other" to whom the journalist (and the audience through mediation) vicariously take the role of and, in doing so, come to briefly take on the point of view of such workers (Mead 1934). This type of mimicry or "imitation" is "at the heart of our ability to "feel into" another person" (Davis 2006, 449) and can operate outside of conscious awareness (450). Through this act of imitating what it is like to work as a healthcare provider caring for Ebola patients, the audience imagines the same embodied movements of healthcare workers and the moments of heightened stress and pressure of removing contaminated items with extreme caution. Such vicarious imitations provide the antecedents to feeling empathy for healthcare workers.

Empathy involves both cognitive and emotional processes. Through empathy, we place ourselves in the shoes of others and orient ourselves toward the world in a manner similar to the one with whom we are empathizing. What is felt when we *do* empathy is not always pity or sadness but can include the whole spectrum of emotions that another's perspective might evoke in us as we place ourselves in their position. This can include fear, of course, as well as anger, sadness, and grief. It involves an imaginative "entering into and sharing the minds of other persons" (Cooley 1922, 132). In the context of media portrayals of Ebola healthcare workers, the feelings of workers as suit-wearers come to be better understood and shared. Over time, though, feeling with "suit-wearers" might become less an antecedent to empathy and more an antecedent to an actual scenario in which the viewer needs to engage in similar protective steps.

Notably, none of the videos in the dataset included examples of journalists "acting out" what it would be like to be a patient suffering from Ebola. Certainly, they include patient stories, and other scholars note that the WHO in particular used social media platforms to emphasize the experiences of survivors and workers alike (Sastry and Lovari 2017). When survivors were invited on news segments as interviewees, most airtime in US and British news outlets focused on Western healthcare workers, journalists, or camera crew who have returned to their home country. These digital practices shape emotions, as audiences take on the role of what it is like to be a healthcare worker, to think and feel what it would be like to be in the suit, pressed for time, and fixated on donning and removing protective equipment with precision. The emotion practices of feeling with healthcare workers might increase sympathy with such workers, but they might also reinscribe patients and victims as sources of fear and as a "them" distinct from "us." These practices can serve as a practical mechanism for anticipating a future in which ordinary citizens might need to wear the type of protective equipment that became ubiquitous in Ebola news coverage.

In the case of COVID-19, the wearing of PPE did become a reality for non–healthcare professionals. While the use of masks in public was more common in countries like China and Hong Kong prior to the outbreak, wearing face masks in public became a mandatory part of governmental efforts to limit the spread of the disease for several countries (Al Jazeera News 2020). Private citizens made and donated cloth masks and social media filled with face mask selfies. Feeling with healthcare workers provided a visceral preparation to what it would be like to use and wear equipment that would otherwise be totally foreign to those outside of the medical field. In the case of Ebola, curiosities about PPE included not only journalists putting on the suits as demonstration but also consumers and manufacturers capitalizing on Ebola interest by developing an Ebola suit as a Halloween costume (Casarez 2014). These curiosities might serve as a precursor to not only feeling empathy for healthcare workers treating Ebola patients but also as an opportunity to act out what steps would be needed should members of the public face a situation in which they themselves need to suit up for protection.

Taking an emotion practice approach allows us to better appreciate the complexity of emotions and the role of political leaders and news media sources in shaping them. Certainly, we can see Dr. Gupta's use of chocolate syrup as a stand-in for blood and *The New York Time*'s stopwatch timer as elements that captivate an audience that is only experiencing the epidemic vicariously. But if we look past these elements, we find a larger picture in which healthcare workers are cast as the main protagonists in the drama of Ebola. In this larger picture, we can see how empathy might be fostered for some but truncated for others. This is not intended to deny the heroic efforts of healthcare workers during Ebola and the COVID-19 outbreak; rather, it highlights the fact that heroizing a single character inevitably blinds us to other victims and other needs. In priming audiences to vicariously suffer with healthcare workers as they put on and remove PPE, audiences engage in acts that can stimulate empathy for healthcare workers but at the expense of empathizing with suffering patients. The emotional capital needed to enact empathy for others is not a limitless resource, as we saw in the reflections of nurses in Chapter 2. Given these limits, it is inevitable that individual consumers and news content producers cannot empathize with all relevant parties. Yet the decisions made about how and for whom to cultivate empathy remain political decisions steeped in inequalities across race and global position.

Conclusion

I began this chapter with a quote from Dr. Tedros Adhanom Ghebreyesus, WHO Director-General, as he responded to the ongoing development of the COVID-19 pandemic. In his initial and some of his follow-up comments, fear remained antithetical to reason and in need of suppression. Yet over the course of the outbreak, we can see subtle changes in how he framed emotions and fear. In February 2020, he argued that "our greatest enemy right now is not the virus itself. It's fear, rumors and stigma. And our greatest assets are facts, reason and solidarity." But at the beginning of March, his framing began to change:

> We understand that people are afraid and uncertain. Fear is a natural human response to any threat, especially when it's a threat we don't completely understand. (March 3, 2020)

> We know people are afraid, and that's normal and appropriate. That fear can be managed and moderated with accurate information. (March 5, 2020)

And on March 20, he emphasized that "It's normal to feel stressed, confused and scared during a crisis. Talking to people you know and trust can help." And in an even more stark contrast to an initial framing of fear as problematic, Dr. Maria van Kerkhove noted in a March 23 WHO virtual conference that:

> It's important that that fear that people have, which is normal, be used in a productive way, turning that fear, turning that energy into ways in which you can keep yourself busy if you have to stay home because of national measures. (World Health Organization 2020d)

Thus, in the WHO's own press conferences over the course of the COVID-19 outbreak, we see shifting and at times contradictory messages about emotions like fear: Is fear normal, even rational? Is it useful?

Taking a practice approach, we can see fear in response to an uncertain situation like a novel virus as a practical orientation to future actions. Fear is the individual and collective body's way of sensing this uncertainty. We can channel, suppress, or demonize this fear in a variety of ways. In Chapter 4, we saw in the case of Ebola that there was indeed some increase in fear and worry discussed on social media as cases of Ebola were reported outside of West Africa, yet the overwhelming response on Twitter was not fear, but humor. This may well be a result of the fact that the virus was contained to only a handful of infections in the English-speaking world. If the outbreak had spread more widely, perhaps we would have seen a shift from humor to more explicit fear. Yet we also see examples of humor in the COVID-19 outbreak, like those mocking the absurdity of empty toilet paper aisles. Social media sites, like Twitter, may be platforms for provocation and entertainment as much as for spreading (mis)information. It is important to keep these multiple emotional functions in mind when debating the types of platform regulations and policies that are needed to combat misinformation.

Political leaders and elites recognize the power of emotions. In their tendency to dismiss the emotional reactions of others as irrational, they work to shore up their own standing as stoic and detached, attempting to transform their emotional capital into political capital. When assuring the public not to fear, political actors embody a stoic habitus that works to transform their skill in managing the emotions of others into increased "prestige, reputation, and status" (Heaney 2019, 234). While disasters, crises, and public health threats are seen as extraordinary, not ordinary, the assumptions about emotion that underlie political decision-making remain quite common. From the WHO Director-General's discussion of fear as antithetical to facts, presidents and PMs calling for calm, and in public health officials' assumption that face masks induce panic, Cartesian assumptions that emotions are dangerously antithetical to practical action abound. The remnants of the Western Enlightenment view of emotions that I highlighted in Chapter 1 continue to haunt discussions and decisions that play out in twenty-first-century health policies, Twitter, and in viral memes as well as viral outbreaks.

By laying bare and critiquing these assumptions, an emotion practice approach promises to help us see how power is enacted both in calls for calm as well as in practices of fear-mongering. Scholars have highlighted a trend toward the "emotionalization" of politics—that is, a trend toward an "audience democracy" (Mair 2013, 44) in which "emotional competence becomes one more, increasingly important, cluster of specific competences, embodied in the habitus of professional politicians in late modernity" (Heaney 2019, 235). Thus, the embodied activation of particular emotional resources (as habitus) becomes an increasingly relevant skill for politicians to use (though this need not be a product of conscious, strategic choice) to shore up political capital during an evolving threat.

In this context, we can again see how emotions operate and shape social life beyond any single emotion or individual feeler. Assumptions about emotions infuse decisions at some of the highest levels and during some of the most critical turning points in the COVID-19 pandemic. Leaders can harness these assumptions by dismissing fear and panic while also shoring up their own reserves of emotional capital—their own claim to enact the "right" emotions and possess the "right" emotional skills for the moment. Showing their calm in the face of a crisis might be praised as bravery and win them some needed political points during a crisis. In tapping into shared assumptions about emotion as problematic, leaders try to find common ground across political divisions and the social hierarchies that stratify nations and regions. In vilifying fear, leaders can generate shared resolve toward defeating a common foe and with it generate the shared emotional energy needed to combat that foe. But in the process, leaders problematically reinforce rules of the game in which they have the most to gain and the least to lose. To be able to feel calm in the face of a crisis is not necessarily a virtue but the ultimate luxury—the ultimate sign of privilege. In setting the feeling rules for others in times of crisis—the expectations of what others *should* feel—leaders attempt to exert control at a time when their governing is most precarious.

Perhaps most critically, when leaders focus on controlling public emotions, they risk being distracted from the urgent task of addressing pressing, life-and-death problems. To solve such problems requires individual energy as well as collective coordination. In that regard, Dr. Tedros Adhanom Ghebreyesus is correct that we need solidarity, but in dismissing fear, political leaders might be ignoring a key source of energy and vigilance. Emotions get us where we *want*, and sometimes *need*, to go. Calling for calm docility in the face of a pandemic seems to be a cheap trick to appear stoic when what we in fact need is leadership that can channel the various emotions of panic, fear, and hope into urgent and effective collective action.

Conclusion

Practical Emotions for a Changing Social World

While writing this book, one singular experience brought together many of the themes I have discussed so far. I had taken to writing in a room in our back garden, usually in the mornings and evenings. One evening in the spring of 2020, I suddenly heard sporadic clapping and hollering and then thunderous applause as my neighbors stood out on their back balconies in the courtyard hooting and clapping in unison. In confusion, I went online to find the reason. A social media initiative had started a day earlier asking the public to give a round of applause at 8 pm on March 17 (Slisco 2020). For whom? For the healthcare workers who were working day and night to meet the challenges of COVID-19. In that moment, much like being at a stadium on game day, people throughout the city of Amsterdam and throughout Europe and the United States used social media to coordinate a moment of gratitude for healthcare workers. They physically moved to their balconies and patios where they could both see and hear each other. What began sporadically became a wave of routinized clapping, whistling, and vocalizations. Out of step with this coordination, I felt confusion and an acute sense of being an outsider. Through these rituals, participants generate collective effervescence and emotional energy, aiming to channel these good vibes to the healthcare workers who were working to contain and treat COVID-19. In this single moment, we can see the importance of generating emotional energy, the utility of social media for coordination, and how the gratitude of the public might be then taken up by nurses who are sorely depleted of emotional resources—resources they need to meet the daily challenges of working in an overburdened healthcare system that exceeded capacity during the pandemic.

If there is one takeaway from this book, it is that emotions are powerful forces that include effort, energy, and habitual practices that straddle the intentional and unintentional. At times, they seem to have their way with us, pushing and pulling us in different directions that are not always easy

Practical Feelings. Marci D. Cottingham, Oxford University Press. © Oxford University Press 2022.
DOI: 10.1093/oso/9780197613689.003.0007

to articulate. But they are also practical. We need them. And particularly in times of crisis and challenge, it can be easy to dismiss them—to tell people to be rational and to stop worrying, panicking, or feeling fear. But this is the wrong approach. Not only is it unlikely to be effective, but in doing so, we might extinguish the very flames of energy that we need to collectively come together and overcome the large societal challenges that threaten our collective well-being. Feeling "gets people where they want to go" (Hochschild 1983, 214). Channeling these emotions toward the practical ends to which they are already oriented, rather than trying to repress, cut off, or stifle them, allows us to tap into a vital energy source when apathy and indifference threaten to keep us stagnant.

Building on Arlie Hochschild's groundbreaking work, numerous studies across the fields of sociology, organizational studies, and management emphasize the management and regulation of emotion. This is important work and not to be minimized. Yet, in fixing our analytical gaze on how emotions are repressed, cultivated to match emotion norms, faked, or generally worked over, we can lose sight of the original situations and relationships from which emotions emerge and the practical, future demands to which they orient our minds, bodies, and collectives. In common vernacular, practical emotions are usually discussed as intuition or "gut feelings." We often fail to recognize that these intuitions are evoked as much from our social environments as from our innards. Our "gut feelings" are always aligned to a particular setting, interaction, and level of power and status within a given context, helping us to navigate a social world filled with ambiguity and limited information.

If Spock, from Star Trek, is the prototype of Enlightenment rationality (Lutz 1998, 60), then Data, from the franchise's 1980's reboot, might be emblematic of a move toward emotions as practical. Data is an android who is devoid of emotion but driven to become a perfect replica of his human creator. In an exchange with Geordi La Forge, Data queries La Forge about how he goes about making decisions:

LA FORGE: "I don't know, Data, my gut tells me we ought to be listening to what this guy's trying to tell us."
DATA: "Your gut?"
LA FORGE: "It's just a . . . a feeling, you know, an instinct. Intuition."
DATA: "But those qualities would interfere with rational judgment, would they not?"
LA FORGE: "You're right, sometimes they do."

DATA: "Then . . . why not rely strictly on the facts?"
LA FORGE: "Because you just can't rely on the plain and simple facts. Sometimes they lie." (Quotes.net n.d.)

And sometimes we simply don't have all the facts needed to be able to make a resolute decision. Instead, we work toward a gut feeling that suggests equilibrium between our limited knowledge of the environment, self, and others. Feelings and intuitions attempt to guide us with the limited information available as we work to meet emerging threats and challenges.

Of course, gut feelings can also "lie." We get it wrong many times. Relying on instinct or intuition alone can be a euphemism for falling back onto our most deep-seated forms of prejudice and stereotypical thinking. Just because emotions are *oriented* toward a practical engagement with the world does not mean that they are infallible. The world to which we are oriented is a flawed, unjust world. Just as reasoning to understand the world is susceptible to misinformation, our gut feelings can get it wrong. From studies of eyewitness accounts, to police shootings of unarmed black men in the United States, we have ample evidence that cultural views of gender and race mold our gut feelings, entrenching social hierarchies that unequally dole out advantages to some and disadvantage, harm, and violence to others (Barrett 2017; Evans and Feagin 2015; Hordge-Freeman 2015). While emotions might be oriented to practical action, what is considered practical and for whom are embedded in histories and contexts marred by inequality and exploitation.

My aim here is not to argue that emotion is a better mode of practical engagement than reasoning, only that feelings are *oriented* toward practical outcomes alongside reasoning. Feelings, in a sense, are how our bodies reason—how we reason nonconsciously alongside conscious reasoning. The fact remains that we will never have all the facts. And we will never have enough certainty to be able to navigate the world solely based on information and our faculties of reason. Thus, when countering prejudice, "fake" news, or conspiracy theories by relying only on bits of facts to try to convince others of their folly, we are destined to fail. We have to appreciate the emotional appeal of digital communities that coalesce around humor and feelings of belonging (Döveling, Harju, and Sommer 2018), even if that belonging depends on habits of distrust and "alternative facts." Faced with a "post-truth" landscape, some scholars continue to pit emotion against reason and feelings against facts in unhelpful ways (McIntyre 2018). Such an approach reproduces the dualistic thinking that has roundly been critiqued by emotion scholars across the disciplines.

A lie is misinformation told with a purpose. And just as facts and reasoning can be hijacked for manipulation, so, too, can emotions. That is always a possibility. But to understand this manipulation, we must understand the socially energizing needs that such manipulation can serve in groups and communities. We must appreciate that the practical needs that feelings are oriented toward are social as well as physiological. Our practical need for emotional energy and group solidarity can be used by others to foster hate and disgust toward outgroups. Sports fans have been known to brawl and behave badly, especially when fans of competing teams mistreat their sacred symbols (Gentry 2020). And the need to conserve emotional resources, as we saw among nurses, can lead to selective "feeling with" certain patients deemed worthy and even disgust for those who are seen as unworthy. In the context of uncertain public health threats, social media users might turn to distasteful jokes that demean rather than to expressions of compassion. Despite the negative ramifications these practices might have for certain groups in society, they remain oriented toward solving the problem of meeting fundamental needs for energizing social connection. We can critique the injustices these acts catalyze, including hate crimes (Ren and Feagin 2021), without dismissing the emotional needs that drive them.

Symbolic interactionism and pragmatism are two schools of thought that heavily influence the emotion practice approach I develop in this book. Both have been critiqued for failing to account fully for the broader social structures that shape the interactions and experiences that they, respectively, emphasize. In developing an emotion practice approach, I turn to work by Pierre Bourdieu and Patricia Hill Collins and key concepts like habitus, emotional capital, field, social location, and social hierarchies along class and race to connect the practices that occur at the individual and interactional levels with the broader social context in which they are embedded. Homophily, or "affective affinity" for others like us (Threadgold 2020), is particularly relevant for understanding how emotion practices are indicative of established social hierarchies, and therefore also critical to their maintenance. Certainly, there are differences in the standards, or emotion norms, to which people are held depending on their gender, race, and social class, but less visible are the nonconscious practices that render certain others (those "like us") more attractive and comfortable to be around, others with whom we more readily "feel with" and "feel for." In an emotion practice approach, social location shapes the feelings rules to which we are all held account (and to which we work to align our feelings) as well as the visceral embodied sensations of comfort and connection with others that can energize us while requiring little effortful management. Next I discuss the relevance of homophily more explicitly for developing an emotion practice approach going forward.

The Role and Limits of Homophily in Emotion Practice

In Chapter 2, I drew on scholarship on *homophily* to explain why nurses conserve their emotional resources in some patient interactions but expend them, sometimes with very little effort, in other interactions. Homophily is the sharing of social location—the degree to which people who we interact with are "like me" or "like us." Skin color, social class, parental status, shared biographical experiences, and many other cues can be used in interactions to nonconsciously judge another as similar or dissimilar to oneself. The degree of felt similarity can then lead to, in the case of nursing, a nurse feeling sympathy or disgust for a particular patient or patient family. But these are not formulaic calculations. Being of the same race or sharing the same social class background or biographical experience is not enough to determine if one will feel an affective affinity for another. The development of those affinities and shared expectations is *the product of past experiences,* a product of being socialized along intersecting social locations such as working or middle class, white, Black, or Latinx, rural or urban, American, or Liberian. The traces of past practices are deeply embedded and embodied in who we are. In selectively finding homophily or shared affinity with certain others, we can more easily navigate interactions with the array of diverse populations we might encounter on a daily basis. In the context of diverse, multicultural life, highlighting the shared humanity of everyone we encounter and working to feel deeply with them might simply be too energy draining of a task. Homophily is an energy-saving strategy for navigating complex social interactions.

Not only do we see homophily play out as an important mechanism for how nurses navigate the difficulties of their job, but we also see this in the controversy surrounding Colin Kaepernick discussed in Chapter 3. The case of Kaepernick and his act of kneeling during the national anthem became a controversy that seemed to split fans and nonfans alike. Kaepernick's kneeling constituted a rupture with past engrained practices and a violation of social norms that suggest standing during the national anthem as the common posture. Part of the conflict his actions elicited fell in line with race as well as political affiliations. Feeling with people from different races and political groups, particularly given the continued de facto segregation of US neighborhoods and schools (Sohoni and Saporito 2009; Schell et al. 2020), is going to be a challenge—and this is especially exacerbated by white supremacist practices in the United States. This is a context in which white people, practically speaking, have little *incentive* to feel with racial minorities because of their relative privilege (Evans and Feagin 2015). Slavery, Jim Crow laws, and segregation of neighborhoods are all systemic problems that allow white people to remain oblivious to the everyday *emotional* and physical realities of being black in America.

Feeling across these divides means scaling the "empathy wall" that Hochschild's (2016) account of political conservatives in Louisiana makes so clear. Scaling this wall will not come easily because *it has not been practiced.* But thinking and feeling with others across racial and political divides is crucial for solving the big challenges of our times. Challenges like climate change, wealth inequality, and the types of public health risks that we see playing out unequally in the COVID-19 pandemic require the collective coordination of practical action that is hampered when we each stay in the well-worn lanes of our own engrained emotion habits. Yet it is important to note that breaking out of these habits can never be simply a matter of thinking our way out of them. We cannot acquire the right emotional capital through a seminar or workshop on empathy or resilience. Following a social practice framework, we have to appreciate that emotional capital is but one key concept in addition to practice, habitus, and field. Change is only possible when the structures that structure habitus (and with it, forms of emotional capital) are also changed. Inner transformation without external transformation provides only a "fantasy of mastery" (Bracke 2016, 58).

In the context of viral fear during the Ebola and COVID-19 outbreaks, we also see social divisions play a role in whose emotions are deemed reasonable and whose emotions are deemed irrational and dangerous. As political leaders and health experts worked to lead during these difficult times, they relied on well-worn practices that emphasize stoicism and set themselves up as the cool rational counterparts to a panic-stricken public. The "public," as a general mass, is both assumed to be panic-stricken and dismissed as irrational and prone to overreacting. In the case of COVID-19, we saw many of the same themes as during the Ebola outbreak, with leaders like President Trump and the WHO's Dr. Tedros Adhanom Ghebreyesus calling for calm and emphasizing fear as a barrier to effective action. Along with these calls were also the confessions and expressions of worry, concern, and even fear among leaders, though these were much less prominent. For example, Dr. Anthony Fauci, speaking a year *before* the COVID-19 outbreak states:

> The thing I'm most *concerned* about as an infectious disease physician and as a public health person is the emergence of a new virus that the body doesn't have any background experience with. . . . It could be something like SARS. SARS was *really quite scary*. Thankfully, it kind of burned itself out by good public health measures. But the thing that *worries most of us* in the field of public health is a respiratory illness that can spread even before someone is so sick that you want to keep them in bed. (Rothschild 2020, emphasis added)

Certainly, the fact that Dr. Fauci's worries and fears are steeped in a lifetime of experience and expertise in the field of public health adds important weight to his voice. But the dichotomy between the elites and the public can make it seem as if political elites have a monopoly on the "right" emotions to have during public health threats. The worries and concerns of political leaders are validated while the fears of the people are seen as dangerous and impractical. Because Dr. Fauci's worries and fears are based on the evidence, calling for calm without recourse to this evidence is not going to be very convincing. This is one of the absurdities of the myth of the panicking public—even if the public is truly panicking, it seems unlikely that rhetoric or placations will effectively minimize such feelings. These feelings point to uncertainties, distrust, and the body poised for action should threats become reality. Rather than dismiss, we must use these feelings to teach, comfort, reassure, and lead through the coordination of effective action that fosters trust.

During the pandemic's unfolding, we also saw critiques of how out of touch elites are when it comes to how ordinary people experience a crisis like COVID-19. One illustration of this is encapsulated in a poignant cartoon from *The New Yorker* in which a figure is seen rowing in a boat precariously perched in turbulent waters. Rain and lightning are featured in the background and sharp-toothed fish in the foreground. Underneath is the text, "This is it . . . the time to finish your novel." Some well-meaning, yet woefully out-of-touch perspectives called for people to use time during the pandemic lockdown to start a novel or learn a new language. This advice shows how misguided we are when we fail to appreciate the heterogeneity of life experiences and conditions. When we fall back on the default settings set by our own context-specific upbringing and the life advantages and disadvantages that we have accrued over the years, we fail to see beyond ourselves. This cartoon also serves as another example of humor shared through social media during a crisis, aligning with the established practices of social media users who turn to energy-generating humor in times of uncertainty.

Social Change in an Emotion Practice Approach

The contexts and uses of emotion that I discuss in this book only begin to scratch the surface of how we might come to see emotions as practical modes of engaging with the world. In Chapters 4 and 5, I detailed dominant framings of epidemic-related fear and responses on social media in the context of Ebola and COVID-19. Yet there are many other angles for examining emotions during what is sure to be a defining historical moment. The COVID-19 pandemic has clearly disrupted "normal" life around the globe. Parents now find themselves homeschooling their children. Disabled and vulnerable groups now confront new risks and uncertainty. And the physicians, nurses, and other healthcare workers responding to this medical crisis are working in conditions unlike anything experienced before. Many find themselves unprepared for this moment, without a reservoir of prior experiences to guide them, leaving them unmoored and overwhelmed. We lack the established practices for taking on these new challenges. Feelings of stress and overwhelm tell us that we need new practices that can build up emotional reserves and new norms for parenting and working that recognize our inherent individual and collective vulnerabilities. Solidarity should never come at a cost borne only by the most vulnerable. "We are all in this together," but some of us are undoubtedly "in" this deeper than others. Giving voice to the vulnerable, making democracy work better, and developing new ways of organizing social life—rather than returning to a past "normal" predicated on exploitation—are all open possibilities during times of upheaval.

In the various contexts in which COVID-19 has restructured life, we can see emotions as providing resources for navigating and coping with uncertainty. Similar to parents with critically ill children (Gengler 2020), we might all find ourselves navigating new sources of uncertainty, worry, and fear during a pandemic. Our habituated practices must change to meet new external demands, and feelings clue us in to the disjuncture between the futures to which we have been attuned and the realities of the world we confront. Simple actions like playing at a park, going to the grocery store, or gathering together as sports fans became at different points fraught moments of uncertainty and possible risk. In facing these risks, emotions need not be dismissed as distractions but can be harnessed as resources alongside factual information for coming to decisions that promise social as well as individual well-being.

Advancing our understanding of how emotions operate in the everyday contexts we encounter is one important aim of the approach I take here. But going forward, we also need to understand these everyday emotions if we are to use emotion practically for tackling large collective problems. We do not live single-issue lives (Lorde 2019), nor do we experience the world only within a single social field (Threadgold 2020). When it comes to issues of war, exploitation, famine, or climate change, we are more often lacking political resolve—the collective confidence and emotional energy needed to take action—than facts, information, or technical abilities. Coordinating collective action requires taking stock of the emotions of divergent actors, assessing the emotional energy gain and loss of different decisions, and putting emotional skills of empathy and negotiation to use.

An emotion practice approach has important implications for thinking about social change. For one, the intimate, interlocking nature of objective conditions with subjective dispositions that is centered in a practice approach implies that any attempt to change one side must attend to the other. Through variable life experiences and objective, external demands, habitus attunes itself in anticipation of similar experiences to those found in the past. This means that there is an inherently status-quo affirming aspect to this concept, and this is partly why Bourdieu's work is often critiqued as deterministic, offering a limited conception of human agency. Yet, in thinking about emotion as energy and effervescence, we can imagine how the emotions of others might be unintentionally caught—whether it is as a nurse caring for others, or in virtual interactions on social media. The more diverse others we encounter, the broader the possible future worlds our calibrated emotional resources will be fine-tuned to tackle.

One metaphor, inspired by Sara Ahmed's (2006) work on paths and orientations, that is helpful for thinking through the types of subtle change implicated in a practice approach is the visual image of desire paths. Change in a practice approach involves an iterative relationship between reflexivity and habit. Much like engrained habits, structured environments provide expected flows of traffic to move from A to B. Sidewalks are devised by land-scape architects, dug and reinforced by construction workers, and paid for and maintained over time by tax dollars. But no matter how well constructed a sidewalk might be, desire paths can emerge as pedestrians make different choices about the best way to get from one point to the next. The emergence of a desire path highlights the incongruence between tradition and changing needs, between established authority, on the one hand, and the power of a single pedestrian, on the other. Regardless of how they began,[1] to see a desire path is to inevitably be confronted with a choice, and because those paths represent the past practices of others, being confronted with choice (the point at which reflexivity emerges) is inherently infused by our relationships to others (past and present) and our feeling about those others and the paths they have taken and thus made.[2] In this way, the relationality of emo-tion is precisely why it is a critical resource for negotiating decision points. Emotions are the distillation and embodiment of our relationships to others and our environment (see Figure 6.1).

Desire paths are part of the social as much as the physical world. Habitus never confronts a single unalterable path, but it can confront established

Figure 6.1. Desire path. Belém, Lisbon, Portugal. April 14, 2015.

Metro Centric. Licensed under the Creative Commons Attribution 2.0 Generic license. https://commons.wikimedia.org/wiki/File:Desire_path_(19811581366).jpg

sanctioned paths alongside alternative, desire paths. These desire paths, as tweaks to structured, or established paths, create moments of choice about how best one might get from A to B or how best one can meet the set of social, physical, and emotional needs that must be practically addressed. These new desires can emerge when the social landscape shifts or when the initial desire paths of others become visible on the horizon. Confronting the past desires of others, we now see that we have a choice—to remain on the established path or take one of possibly many alternative paths worn to varying degrees by the footfalls of those who walked before. The "sensing" of these new paths suggests that past internalized structures for structuring the world become slightly out of sync with that landscape, leading to a shift in both the objective conditions and internal dispositions that make subtle social change feasible.

Protests and social movements as more dramatic forms of social change are one mechanism for jolting people from their established practices—the established practices exemplified in solid concrete and cobblestone. Such a jolting might be experienced as disorienting and uncomfortable, both to participants and to outsiders. It does not feel good to be forced from an established path onto a muddy grass one. That does not mean that more dramatic disruptions are not necessary—in many ways they are—but it is only in retrospect that we hold up resisters to the status quo as heroes. The trailblazers of new desire paths have to muddy an otherwise pristine green space and bend and trample a lot of grass in the process. And when we follow in the muddy, desire paths of others, we, too, contribute to the ongoing re-creations of those very paths that now seem much more practical for getting us where we want to go. In the end, enough people might recognize the value of a desire path and decide to add in stepping-stones or pavement, completing the cycle of structured path, being deviated from, to ultimately become its own structured path. The force of our desires—the force of our emotions—permeates this process.

As the pandemic disrupts everyday routines, new practices can chart new paths. As huge swaths of the public now work from home (or live at work, as it were), front and back stages (Goffman 1959) collapse and take new forms as digital interactions compete with bodily co-presence. With "private" spaces altered, private emotions might have no place to go but to the (digital) streets. As new risks move from public spaces to homes, safe havens are threatened and the need to act takes hold and might overwhelm. With new options for remote work and flexibility in the workplace, workers might resist a return to the old routines (Duffy 2021). At no other time have the public and private domains seemed so porous and artificial. Future research needs to attend to the emotion practices that flow between domains (through stocks of emotional capital; Cottingham et al. 2020) and the practices that emerge when those domains break down, as well as the policies that emerge from political actors working to transform emotional capital into political capital.

In thinking about processes of social change, we often think of individual change agents rather than their accumulated experiences or the structural disruptions they encounter as fundamental causes. Highlighting this individualistic bias, Threadgold writes:

> As subversive innovators, such figures can become leaders of change, developing symbolic capital and producing new forms, products, styles, tastes and genres that will eventually become toxic. This subversive innovator perspective critiques the individual connotations of the notion of genius, showing how they are always products of the conditions of the field, regardless of how revolutionary, idiosyncratic or shocking their practices may be. (Threadgold 2020, 118)

The current moment opens up new possibilities for social actors to break out of past practices and for subversive innovators to emerge. The nurse who decides to protest rather than clock-in, the players who decide to kneel rather than stand for the national anthem, the social media users who engage in playful disruption to develop empathy rather than xenophobia. All three can be signs of rupture with well-worn habits and the development of new practices that themselves might become part of the status quo. For these disruptions to solidify into new practices, though, and become engrained in the habitus of their carriers, they must ultimately prove useful. Disrupted practices, if they are to stick around, must get us where we want to go. And even if disrupted practices emerge and gain traction, they are likely to be steeped in contradictions and ambiguity (Threadgold 2020, 130).

As large disruptions to the status quo are invariably accompanied by discomfort and negative emotions (including fear, anxiety, and confusion), it is not too surprising that social change occurs in a dialectic in which habitus adjusts slowly, taking on subtle changes in novel moments, but also simultaneously reasserting engrained habits that just *feel* right. In this way, progress can seem to occur in a fashion of two steps forward and one step back, in a cycle of stretching but reaching the limits of elasticity that then snap us back to familiar terrain. During that snap, we inevitably feel as though we are propelled backward. Yet, in stretching each time, the internalized habitus is being reconstituted to stretch further to meet the next set of external demands.

I have argued in this book that an approach to emotion as a form of practice helps to overcome lingering dualisms in social theory and commonsense thinking about emotions. But there are limitations to an emotion practice approach. For one, thinking of the social world, and emotions, in terms of practices is a radical shift from the individualistic and physiology-based frameworks that tend to predominate our understanding of emotions. This is not meant to discount more biological/physiological accounts or frame emotions as somehow disembodied, but rather, to serve as a corrective to the reductionist tendencies of biomedical framings of emotion. I see compatibility between an emotion practice approach and approaches in other disciplines that highlight the simultaneously social, physiological, and neurological underpinnings of emotion. For example, Lisa Feldman Barrett's (2017) development of a theory of constructed emotion is compatible with arguments I have made here, though her work is embedded in the fields of psychology and neuroscience. As she herself notes, much of our commonsense thinking about emotion is the product of stereotypes that frame discrete emotions as singular and universal. Notably, recent research in psychology and neuroscience finds that prior claims about the universality of emotions like fear and anger are actually a product of research design and researchers influencing participant responses (Barrett 2012).

A second limitation is that, because an emotion practice approach centers concepts like habitus, social location, and capital, it might be dismissed as redundant with Bourdieu's original development of these concepts and his overall theoretical contribution. In my own use of these terms, I tend to retain the simple use of habitus rather than use the term "emotional habitus" as other scholars have done (Gould 2009), while using "emotional capital" rather than the more general "cultural capital" from Bourdieu's (1986) original typology. I would again return to the general point I made in Chapter 1 that, despite valiant efforts in the past to deconstruct the dualism between reason and emotion and the privileging of the former above the latter, these dualisms remain entrenched in scholarly and lay conceptions of emotion. These entrenched dualisms have wide-ranging negative implications—the starkest being our failure to act quickly and collectively to meet the challenges of COVID-19. If we are to finally do away with problematic dualisms, we may have to sprinkle "emotion" and "emotional" more liberally into our terminology, along with analyses that shift conceptualization of so-cial life toward *emotion* practices, intertwining modes of engagement, and thinking/feeling processes as overlapping. At the same time, we have to counter assumptions that emotions are private, individual things that point us solely toward self-help and therapeutic interventions. These assumptions are embedded in our language, habits, and commonsense understanding of the world. But collective global challenges might be the very thing that dislodges many unhelpful habits, ways of thinking, and the faulty gut feelings that exacerbate rather than solve such problems.

A Social World Filled with Emotion Practices

I have argued that emotions are practical ways of engaging with the world. Rather than conceptualize emotion and reason as mutually exclusive, feeling and thinking are intertwined modes of action, both forged in the repeti-tion of past practices and oriented toward future, smoother engagements in which physiological and social needs are met. To say that emotions are practices and practical is not to see them as always strategic calculations of knowing actors, but to illustrate how our acts span the conscious and the nonconscious—how our acts are done, and in doing them repeatedly, come to be habitual forces that pull us along, sometimes unwittingly, through the types of social life to which they have been attuned. These practices get into the body and not just the mind. A sports fan marked with the team's logo, a nurse's aching feet after a twelve-hour shift, and the social media user's re-peated scrolling, liking, and sharing all highlight the mindful embodiment of practices both fleshy and digital.

The habituated dispositions of nurses, sports fans, Twitter users, elites and politicians, and the environments for which they are calibrated precede each feeling act. Emotions are practical, embodied calculations haunted by past practices and predictive of future demands. They help sports fans connect with family and their city, they clue nurses into the ambiguous and complex demands of the job, and they can serve to unite disparate groups through digital spaces. By conceptualizing emotions as embodied resources that include both energy and effortful management, we can integrate influen-tial strands of the sociology of emotion with concepts from practice theory aimed at straddling the conscious and nonconscious and objective and sub-jective. Of course, emotions can overwhelm us and might at times seem to get in our way. But this indicates a point of friction that needs to be smoothed out (through self, collective, or environmental change), or perhaps it is an indication that an easy path needs to be traded for a more challenging one. Emotions contain within them the seeds of action and change but can also indicate comfort and contentedness when selves and contexts align.

By tracing emotions through the disparate spaces of sports bars and stadiums, hospital beds and hallways, on social media sites, and in the framing of epidemics, we can see social actors (nurses, sports fans, social media users, and political actors) in more complex, holistic ways. Sports fans are not simply "crazed" fanatics, nurses are not endlessly selfless heroines, and social media users can be appreciated as more than mere reactionary pawns or malicious trolls. In this framework, the placations as well as fear-mongering practices of political actors can be better understood. Homing in on the routine and generative practices of these groups pushes us beyond stereotypes that link each to a limited set of discrete emotions and tendencies. The result is a more humanizing portrait of each of these social players. In the process, we also refine an emotion practice approach that can account for how we use or conserve emotional resources, rather than simply managing them, and how we draw from and invest in the emotional potency of cultural symbols. Yet, in developing an emotion practice approach, we can see how uses of emotional capital are embedded in class-based and racial hierarchies—hierarchies that predict who we will feel with and against, while also transforming the bodily capital of some into the emotional capital of others.

In moving to the digital sphere of social media, I applied an emotion practice approach to digital interactions that span geography and traditional social divisions. Emotion management and interaction ritual theory have been developed as part of symbolic interactionist tradition—a tradition in which the in-person interactions of individuals are of utmost importance for the development of emotions and selves (Shott 1979). In both the public tweets responding to Ebola in 2014 and in the responses of political actors to Ebola and COVID-19, an emotion practice approach helps to explain how symbols, emotional capital, and political capital intermix through digital communications no longer confined to face-to-face interactions. Yet, while communication is increasingly digital, the habitus of political leaders affirms again and again an antiquated view of emotions as volatile and problematic. This outdated view of emotion hampers our ability to harness all resources, including emotional ones, to meet the present and impending challenges of our times.

By integrating prominent theories in the sociology of emotion with a social practice perspective, this book puts forth a distinct emotion practice approach to understanding the enduring role of emotions in social life. It offers one set of conceptual tools for overcoming difficult dualisms in scholarly and lay conceptions of emotion—conceptions that frame emotion as synonymous with base, asocial impulses incompatible with practical action. In demonstrating how emotions operate as practical engagements with the social world, concepts like habitus, emotional capital, field, and social location are relevant for tracing the embodied dispositions and resources that individuals bring to each social encounter, be it a draining or energizing one. In folding emotional energy, knowledge of feeling rules, and the skills of effective emotion management into the concept of emotional capital, this concept becomes a linchpin for integrating important advances in the sociology of emotion since the 1970s. Such conceptual developments, along with the empirical picture they illuminate—be it in the domains examined here or others going forward—provide what I hope will be useful insights for advancing the sociological treatment of emotion in the decades to come.

METHODOLOGICAL APPENDIX
Capturing Emotions

Emotions are tricky to study. Scholars often rely on what people can name and describe in interviews and public documents, or what they can meaningfully translate into established survey questions—what Summers-Effler et al. (2015, 454) refer to as "secondary/reflexive experiences [that] require deliberate reflexivity." As a result, scholars might end up studying the words people use to label emotions more than their raw, experienced sensations. Efforts to capture raw experiences might turn to biomarkers of arousal or other measures using biomedical equipment (Rogers and Robinson 2014), but these also carry limitations, as pupil dilation, heart rate, and skin temperatures are not measures of a singular emotion and such methods risk reductionism—reducing complex emotional experiences to what we can easily measure. Like other social constructionist approaches to emotion, I see interpretation and embodied sensation as nearly impossible to fully disentangle. Even if we could successfully disentangle them, the results would be an artifact of the research process itself rather than emblematic of "real," everyday emotional experiences.

I try to overcome some of these limitations by drawing on a diverse range of methods in the three empirical contexts I study. These methods include taking the self-reports of individuals seriously, but they also include putting myself in the same spaces as participants to try to feel along with them. Such an approach is common in anthropology and sociology. Often such ethnographic work is not in one's own native environment, but in the anthropological tradition, researchers seek out exotic places in which to embed themselves and learn about the culture and society of another group. I was not seeking out exclusively exotic cases; rather, I was hoping to study emotions in both common and extraordinary contexts through the lens of both ordinary folks who work as nurses, who participate as sports fans, and who interact on social media platforms as well as in the rhetoric of public figures and leaders.

I do not identify as a nurse, sports fan, or a particularly dedicated social media user. There is a tension between my own identities and the identities of those included in this research. I worked to attune myself to different work, leisure, and social media practices than the ones I myself have adapted. To deal with this tension, I adopted a variety of methods for collecting different types of data. This includes data gathered through participant observation, informal and formal interviewing, audio diaries, and content analysis of news articles, cultural objects, and user content on social media. These methods of gathering data are intended to help us confront the experiences, reflections, and meanings of these different identities by those who actually live them. Rather than speculate from a distance, the data gathered through these methods can bring us into close contact with the people who identify with and walk out life on different paths than our own. This does not mean that we gain a perfect picture of their lives. There will always be parts of our individual and collective experiences that escape data collection methods. Even our most basic attempt to translate experiences into words will be imperfect (Gould 2009). But these methods give us an approximation that is an improvement over and above armchair speculation.

Examining the Underside of Nursing

In the first empirical context, I turn to the case of nursing in order to understand how nurses confront the particularly challenging emotional demands of their job. Many jobs have distinct affective requirements (Bulan, Erickson, and Wharton 1997) and some fascinating work on nurses has used an ethnographic approach, involving shadowing nurses or even documenting what it is like to practice as a nurse (Theodosius 2008). As a collaborator on a project studying nurses, we built on this prior work by using one method that has only been used sporadically in emotion research: audio diaries. Asking participants to keep an audio diary for each of six consecutive shifts was a tall order—particularly for a workforce that is already stressed and overtaxed. By gaining the trust and buy-in of nurse management at two hospitals and meeting regularly with a group of nurse advisors, the project principal investigator[1] was able to entice nurses to participate in the survey, audio diary, and interview phases of the larger project on nurses' emotions on the job. Certainly, paying nurses for their time helped as well. This project received ethical approval from the Institutional Review Board at the University of Akron.

Nurse diaries offer us richly detailed accounts of their experiences and reflections that are not fully controlled by researcher prompting. When introducing nurses to the project and demonstrating the technical features of the voice recorders, we gave generic advice to record anything pertaining to their emotions throughout the day—this could be done in the moment while working or it could be recorded after the fact on their way home from work, in the car, or at home. Each nurse could choose when and what to record. Some made long recordings as they vented about their day on the drive home. Some made short ten-minute recordings that focused on the events of the day but without much emotional reflection. The method requires that the researchers give up a degree of control over what is said. Without us being present when nurses made recordings, we could not follow up with specific questions or find out more about whom they interacted with. But this lack of control on our part led, we believe, to a trove of emotional reflections and experiences from nurses as they navigated through hospital corridors, from bedside to bedside and on their way to and from work (Cottingham and Erickson 2020a).

The project solicited participation from all full-time registered nurses at two hospitals in two Midwestern US cities. In total, forty-eight nurses participated in the audio diary phase of the project and twenty-one nurses participated in follow-up interviews. The majority of participants were white women, but we aimed to diversify the sample by reaching out to men and nurses of color specifically. In the end, ten white men, nine women of color (seven African American and two Asian American), and one African American man participated in the diary phase. After they completed their diaries for six consecutive shifts, the research team transcribed the entries and one member met up with some of the nurses to ask follow-up questions about what they had recorded. These follow-up interviews focused on how they reflect back on the experiences they described in their diaries and probed for further reflections on the emotional demands of nursing and how they manage their emotions on the job.

These diaries and interviews were transcribed first by a transcription company and then checked twice by members of the research team. Transcription is never a straightforward process (Bird 2005), and audio diaries presented new challenges. We encountered a variety of background noises (traffic, beeping machinery, and side conversations with coworkers), run-on sentences, verbal fillers, and verbalizations like sobbing, shaking voices, laughter, sighs, and inhales that are not easy to transfer to text. Introducing structured sentences and paragraphs involved elements of interpretation before we formally uploaded the transcripts to a qualitative analysis program. People do not typically speak in complete sentences, much less when they are trying to think and feel their way through complex and ambiguous emotional experiences. As a result, we included a number of checks on the transcription process, with two members of the research team tasked with verifying a transcript against the recording after we received an initial version from the transcription company.

In analyzing the data, I developed a code structure that included deductive codes based on prior work in the study of emotions among nurses (*work-family spillover, surface acting,* and *deep acting* are some examples) as well as inductive codes that seemed to closely match the responses of our nurses (*mixed emotions, the mood of the unit, déjà vu, catching the emotions of others,* and *empathy/compassion limits* are some examples). The goal with this mix of inductive and deductive coding is to identify areas where prior theorizing has limited reach in making sense of the rich and context-dependent reflections of nurses in our sample. Thus, the analysis proceeds in a more abductive rather than purely inductive manner (Timmermans and Tavory 2012). This allows us to see where an emotion management perspective is limited and turn to other theories and concepts to compensate. In doing so, we develop a hybrid theory of emotion practice that tries to compensate for the relative limitations of emotion management theory, on the one hand, and poststructuralist approaches to social practice, on the other. I used Dedoose, a web-based qualitative analysis program, for this analysis.

There are, of course, limitations inherent to our research design and to an abductive, hybrid approach to analyzing qualitative data. For one, our data collection required active participation and commitment from nurses—nurses who are already likely taxed and exhausted from the demanding work they perform. This means that participants at the most extreme levels of exhaustion and stress would be less likely to participate and their experiences might be missed by this method of data collection. Secondly, as I outline in Chapter 2, emotion management theory, interaction ritual theory, and poststructuralist conceptions of social practice emphasize different aspects about how the world works and how to develop knowledge about its workings. Merging approaches in a haphazard way can lead to a new hybrid theory that violates the assumptions of both traditions—a Frankenstein theory that lacks internal coherence and symmetry. Grand theories of the social world might have a beauty in their simplicity—a framework that is built from foundational assumptions up to real-world postulates in a seamless manner. But grand theorizing can appear sealed off from the messiness of everyday living. An emotion practice approach, as I have argued, is a way to try to return to historical developments in the traditions of symbolic interactionism and poststructuralism and create connections across what seem like vast differences. It might have a touch of a Frankenstein aesthetic. It might not be pretty, but the point is its utility—that it is useful in explaining emotions in and across the social arenas of work, leisure, and digital life I examine in this book.

Feeling with Sports Fans

In turning to the context of sports fandom, I took a different approach to data collection in order to capture the emotions, symbols, and meanings of being a fan. In studying sports fans, I was studying a group that I was familiar with but not a group to which I strongly identified. I grew up in western Pennsylvania and had a working knowledge of the game, the teams, and some of their histories and rivalries. My approach to studying sports fans was a combination of participating in fan activities, observing others in fan contexts, informal interviews, and gathering and analyzing journalistic accounts of Steelers fans. In participating in tailgating, watching games with my informant at sports bars, and watching a game at Heinz Field, I was able to meet the first ritual ingredient identified by Collins—physical co-presence—and as a result, I could interrogate my own embodied sensations and interpretations, albeit as a newcomer versed in knowledge about the sport, but without a strong fan identity. Through informal conversations with fellow tailgaters and my informant, I was able to learn more about how fans understand these practices and how they linked to family and city life. By turning to journalistic accounts of fan behavior, I was able to supplement what I could learn from talking to individuals in particular situations and trace the use of important fan symbols outside of tailgating and watching games. This study received ethical approval from the Institutional Review Board at Indiana University of Pennsylvania.

I chose to study fans of this American football team for a couple of reasons. Most pragmatically, this was a team I grew up hearing about and I was already familiar to an extent with the city, the team, and its fan base. I grew up north of Pittsburgh, listening to Myron Cope on the radio during Sunday drives after church. Traveling to see a baseball game at the then Three Rivers Stadium is one of my first memories of being in the "big" city. I had returned to living in the area after being away for five years and, in returning, the influence of sports on the city took on a strange rather than familiar quality. I became intrigued by the way the city seemed to transform during the football season.

During the course of the project, I also learned that Steelers fans are, according to some sources, seen as unusual in their devotion. ESPN ranked fan bases for the NFL (National Football League) in 2008 and determined that the Steelers and the Packers (of Green Bay, Wisconsin) were the top fans because of their loyalty, devotion, commitment to attendance (even at away games), and the connection that the teams have to their home town (Mosley 2008). Part of this connection to the city is because the Steelers franchise was one of the first in the NFL and the Rooney family has owned them for the duration of their existence (a rarity among team franchises). This creates a degree of continuity in spite of the fact that beloved players routinely cycle out of the roster as they become injured, traded, or retire. As James Walker notes in the decision to rank Steelers fans as number one: "No team is as woven into the fabric of a city" (Mosley 2008). While this suggests a degree of exceptionalism among Steelers fans, the connection between city and fan base was echoed in many of the rationales for fan base ranking: "Cleveland is a football-crazed town year-round" and "No other team dictates a city's [Philadelphia] mood like the Eagles" (Mosley 2008). This does not necessarily mean that the fans I observed in Pittsburgh were wholly different from the fans of other teams, but it does suggest that if I was going to be able to empirically capture fan emotions in and beyond the peak moments of a game, then a good place to start would be with Pittsburgh Steeler fans.

When beginning the project, I connected with a fan who could act as my informant and guide me through the experiences of tailgating and watching games. This gave me entrée into a group of dedicated tailgaters who readily welcomed me to their gatherings in the parking lot near Heinz Field prior to home games. Additionally, we visited sports bars near the stadium and one farther from the stadium center in the Mt. Washington area, which is known for its panoramic view of the three rivers at the heart of the city. Though not planned, I was also able to attend a game in December with my informant when fans at a sports bar fortuitously gave us free tickets to the game. In participating with fans, I was able to align myself with them so that my awareness of the social context was "aligned closely with subjects' awareness" (Summers-Effler, Van Ness, and Hausmann 2015, 458). While I took notes of my observations and informal conversations with fans, I was also mindful of how I felt in these spaces. I relayed these in my field notes along with my observations.

In addition to observing while tailgating, at a game, and in sports bars, I also collected a database of news articles covering the Steelers fan base. An initial query led me to discover several notable cases of Steelers-themed funerals. From there, I wondered if there were also examples of weddings, and this expanded to include other ways that Steelers symbols are incorporated into the city, such as the team's impact on the schedules of professionals and hoteliers, and reactions of politicians, hospitals, and companies that tried to capitalize on the emotionally rich symbols of fandom. The school and mass closings that followed the Steelers Super Bowl win in 2009 were serendipitous, as much of these data points would have been absent if the team had not done so well in the particular football season I had chosen to study fans. I continued to read sports commentary and news articles specific to Steelers fans and to controversies in the NFL, including the recent controversy surrounding Colin Kaepernick's protest of racial injustices in the criminal justice system. Search counts for Steelers-themed wedding items and fan tattoos were all done in 2020 and 2021.

Like the use of audio diaries in the nursing project, there are limitations to my research design in studying sports fans. Importantly, my focus on public spaces where fans congregate meant that I could not easily observe the type of family dynamics that my informant highlighted as influential in fan identity and interactions. Future research might combine public observation with observations in more intimate spaces like family gatherings in homes as family and friends prepare for and watch games.

Tracing Emotions Online with #Ebola

Chapters 4 and 5 in this book are based on a third project that centered on the types of emotions endemic to news coverage and social media reactions to the 2014–2016 Ebola epidemic. This project focused on how emotions are framed, spread, and discussed in these digital spaces. I was particularly interested in this topic after reading a retrospective statement by the then WHO Director-General, Dr. Margaret Chan, who claimed that information technology and social media had allowed fear to spread faster than the Ebola virus (Chan 2015).

In order to assess the types of emotions and the way in which emotions were discussed in the context of the Ebola outbreak, I archived a database of three different sources of data: (1) news headlines retrieved from Lexis-Nexis, (2) online videos from the top three global news brands (CNN, The New York Times, and the BBC, Newman 2015); and (3) Twitter data collected the week before and the week after the first reported US case of Ebola. In a preliminary assessment of the Lexis-Nexis database, October 2014 emerged as the month of peak Ebola coverage in English-language news outlets. This correlated with the first reported US case of Ebola, which was documented on September 30, 2014 (Centers for Disease Control and Prevention 2014). Tracing emotions in the context of these digital practices involved interpretively categorizing text according to emotional appeals (Altheide 1987; Loseke 2009), as well as descriptively measuring variations in types of emotions referenced. This project received approval from the ethical review board at the Amsterdam Institute for Social Science Research at the University of Amsterdam.

News Headlines on the Ebola Outbreak

The first type of data to address the role of emotions in Ebola coverage is English-language headlines published before and during peak coverage of Ebola. The LEXIS-NEXIS database (now Nexis Uni) offers access and advanced search capabilities for collecting this data (Bail 2014). Several different datasets were developed using the Nexis Uni search function. Because personal protective equipment (PPE) had such a qualitatively important role in how news videos seemed to present the outbreak, one dataset focused on the use of emotions in discussing both Ebola and a number of items, including gloves, hazmat suits, boots, and face masks. Two additional news headline datasets were created to assess the use of emotions in all Ebola-related news, particularly as it might vary across news source, between May 1, 2014, and January 31, 2015. Inspired by WHO Director-General Chan's claim that social media had allowed fear to spread more readily than traditional news sources, I developed one dataset of 750 of the top most relevant, English-language headlines from traditional newspapers sources and a second dataset of 750 of the top most relevant, English-language headlines from video, blog, and web-based sources. Each of these subsamples represents roughly 2 and 1 percent, respectively, of the total number of headlines.

In my analysis of these data, I focused on direct references to specific emotions of fear (terror, panic, shock), compassion, hope, and references to concern and worry. This allows for a descriptive assessment of which emotions were used by news sources just before and during peak coverage of the epidemic. The aim of this method was to descriptively examine the vast range of emotions across traditional news sources. Results are thin (based only on article titles), but they span a longer timeframe than the news videos and social media datasets discussed next.

News Video Coverage of Ebola

To complement the more exhaustive datasets of Ebola headlines, the second source of data was online video media produced by the top three international news outlets (BBC, CNN, and *The New York Times*, according to the Reuters Institute, Newman 2015) before and during peak global news coverage (September 23–October 31). Decline in print-based revenue has caused significant decline in international reporting in print sources (Jurkowitz 2014). Digital news consumption has overtaken traditional newspapers and is close to overtaking television sources among Americans (Pew Research Center 2012). Digital reporting offers new modes of storytelling that merge audio, video, and graphics. Such modes are ripe for exploring the distinct emotion practices of epidemic coverage. I downloaded video data from online news sites using screen and audio capture software. This data set included eighty-four videos ranging in length from one to ten minutes, with an average of three minutes. Working with a research assistant, we developed a code book of inductive and deductive codes. We applied these codes to excerpted video data using the qualitative analysis software Atlas.ti.

My analysis of the video content used a similar abductive approach noted earlier that formulates hunches and seeks out surprising findings by relating data to the theoretical framework of emotion practice (Timmermans and Tavory 2012). More specifically, the analysis asked how emotions emerge in relation to people (healthcare workers), objects (hazmat suit, gloves), and activities (international travel), pointing to distinct forms of digital emotion practice. The analysis involved coding the data for emergent themes, using the strategies of initial and in vivo coding (Saldaña 2013). Positioning of victims and healthcare workers (Bleiker et al. 2013) and use of symbolic codes (Loseke 2009)—such as the hazmat suit—were analyzed in particular for the emotions they can convey. In coding the video data, we also attended to the mood portrayed in the use of particular images, graphics, and music embedded in the videos (Rose 2004) in order to understand how all three elements converge to create emotional meanings (Altheide 1987). In-depth, interpretive analysis can provide rich understanding (Tracy 2010) of emotions in the context of news coverage.

Twitter Responses to Ebola

The third data source used to understand epidemic emotions was social media. Twitter provides real-time data "that is both fine-grained and massively global in scale" (Golder and Macy 2011). While health scholars have used Twitter for surveillance (Odlum and Yoon 2015), only recently has critical scholarship used Twitter to address sociological questions (Bail 2014; Brownlie and Shaw 2019). I again took September 30, 2014—the day of the first US Ebola case—as a focal point, sampling tweets before and after that date. Sifter, a Twitter archive service, estimated 705,000 tweets the week before September 30 (September 23, 2014–September 29, 2014) and 6,118,000 the week after (September 30, 2014–October 6, 2014). This growth rate of 768 percent suggests that this date was indeed a turning point in the Ebola conversation among English-language users on Twitter. Drawing a sample of 1 percent of tweets posted in the week before and after September 30 allows for broad variation in the type of tweets captured while also remaining small enough to allow for interpretive coding that can account for direct and indirect references to emotions from both organizations and individuals. The total sample size is roughly 50,000 tweets.

In analyzing the Twitter dataset, clear emotion references require only simple search functions to isolate emotion words (afraid, panic, shock, etc.). However, more nuanced communication of emotion required interpretation within the project team. References, say, to a broken heart, tears, and avoiding public space, may all communicate emotions indirectly. Given the nature of the data, research assistance was critical in assuring that the analysis was internally valid (Seale 1999) and that specific Twitter subcultural knowledge needed to interpret tweets was leveraged as much as possible. The project team met weekly to first code a subset of tweets and develop the codebook. This codebook included specific, discrete emotions (fear, worry, anger, compassion, doubt/confusion) as well as humor, references to governments (including government agencies such as the CDC and health ministries), and references to international and nonprofit agencies (WHO, UNICEF, the Gates Foundation). We continued to meet regularly to discuss examples of questionable tweets or raise questions about the code descriptions. The codebook was continuously refined and updated as a result of these discussions, and I and a research assistant worked through any cases that were unclear or ambiguous.

In the end, the code descriptions for the social media data sought to take a more comprehensive view of emotions. Rather than only look for direct words referencing emotions, we also included uses of emojis (laughing), the visuals shared with tweets (images of zombies, references to Ebola as a "nightmare," or the work of "Satan," for example, connoted fear), and compassion was assigned to a tweet in cases where victims or healthcare workers were discussed in humanizing ways (by reference to their biographies, challenges, and through use of close-up images of their faces). The goal of the analysis of social media data was not to say definitively that users were feeling a particular discrete emotion; rather, the goal was to assess the emotional tenor of the textual content, images, and videos shared through Twitter in relation to Ebola.

Following the development of the Twitter codebook, we took a smaller random subset of tweets from week 1 and week 2 in order to calculate the level of interrater reliability (IRR)—that is, the level of agreement between two raters. We generated a random subsample of 1,000 tweets from week 1 and 1,200 from week 2. Two raters (the PI and a research assistant who had assisted with developing the codebook from the beginning) independently applied codes to this smaller subset using the most updated version of the codebook. After calculating the observed agreement between the two raters, we then calculated the agreement based on chance and Cohen's kappa—a statistic that weights the observed agreement based on chance (Viera and Garrett 2005). Fear and humor, the two themes taken up in greatest detail in Chapters 4 and 5, were each rated as having substantial agreement between the two raters. For fear, $k = 0.79$ in week 1 and $k = 0.72$ in week 2. For humor, $k = 0.73$ in week 1, and $k = 0.75$ in week 2. In terms of quantifying the classification of tweets according to these codes, we took the average of the two independent raters. Fear was identified in 10 percent of tweets in week 1 and 16.2 percent in week 2. Humor was identified in 6.2 percent of tweets in week 1 and 38.1 percent of tweets in week 2.

With the COVID-19 pandemic developing during the analysis and writing up of the Ebola findings, I focused on areas of overlap and distinction in the role of emotions in the two outbreaks. I followed the WHO press releases and reports closely between February and May 2020. I was particularly tuned into the reporting in *The New York Times*, the BBC, and CNN because these were the primary sources I used in my analysis of video coverage of Ebola, but I also searched more widely for coverage of the COVID-19 pandemic in order to be able to follow the developments of a particular aspect of the outbreak closely. For example, the BBC did not do the type of detailed investigative reporting into policies for preventing the spread of COVID-19 in US prisons in the way that sources like NPR did. In the case of stories and developments where the links between policy and assumptions about emotion were apparent, I turned to other news sources, as cited in Chapter 5.

Ethical Considerations

I received ethical approval from the review boards at the three different universities where I was affiliated for each of these projects. In the project on nursing, the project was also reviewed and approved by institutional review boards at the two hospital systems where we collected data from nurse participants. Assuring confidentiality of participants was one of the principal ways that we aimed to safeguard the ethical treatment of participants in these projects. For the nursing project, we swapped in pseudonyms for not only nurse names but also the names of hospitals, cities, patients, managers, and physicians where relevant before uploading the data to any web-based analysis program. In studying sports fans, I have masked the identity of my informant and the fellow tailgaters and sports bar attendees that I met over the course of the research.

While news media is public data and aimed at public dissemination, Twitter data are more ambiguous and blur the line between private and public settings (McKee 2013). As eliciting informed consent from Twitter users would prove logistically impossible, this raised questions about how user information should be handled. While some scholars recommend de-identifying all social media data (Hays and Daker-White 2015), this would eliminate potentially meaningful qualitative information about the status, position, and influence of the individual and organizational users that make up Twitter's user base. Twitter accounts can be created and used to represent organizations (such as the WHO, CDC, or corporations), and de-identifying the dataset would remove relevant information for understanding how emotions might spread through influential social media users, including political figures, celebrities, and corporations such as the NFL during the epidemic.

Yet the aim of the research is not to single out any one individual user, but rather to highlight larger patterns and trends over the two-week window of the epidemic in which social media data were sampled. The number of "followers" that an individual has can partially provide insight into the influence they hold over the larger social media conversation about Ebola. Twitter user IDs can themselves be pseudonyms already developed by the user, so the likelihood of an individual who does not want to be identified being discovered retroactively through published research findings is further limited.

Generally, I aimed to mask the identities of those with little power but hold accountable those individuals and organizations that do wield power/influence over the social media conversation surrounding the epidemic. While de-identifying the data would likely take care of the first concern, it would also mask the potential influence of public figures and government and public health organizations. Calls from certain US politicians for airport closures, for example, are qualitatively different than when the same expressions come from a private citizen. In disseminating the findings, then, I mask the Twitter handle and user name for all social media users who are not public figures or organizations. Public figures include politicians, public intellectuals, corporations, journalists, and celebrities.

Studying emotion is never a straightforward process. The aforementioned procedures are not perfect for capturing emotion in an objective sense, but they try to strike a balance between recognizing the "fuzzy," inherently subjective nature of emotions and also trying to pin down something precise about how feelings of elation, exhaustion, humor, and fear take form in different contexts. Not content to simply identify their presence, these methods also aim to capture the processes that shape the emergence of certain emotions (and their combination) as well as what these feelings catalyze in terms of action, reflection, and in constructing the type of social world in which we find ourselves.

Collecting audio diaries, participating in leisure activities directly, tracing symbols in and outside of their original contexts, and analyzing the plethora of digital media now produced and consumed online are all distinct ways of trying to capture emotions in their lived and messy reality. While each project mentioned here has strengths and limitations, future research on emotion should develop better methods for capturing emotion across social domains. Ethnographic methods are the classic approach used to follow individuals and groups across work, family, leisure, and civic pursuits in order to identify social practices as they unfold. Going forward, research that combines audio diaries with ethnographic observation and digital and offline experiences might be particularly useful for examining how emotions move across these arenas and the impact their movement has on well-being, inequality, and meaning making.

Notes

Introduction

1. See, for example, the work of Diefendorff in psychology (Diefendorff et al. 2011; Diefendorff, Croyle, and Gosserand 2005) and Krishnan in organizational studies (Krishnan et al. 2021).
2. https://www.statista.com/statistics/804812/top-tv-series-usa-2015/
3. Coming from a poststructuralist tradition within French sociology, Bourdieu also holds different ontological assumptions (Swartz 1997). Stated simply, the central role of agents and actors in symbolic interactionism seems at odds with Bourdieu's attempt to move beyond an agentic/deterministic gridlock (Shilling 2012). I can't fully overcome this tension here, but I hope to push both approaches toward something of a compromise—a compromise that might allow us to integrate all three into a cohesive theory of emotions as practical engagements with the world (Scheer 2012). Such engagements inevitably span the nonconscious and the strategic.

Chapter 1

1. This Cartesian way of viewing the world privileges rationality and is carried forward into political philosophy: "Human beings are rational, sociable agents who are meant to collaborate in peace to their mutual benefit. Since the seventeenth century, this idea increasingly has come to dominate our political thinking and the way we imagine our society" (C. Taylor 2002, 92). This way of thinking has led to a "human self-understanding as disembodied beings, as agents of disengaged discipline capable of dispassionate control" (McKenzie 2016, 122).
2. Manicheism, for example, was a dualistic Gnostic belief system that divided the world and the cosmos between good and evil (Lange et al. 2011).
3. This oppositional, or dualistic thinking, is challenging to overcome because it is so rooted in our language. But contemporary thinkers have worked to break out of it, though to do so usually means introducing new, sometimes cumbersome, terms. My aim is to avoid jargon as much as possible in this text and to define and clarify terms as I use them.
4. Bourdieu's conception of social practice does not ignore feelings and emotions outright, but they are not the main focus of investigation. Similarly, Alexander's focus on cultural practices certainly emphasizes the "irrational" and "expressive" features of symbolic action (Alexander, Gieson, and Mast 2006). So why should we put emotion

in the center rather than simply adopt a new focus on social or cultural practice? If one of the underlying problems of Enlightenment thinking as it currently haunts our attempts to understand social life is the problem of dualistic thinking (which pits reason against emotion), then turning to practice and dropping emotion altogether seems like it would be the best path forward.

But I disagree. In the rush to move "beyond" these dualisms, there has not been sufficient attention to, nor a critical revaluing of those parts of the dualism that have been and remain dominated by their more highly valued counterpart. Rushing to "go beyond" these dualisms often means ignoring the lengthy history of symbolic abuse (used to justify physical abuse) they have exacted and continue to exact when these assumptions go unexamined. I believe we need to sit with emotion for a bit longer. This means privileging emotion's role in social life—attending to its dynamics and complexities directly rather than always in explicit conversation with other, presumed to be more important matters such as action, behavior, cognition, and material conditions. Certainly, the relationships between emotion and these other matters have been and should continue to be explored. But in focusing on emotion, we need to first appreciate what has been lost in the dualistic thinking that still pervades lay approaches to social life.

5. Bourdieu himself notes the similarities between his approach and Dewey's: "I would say that the theory of practical sense presents many similarities with theories, such as Dewey's, that grant a central role to the notion of habit, understood as an active and creative relation to the world, and reject all the conceptual dualisms upon which nearly all post-Cartesian philosophies are based: subject and object, internal and external, material and spiritual, individual and social, and so on" (Bourdieu and Wacquant 1992, 122). Rather than see this overlap as a lack of originality, I see it as a sign of the pressing need to move toward synthesis and application in developing a post-Cartesian conception of emotion.

6. We might see parallels with Hochschild's discussion of *templates*: "When an emotion signals a message of danger or safety to us, it involves a reality newly grasped on the template of prior expectations. A signal involves a juxtaposition of what we see with what we expect to see—the two sides of surprise. The message 'danger' takes on its meaning of 'danger' only in relation to what we expect" (1983, 231).

7. Because of practice theory's emphasis on the ongoing, social-life-in-flux dynamic between habitus, capital, and field, I do not make clean, analytical distinctions among concepts like sensations, sentiments, affect, feeling, emotion, and mood. Following Deborah Gould, naming and defining these as distinct can be useful, but it also risks reification. "In practice, affect and emotions usually are simultaneously in play and can be difficult to distinguish" (Gould 2009, 22). I use these terms to capture the spectrum of modes of engagement and ambiguity that a practice approach helps us confront.

8. In other words, emotions are inherently relational (Burkitt 2017). As Katz (2012, 18) puts it, "Emotions and feelings are ways of gasping, appreciating, and corporeally reflecting on the very structuring of life into social forms."

Chapter 2

1. All participant names are pseudonyms.
2. In attending to the nonconscious as well as the conscious, an emotion practice perspective provides a more comprehensive, sociological basis for emerging research in psychology on implicit bias—biases which have been documented in the context of healthcare ("Implicit Bias in Health Care" 2016).

Chapter 3

1. My thanks to Becky Erickson for this brilliant connection.
2. A pseudonym.
3. This can also be seen in the classic work of Howard Becker (1953) in which he shows how practices (or "experiences," as he puts it) of "getting high" are learned rather than inevitable interpretations of drug use.
4. The iconic Terrible Towel found its way to the International Space Station in 2019, as discussed in this segment by WTAE-TV Pittsburgh: https://youtu.be/WC_Cu4Go G2E. The description reads: "You can find a Pittsburgh Steelers fans [sic] anywhere— even in space! Dr. Andrew Morgan pulled out a Terrible Towel on the International Space Station, where he is learning more about the body's response to weightlessness as part of NASA's mission to return to the moon in 2024."
5. Studies of young people's sports participation in the United States find that football has one of the highest rates of concussion compared to other youth sports (O'Connor et al. 2017; Rosenthal et al. 2014).
6. The city of Pittsburgh, Pennsylvania, is majority (65 percent) white ("Data USA: Pittsburgh, PA" 2018). The fan base for the Steelers is estimated to be 64 percent white (second only to the Green Bay Packers in terms of largest percentage of a white fan base) (Silverman 2020). African Americans make up 59 percent of NFL players ("Share of African Americans in the National Football League in 2019, by Role" 2019).

Chapter 4

1. There are inconsistencies in the precise date for Romero; see Kaner and Schaack (2016) and World Health Organization (2014).
2. Similar, perhaps, to how conservatives in Hochschild's (2016) study of polarized politics in Louisiana rebel against what they see as politically correct feeling rules that frame refugees and migrants as sympathetic characters worthy of compassion.
3. ESPN stands for Entertainment and Sports Programming Network.

4. Giselinde Kuipers highlights the prevalence of this "safety valve" theory in early conceptions of humor: "The discharge of tension is still one of the main functions humor is believed to fulfill, and as such the relief theory has had great influence on modern humor scholarship, mostly via Sigmund Freud (1905/1876). However, 'pure' relief theorists, explaining humor and laughter as release of tension or 'safety valve,' cannot be found anymore in humor scholarship these days" (2008, 362).

5. We can see this rational choice thinking in research by computer scientists who track bots and the spread of misinformation online (V. A. Young 2020). In decrying the problematic conspiracy theories that are perpetuated through bot accounts on sites like Twitter, Kathleen Carley notes their link with irrationality: "Carley said that spreading conspiracy theories leads to more extreme opinions, which can in turn lead to more extreme behavior and less rational thinking" (V. A. Young 2020). Spreading harmful misinformation is clearly a problem, but assuming one group is rational and the other is not because of their belief in conspiracy theories reinforces unhelpful dualistic thinking about emotions and reason.

Chapter 5

1. For example, we can see this in nursing when the administration of certain interventions such as inserting an NG (nasogastric) tube requires that the patient's body be in a relaxed state (Theodosius 2008, 158–59).

2. This type of reasoning is also relevant for discussions of vaccine hesitancy. Rather than assume emotions of hesitancy or distrust are illogical, we can instead see them as signals of a problematic system rather than problems in and of themselves. Emotions of distrust or fear are signs of more pervasive social breakdown.

3. Interestingly, "hoarding" in the Dutch language is *hamsteren*, a term that alludes to the burrowing actions of an animal like a hamster (van Kesteren 2020). The dehumanizing implication being that such actions are more suitable for an animal.

4. Freud's treatment of emotion is described in phases. His view of emotion as catharsis or a "safety-valve" theory preceded his later focus on the "signal function" of emotion (Hinton, Fessler, and Quinn 1999).

5. While feeling rules and emotion norms are two similar concepts developed by Arlie Hochschild, her application of these terms tends to primarily focus on their relevance for navigating individual and group encounters. Emotion discourse, in Loseke's use of the term, tries to address how specific story archetypes like that of "victim" and "hero" are circulated through dominant speech and text (in the context of Loseke's research, that of presidential speeches) to understand how these translate into emotions that convince an audience that a leader's actions are justified.

6. As of January 14, 2022: https://www.worldometers.info/coronavirus/.

7. There are many parallels to the way the COVID-19 pandemic has unfolded. Science, even the natural sciences, is a messy, human affair. Dr. Gupta in this quote begins to suggest that some of the fear during the Ebola outbreak was not irrational, but a

rational response to the suspicious ways in which politicians translate emerging scientific knowledge into policies. See Stevens (2020) for a summary of these practices in the context of COVID-19 in the United Kingdom.

8. Blackburn says, "We have to give the American people confidence that they can trust us" (Gupta 2014b).

9. Vaz suggests that "any action that will reassure the public" is important to consider (Coburn 2014).

10. In the supermarket, Rutte states, "We hebben zoveel dat we tien jaar kunnen poepen" (RTL Nieuws 2020).

11. One company estimates 40 percent more toilet paper ("Statement on Georgia-Pacific's Response to COVID-19" 2020).

Conclusion

1. It is amusing to think about how a given desire path began. Was it a group of late-night revelers eager to rebel, an earnest student late for class, a father trying to get a fussy child home as soon as possible? Or, more scandalous, was it a disgruntled worker who helped build the structured path in the first place?

2. See Burkitt (2012) for further discussion of how reflexivity is infused with emotion.

Methodological Appendix

1. The research reported here uses data from a larger study, "Identity and Emotional Management Control in Health Care Settings," which was funded by the National Science Foundation (SES-1024271) and awarded to Rebecca J. Erickson (principal investigator) and James M. Diefendorff (co-principal investigator).

References

Ahmed, Sara. 2002. "Affective Economies." *Social Text* 22 (79): 117–39.

Ahmed, Sara. 2006. "Orientations: Toward a Queer Phenomenology." *GLQ: A Journal of Lesbian and Gay Studies* 12 (4): 543–74. http://muse.jhu.edu/journals/glq/summary/v012/12.4ahmed.html.

Al Jazeera News. 2020. "Which Countries Have Made Wearing Face Masks Compulsory?" *Al Jazeera*, August 17, 2020. https://www.aljazeera.com/news/2020/8/17/which-countries-have-made-wearing-face-masks-compulsory.

Alexander, Jeffrey C., Bernhard Gieson, and Jason L. Mast, eds. 2006. *Social Performance: Symbolic Action, Cultural Pragmatics and Ritual*. Cambridge: Cambridge University Press.

Altheide, David L. 1987. "Reflections: Ethnographic Content Analysis." *Qualitative Sociology* 10 (1): 65–77. http://link.springer.com/article/10.1007/BF00988269.

Altheide, David L. 2009. "Moral Panic: From Sociological Concept to Public Discourse." *Crime, Media, Culture: An International Journal* 5 (1): 79–99. https://doi.org/10.1177/1741659008102063.

Altheide, David L. 2013. "Media Logic, Social Control, and Fear." *Communication Theory* 23 (3): 223–38. https://doi.org/10.1111/comt.12017.

The Associated Press. 2020. "'Stay Calm, It Will Go Away:' Trump Plays Down Coronavirus Threat." *The New York Times*, March 10, 2020. https://www.nytimes.com/video/us/politics/100000007026448/trump-coronavirus.html.

Axelrod, Joshua. 2017. "This Packers-Theme Wedding Is Cute, but Let Steelers Fans Show You How It's Done." *Pittsburgh Post-Gazette*, June 21, 2017, sec. Sports. https://www.post-gazette.com/sports/steelers/2017/06/21/Steelers-wedding-Green-Bay-Packers-football-fandom/stories/201706210159.

Bail, Christopher A. 2014. "The Cultural Environment: Measuring Culture with Big Data." *Theory and Society* 43 (3–4): 465–82. https://doi.org/10.1007/s11186-014-9216-5.

Bakhamis, Lama, David P. Paul, Harlan Smith, and Alberto Coustasse. 2019. "Still an Epidemic: The Burnout Syndrome in Hospital Registered Nurses." *The Health Care Manager* 38 (1): 3–10. https://doi.org/10.1097/HCM.0000000000000243.

Barbalet, Jack. 1993. "Confidence: Time and Emotion in the Sociology of Action." *Journal for the Theory of Social Behaviour* 23 (3): 229–47. https://doi.org/10.1111/j.1468-5914.1993.tb00239.x.

Barbalet, Jack. 1998. *Emotion, Social Theory, and Social Structure: A Macrosociological Approach*. Cambridge: Cambridge University Press. https://search.ebscohost.com/login.aspx?direct=true&db=e000xww&AN=55629&site=ehost-live&scope=site.

Barbalet, Jack. 2002. "Introduction: Why Emotions Are Crucial." *The Sociological Review* 50 (2 Suppl.): 1–9. https://doi.org/10.1111/j.1467-954X.2002.tb03588.x.

Barbalet, Jack. 2004. "William James: Pragmatism, Social Psychology and Emotions." *European Journal of Social Theory* 7 (3): 337–53. https://doi.org/10.1177/1368431004044197.

Barbalet, Jack. 2006. "Emotional Payoffs of Ritual." *European Journal of Sociology /
Archives Européennes de Sociologie / Europäisches Archiv Für Soziologie* 47 (3): 446–51.
www.jstor.org/stable/23998957.

Baron, Sherry L., Misty J. Hein, Everett Lehman, and Christine M. Gersic. 2012. "Body
Mass Index, Playing Position, Race, and the Cardiovascular Mortality of Retired
Professional Football Players." *The American Journal of Cardiology* 109 (6): 889–96.
https://doi.org/10.1016/j.amjcard.2011.10.050.

Barrett, Lisa Feldman. 2012. "Emotions Are Real." *Emotion* 12 (3): 413–29. https://doi.
org/10.1037/a0027555.

Barrett, Lisa Feldman. 2017. *How Emotions Are Made: The Secret Life of the Brain.*
Boston: Houghton Mifflin Harcourt.

Barrios, Roberto E. 2017. *Governing Affect: Neoliberalism and Disaster Reconstruction.*
Anthropology of Contemporary North America. Lincoln: University of Nebraska Press.

Beck, Ulrich. 1992. *Risk Society: Towards a New Modernity.* London: Sage.

Becker, Howard S. 1953. "Becoming a Marihuana User." *American Journal of Sociology* 59
(3): 235–42.

Belson, Ken. 2019. "Only Three N.F.L. Head Coaches Are Black. 'It's Embarrassing.'" *The
New York Times*, December 31, 2019. https://www.nytimes.com/2019/12/31/sports/
football/rooney-rule-nfl-coach.html.

Bericat, Eduardo. 2016. "The Sociology of Emotions: Four Decades of Progress." *Current
Sociology* 64 (3): 491–513. http://csi.sagepub.com/content/early/2015/06/10/00113
92115588355.abstract.

Bird, Cindy M. 2005. "How I Stopped Dreading and Learned to Love Transcription."
Qualitative Inquiry 11 (2): 226–48. https://doi.org/10.1177/1077800404273413.

Birrell, Susan. 1981. "Sport as Ritual: Interpretations from Durkheim to Goffman." *Social
Forces* 60 (2): 354–76.

Bleiker, Roland, David Campbell, Emma Hutchison, and Xzarina Nicholson. 2013. "The
Visual Dehumanisation of Refugees." *Australian Journal of Political Science* 48 (4): 398–
416. https://doi.org/10.1080/10361146.2013.840769.

Blix, Stina Bergman, and Åsa Wettergren. 2018. *Professional Emotions in Court: A
Sociological Perspective.* 1st ed. London: Routledge.

Bolton, Sharon C. 2001. "Changing Faces: Nurses as Emotional Jugglers." *Sociology of
Health & Illness* 23 (1): 85–100.

Bourdieu, Pierre. 1986. "The Forms of Capital." In *Handbook of Theory of Research for the
Sociology of Education*, edited by J. E. Richardson, 241–58. New York: Greenwood Press.

Bourdieu, Pierre. 1990. *The Logic of Practice.* Translated by R. Nice. Stanford, CA: Stanford
University Press.

Bourdieu, Pierre. 1996. *Distinction: A Social Critique of the Judgement of Taste.* Translated
by R. Nice. London: Routledge.

Bourdieu, Pierre. 1998. *Practical Reason: On the Theory of Action.* Stanford, CA: Stanford
University Press.

Bourdieu, Pierre, and Loïc J. D. Wacquant. 1992. *An Invitation to Reflexive Sociology.*
Chicago: University of Chicago Press.

Bracke, Sarah. 2016. "Bounce Back. Vulnerability in Times of Resilience." In *Vulnerability
in Resistance. Towards a Feminist Theory of Resistance and Agency*, edited by J. Butler, Z.
Gambetti, and L. Sabsay, 52–75. Durham, NC: Duke University Press.

Brah, Avtar, and Ann Phoenix. 2004. "Ain't I a Woman? Revisiting Intersectionality."
Journal of International Women's Studies 5 (3): 75–86.

Brownlie, Julie, and Frances Shaw. 2019. "Empathy Rituals: Small Conversations about Emotional Distress on Twitter." *Sociology* 53 (1): 104–22. https://doi.org/10.1177/0038038518767075.

Brubaker, Jed R., Gillian R. Hayes, and Paul Dourish. 2013. "Beyond the Grave: Facebook as a Site for the Expansion of Death and Mourning." *The Information Society* 29 (3): 152–63. https://doi.org/10.1080/01972243.2013.777300.

Brubaker, Rogers. 1985. "Rethinking Classical Theory: The Sociological Vision of Pierre Bourdieu." *Theory and Society* 14 (6): 745–75.

Brubaker, Rogers. 2020. "Digital Hyperconnectivity and the Self." *Theory and Society* 49 (5–6): 771–801. https://doi.org/10.1007/s11186-020-09405-1.

Bulan, Heather Ferguson, Rebecca J. Erickson, and Amy S. Wharton. 1997. "Doing for Others on the Job: The Affective Requirements of Service Work, Gender, and Emotional Well-Being." *Social Problems* 44 (2): 235–56.

Bureau of Labor Statistics. 2020. "Healthcare Occupations." https://www.bls.gov/ooh/healthcare/home.htm.

Burkitt, Ian. 2012. "Emotional Reflexivity: Feeling, Emotion and Imagination in Reflexive Dialogues." *Sociology* 46 (3): 458–72. http://soc.sagepub.com/content/46/3/458.short.

Burkitt, Ian. 2017. "Decentring Emotion Regulation: From Emotion Regulation to Relational Emotion." *Emotion Review* 10 (2): 167–73. https://doi.org/10.1177/1754073917712441.

Business Insider US. 2020. "North Dakota's GOP Governor Grew Emotional Discussing the Partisan Divide over Face Masks, Asking Residents to 'Dial up Your Empathy.'" *Business Insider*, May 23, 2020. https://www.businessinsider.nl/north-dakota-governor-grew-emotional-talking-about-face-mask-politics-2020-5?international=true&r=US.

Calhoun, Craig. 2004. "A World of Emergencies: Fear, Intervention, and the Limits of Cosmopolitan Order." *The Canadian Review of Sociology* 41 (4): 373–95. https://doi.org/10.1111/j.1755-618X.2004.tb00783.x.

Callard, Felicity, and Elisa Perego. 2021. "How and Why Patients Made Long Covid." *Social Science & Medicine* 268: 1–5. https://doi.org/10.1016/j.socscimed.2020.113426.

Casarez, Jean. 2014. "Ebola Seeps into Pop Culture." CNN, October 17, 2014. https://edition.cnn.com/videos/us/2014/10/17/dnt-casarez-ebola-in-pop-culture.cnn.

CBS Broadcasting. KDKA. 2009. "Black & Gold Wedding Bells Ring for Local Couple." January 31, 2009. Pittsburgh, Pennsylvania.

Centers for Disease Control and Prevention. 2014. "Cases of Ebola Diagnosed in the United States." http://www.cdc.gov/vhf/ebola/outbreaks/2014-west-africa/united-states-imported-case.html.

Chan, Margaret. 2014. "WHO Director-General Briefs Geneva UN Missions on the Ebola Outbreak." World Health Organization. https://www.who.int/dg/speeches/2014/ebola-briefing/en/.

Chan, Margaret. 2015. "WHO Director-General Addresses Princeton - Fung Global Forum on Lessons Learned from the Ebola Crisis." Presented at the Princeton—Fung Global Forum, Dublin, Ireland, November 2. http://who.int/dg/speeches/2015/princeton-ebola-lessons/en/.

Chow, Denise. 2020. "Pandemic Decision-Making: Why Humans Aren't Wired to Understand the Coronavirus." NBC News, April 9, 2020. https://www.nbcnews.com/science/science-news/people-often-think-their-gut-s-not-ideal-pandemic-n1179

926?cid=sm_npd_nn_tw_ma&fbclid=IwAR1r8NPXvELhB4ZQdW48Y7Yw2a1rLws pKU6wj4alAbQk76lhVLmbUm--rNM.

The Citizens' Voice. 2015. "Eleanor Miriam Gallagher," January 16, 2015. https://www. legacy.com/us/obituaries/citizensvoice/name/eleanor-gallagher-obituary?pid= 173870846.

Clarke, Lee. 2002. "Panic: Myth or Reality?" *Contexts* 1 (3): 21–26. https://doi.org/ 10.1525/ctx.2002.1.3.21.

Clarke, Lee, and Caron Chess. 2008. "Elites and Panic: More to Fear than Fear Itself." *Social Forces* 87 (2): 993–1014. https://doi.org/10.1353/sof.0.0155.

CNN. 2014. "Who Is 'Clipboard Man' with Ebola Nurse?," October 16, 2014. https:// edition.cnn.com/videos/health/2014/10/16/ath-cohen-clipboard-man-with-ebola-nurse.cnn.

Coburn, Jo. 2014. "Ebola: MP Keith Vaz Calls for UK Passenger Screening." BBC, October 9, 2014, sec. Daily Politics. https://www.bbc.com/news/av/uk-politics-29556719/ ebola-mp-keith-vaz-calls-for-uk-passenger-screening.

Cohen, Stanley. 2002. *Folk Devils and Moral Panics: The Creation of Mods and Rockers*. 3rd ed. London: Routledge.

Collins, Patricia Hill. 1986. "Learning from the Outsider Within: The Sociological Significance of Black Feminist Thought." *Social Problems* 33 (6): S14–32. https://doi. org/10.2307/800672.

Collins, Patricia Hill. 2000. *Black Feminist Thought: Knowledge, Consciousness, and the Politics of Empowerment*. New York: Routledge.

Collins, Patricia Hill. 2012. "Social Inequality, Power, and Politics: Intersectionality and American Pragmatism in Dialogue." *The Journal of Speculative Philosophy* 26 (2): 442–57.

Collins, Randall. 1981. "On the Microfoundations of Macrosociology." *The American Journal of Sociology* 86 (5): 984–1014.

Collins, Randall. 2004. *Interaction Ritual Chains*. Princeton, NJ: Princeton University Press.

Collins, Randall. 2009. "The Micro-Sociology of Violence." *British Journal of Sociology* 60 (3): 566–76. https://doi.org/10.1111/j.1468-4446.2009.01256.x.

Cook, Bob. 2014. "Should Players Be Required To 'Take A Knee' When A Fellow Competitor Gets Injured?" *Forbes*, October 14, 2014, sec. Lifestyle. https://www.forbes. com/sites/bobcook/2014/10/14/should-players-be-required-to-take-a-knee-when-a-fellow-competitor-gets-injured/?sh=24f5fd525300.

Cooley, Charles Horton. 1922. *Human Nature and the Social Order*. Brunswick, NJ: Transaction.

Cottingham, Marci D. 2012. "Interaction Ritual Theory and Sports Fans: Emotion, Symbols, and Solidarity." *Sociology of Sport Journal* 29 (2): 168–85.

Cottingham, Marci D. 2015. "Learning to 'Deal' and 'De-Escalate': How Men in Nursing Manage Self and Patient Emotions." *Sociological Inquiry* 85 (1): 75–99. https://doi.org/ 10.1111/soin.12064.

Cottingham, Marci D. 2016. "Theorizing Emotional Capital." *Theory and Society* 45 (5): 451–70. https://doi.org/10.1007/s11186-016-9278-7.

Cottingham, Marci D. 2019. "Emotion, Sociology Of." In *Core Concepts in Sociology*, edited by J. Michael Ryan, 90–92. Oxford: John Wiley & Sons.

Cottingham, Marci D., and Lana Andringa. 2020. "'My Color Doesn't Lie': Race, Gender, and Nativism among Nurses in the Netherlands." *Global Qualitative Nursing Research* 7: 1–11. https://doi.org/10.1177/2333393620972958.

Cottingham, Marci D., Jamie J. Chapman, and Rebecca J. Erickson. 2020. "The Constant Caregiver: Work–Family Spillover among Men and Women in Nursing." *Work, Employment and Society* 34 (2): 281–98. https://doi.org/10.1177/0950017019885084.

Cottingham, Marci D., and Janette S. Dill. 2019. "Intergenerational Dynamics among Women and Men in Nursing." In *Gender, Age and Inequality in the Professions: Exploring the Disordering, Disruptive and Chaotic Properties of Communication*, edited by M. Choroszewicz and T. L. Adams, 58–75. Routledge Studies in Gender and Organizations. Philadelphia: Taylor & Francis.

Cottingham, Marci D., and Rebecca J. Erickson. 2020a. "Capturing Emotion with Audio Diaries." *Qualitative Research* 20 (5): 549–64. https://doi.org/10.1177/146879411 9885037.

Cottingham, Marci D., and Rebecca J. Erickson. 2020b. "The Promise of Emotion Practice: At the Bedside and Beyond." *Work and Occupations* 47 (2): 173–99.

Cottingham, Marci D., Rebecca J. Erickson, and James M. Diefendorff. 2015. "Examining Men's Status Shield and Status Bonus: How Gender Frames the Emotional Labor and Job Satisfaction of Nurses." *Sex Roles* 72 (7–8): 377–89. https://doi.org/10.1007/s11 199-014-0419-z.

Cottingham, Marci D., and Jill A. Fisher. 2017. "From Fantasy to Reality: Managing Biomedical Risk Emotions in and through Fictional Media." *Health, Risk & Society*, 19: 284–300. https://doi.org/10.1080/13698575.2017.1350638.

Cottingham, Marci D., Austin H. Johnson, and Rebecca J. Erickson. 2018. "'I Can Never Be Too Comfortable': Race, Gender, and Emotion at the Hospital Bedside." *Qualitative Health Research* 28 (1): 145–58.

Crenshaw, Kimberle. 1991. "Mapping the Margins: Intersectionality, Identity Politics, and Violence against Women of Color." *Stanford Law Review* 43 (6): 1241–99.

"Cuban Doctors Train, Then Fight Ebola in Africa." 2014. CNN. https://edition.cnn.com/ 2014/10/11/world/americas/cuba-doctors-ebola-preparadeness/index.html.

Damasio, Antonio R. 1994. *Descartes' Error*. New York: HarperCollins.

"Data USA: Pittsburgh, PA." 2018. https://datausa.io/profile/geo/pittsburgh-pa/#:~:text= The%20population%20of%20Pittsburgh%2C%20PA%20is%2064.9%25%20Wh ite%20Alone%2C,%2C%20and%205.56%25%20Asian%20Alone.

Davey, Graham C. L. 2011. "Disgust: The Disease-Avoidance Emotion and Its Dysfunctions." *Philosophical Transactions of the Royal Society of London. Series B, Biological Sciences* 366 (1583): 3453–65. https://doi.org/10.1098/rstb.2011.0039.

Davis, Mark H. 2006. "Empathy." In *Handbook of the Sociology of Emotions*, edited by J. E. Stets and J. H. Turner, 443–66. New York: Springer. http://link.springer.com/chapter/ 10.1007/978-0-387-30715-2_20.

Davis, Jenny L., Tony P. Love, and Gemma Killen. 2018. "Seriously Funny: The Political Work of Humor on Social Media." *New Media & Society* 20 (10): 3898–916. https://doi. org/10.1177/1461444818762602.

De Keere, Kobe. 2020. "Als in Een Film: Waarom Een Wereld in Crisis Soms Niet Helemaal Echt Lijkt." *Tijdschrift Sociologie* 1: 67–74.

Dewey, John. 1946. *The Public and Its Problems*. Chicago: Gateway Books.

Diefendorff, James M., Meredith H. Croyle, and Robin H. Gosserand. 2005. "The Dimensionality and Antecedents of Emotional Labor Strategies." *Journal of Vocational Behavior* 66 (2): 339–57. https://doi.org/10.1016/j.jvb.2004.02.001.

Diefendorff, James M., Rebecca J. Erickson, Alicia A. Grandey, and Jason J. Dahling. 2011. "Emotional Display Rules as Work Unit Norms: A Multilevel Analysis of Emotional Labor among Nurses." *Journal of Occupational Health Psychology* 16 (2): 170–86. https://doi.org/10.1037/a0021725.

Dijk, Jan A. G. M. van. 2006. "Digital Divide Research, Achievements and Shortcomings." *Poetics* 34 (4–5): 221–35. https://doi.org/10.1016/j.poetic.2006.05.004.

Döveling, Katrin, Anu A. Harju, and Denise Sommer. 2018. "From Mediatized Emotion to Digital Affect Cultures: New Technologies and Global Flows of Emotion." *Social Media + Society* 4 (1): 1–11. https://doi.org/10.1177/2056305117743141.

Duffy, Kate. 2021. "Nearly 40% of Workers Would Consider Quitting If Their Bosses Made Them Return to the Office Full Time, a New Survey Shows." *Business Insider*, June 2, 2021. https://www.businessinsider.com/quit-job-flexible-remote-working-from-home-return-to-office-2021-6?international=true&r=US&IR=T.

Durkheim, Emile. 1915. *The Elementary Forms of Religious Life*. New York: Macmillan.

Duyvendak, Jan Willem. 2011. *The Politics of Home: Belonging and Nostalgia in Western Europe and the United States*. London: Palgrave Macmillan.

Dvorchak, Robert. 2006. "In Pittsburgh, a Confluence of Funeral and Football: 'The Best Way to Approach the Day Is in the Tradition of an Irish Wake.'" *Pittsburgh Post-Gazette*, September 7, 2006. https://www.post-gazette.com/local/city/2006/09/07/In-Pittsburgh-a-confluence-of-funeral-and-football/stories/200609070361.

"Ebola Crisis: Fears Quarantine Could Deter Ebola Workers." 2014. BBC. https://www.bbc.com/news/av/world-29776435/ebola-crisis-fears-quarantine-could-deter-ebola-workers.

Einboden, Rochelle. 2020. "SuperNurse? Troubling the Hero Discourse in COVID Times." *Health: An Interdisciplinary Journal for the Social Study of Health, Illness and Medicine* 24 (4): 343–47. https://doi.org/10.1177/1363459320934280.

Elias, Norbert, and Eric Dunning. 1986. *Quest for Excitement: Sport and Leisure in the Civilizing Process*. Oxford: Basil Blackwell.

Emirbayer, Mustafa, and Chad Alan Goldberg. 2005. "Pragmatism, Bourdieu, and Collective Emotions in Contentious Politics." *Theory and Society* 34 (5–6): 469–518. http://link.springer.com/article/10.1007/s11186-005-1619-x.

"Emoji Statistics." n.d. Emojipedia. Accessed June 21, 2021. https://emojipedia.org/stats/.

Erickson, Rebecca J. 2005. "Why Emotion Work Matters: Sex, Gender, and the Division of Household Labor." *Journal of Marriage and Family* 67 (2): 337–51.

Erickson, Rebecca J. 2007. "Where the Ritual Is: Examinations of a Microfoundational Mo(ve)Ment." *Contemporary Sociology* 36 (3): 209–11. http://www.jstor.org/stable/10.2307/20443766.

Erickson, Rebecca J., and Wendy J. C. Grove. 2007. "Why Emotions Matter: Age, Agitation, and Burnout among Registered Nurses." *Online Journal of Issues in Nursing* 13 (1): 1–13.

Erickson, Rebecca J., and Wendy J. C. Grove. 2008. "Emotional Labor and Health Care." *Sociology Compass* 2 (2): 704–33. https://doi.org/10.1111/j.1751-9020.2007.00084.x.

Erickson, Rebecca J., and Christian Ritter. 2001. "Emotional Labor, Burnout, and Inauthenticity: Does Gender Matter?" *Social Psychology Quarterly* 64 (2): 146. https://doi.org/10.2307/3090130.

Erickson, Rebecca J., and Clare Stacey. 2013. "Attending to Mind and Body: Engaging the Complexity of Emotion Practice among Caring Professionals." In *Emotional Labor in the 21st Century: Diverse Perspectives on Emotion Regulation at Work*, edited by Alicia A. Grandey, J. M. Diefendorff, and D. E. Rupp, 175–96. New York: Routledge.

Evans, Louwanda. 2013. *Cabin Pressure: African American Pilots, Flight Attendants, and Emotional Labor*. Lanham, MD: Rowman and Littlefield.

Evans, Louwanda, and Joe R. Feagin. 2015. "The Costs of Policing Violence: Foregrounding Cognitive and Emotional Labor." *Critical Sociology* 41 (6): 887–95. https://doi.org/ 10.1177/0896920515589727.

Evans, Louwanda, and Wendy Leo Moore. 2015. "Impossible Burdens: White Institutions, Emotional Labor, and Micro-Resistance." *Social Problems* 62 (3): 439–54. https://doi. org/10.1093/socpro/spv009.

Feagin, Joe, and Zinobia Bennefield. 2014. "Systemic Racism and U.S. Health Care." *Social Science & Medicine* 103 (February): 7–14. https://doi.org/10.1016/j.socsci med.2013.09.006.

Feldman, Martha S., and Wanda J. Orlikowski. 2011. "Theorizing Practice and Practicing Theory." *Organization Science* 22 (5): 1240–53. https://doi.org/10.1287/orsc.1100.0612.

Fielding-Singh, Priya. 2017. "A Taste of Inequality: Food's Symbolic Value across the Socioeconomic Spectrum." *Sociological Science* 4: 424–48. https://doi.org/10.15195/ v4.a17.

Fine, Gary Alan. 2005. "Interaction Ritual Chains (Review)." *Social Forces* 83 (3): 1287–88. http://muse.jhu.edu/journals/sof/summary/v083/83.3fine.html.

Fine, Gary Alan, and Ugo Corte. 2017. "Group Pleasures: Collaborative Commitments, Shared Narrative, and the Sociology of Fun." *Sociological Theory* 35 (1): 64–86. https:// doi.org/10.1177/0735275117692836.

Fine, Gary Alan, and Michaela DeSoucey. 2005. "Joking Cultures: Humor Themes as Social Regulation in Group Life." *Humor—International Journal of Humor Research* 18 (1): 1–22. https://doi.org/10.1515/humr.2005.18.1.1.

Fisher, Jill A. 2002. "Tattooing the Body, Marking Culture." *Body & Society* 8 (4): 91–107. https://doi.org/10.1177/1357034X02008004005.

Francis, Linda E. 1994. "Laughter, the Best Mediation: Humor as Emotion Management in Interaction." *Symbolic Interaction* 17 (2): 147–63.

Francis, Linda E. 1997. "Ideology and Interpersonal Emotion Management: Redefining Identity in Two Support Groups." *Social Psychology Quarterly* 60 (2): 153–71.

Francis, Linda E., Kathleen Monahan, and Candyce Berger. 1999. "A Laughing Matter? The Uses of Humor in Medical Interactions." *Motivation and Emotion* 23 (2): 155–74. https://doi.org/10.1023/A:1021381129517.

Freud, Sigmund. 1961. *Civilization and Its Discontents*. New York: Norton.

Frey, James H., and D. Stanley Eitzen. 1991. "Sport and Society." *Annual Review of Sociology* 17: 503–22.

Frijda, Nico H. 2004. "Emotions and Action." In *Feelings and Emotions: The Amsterdam Symposium*, edited by A. S. R. Manstead, N. H. Frijda, and A. Fischer, 158–73. Cambridge: Cambridge University Press.

Furedi, Frank. 2007a. *Invitation to Terror: The Expanding Empire of the Unknown*. New York: Continuum.

Furedi, Frank. 2007b. "The Only Thing We Have to Fear Is the 'Culture of Fear' Itself." *Spiked*, April 4, 2007. Retrieved from https://www.spiked-online.com/2007/04/04/the-only-thing-we-have-to-fear-is-the-culture-of-fear-itself/.

Furedi, Frank. 2011. "The Objectification of Fear and the Grammar of Morality." In *Moral Panics and the Politics of Anxiety*, edited by Sean Patrick Hier, 90–103. London: Routledge.

Furedi, Frank. 2018. *How Fear Works: Culture of Fear in the Twenty-First Century.* Bloomsbury.

Gantt, Paul, and Ron Gantt. 2012. "Disaster Psychology: Dispelling the Myths of Panic." *Professional Safety* 57 (8): 42–49.

Garland, David. 2008. "On the Concept of Moral Panic." *Crime, Media, Culture: An International Journal* 4 (1): 9–30. https://doi.org/10.1177/1741659007087270.

Gengler, Amanda M. 2020. "Emotions and Medical Decision-Making." *Social Psychology Quarterly* 83 (2): 174–194.

Gentry, Jack. 2020. "Keith Bulluck Tells the Tale of the Terrible Towel Trouble." *A to Z Sports: Nashville*, September 30, 2020. https://atozsportsnashville.com/keith-bulluck-tells-the-tale-of-the-terrible-towel-trouble/.

Glassner, Barry. 1999. *The Culture of Fear: Why Americans Are Afraid of the Wrong Things.* New York: Basic Books.

Goffman, Erving. 1959. *The Presentation of Self in Everyday Life.* Garden City, NY: Doubleday.

Golder, Scott A., and Michael W. Macy. 2011. "Diurnal and Seasonal Mood Vary with Work, Sleep, and Daylength Across Diverse Cultures." *Science* 333 (6051): 1878–81. https://doi.org/10.1126/science.1202775.

Google.com. 2015. "Google Trends." 2015. http://www.google.com/trends/topcharts#vm=cat&geo=US&date=2014&cid.

Gordon, Steven L. 1989. "The Socialization of Children's Emotions: Emotional Culture, Competence, and Exposure." In *Children's Understanding of Emotion*, edited by C. Saarni and P. L. Harris, 319–49. Cambridge: Cambridge University Press.

Gould, Deborah B. 2009. *Moving Politics: Emotion and ACT UP's Fight Against AIDS.* Chicago: University of Chicago Press.

Graeber, David. 2015. *The Utopia of Rules: On Technology, Stupidity, and the Secret Joys of Bureaucracy.* London: Melville House.

Grandey, Alicia A., and Allison S. Gabriel. 2015. "Emotional Labor at a Crossroads: Where Do We Go from Here?" *Annual Review of Organizational Psychology and Organizational Behavior* 2 (1): 323–49. https://doi.org/10.1146/annurev-orgpsych-032414-111400.

Gupta, Sanjay. 2014a. "Are Ebola Fears the Media's Fault?" CNN, October 18, 2014. https://edition.cnn.com/videos/bestoftv/2014/10/18/rs-are-ebola-fears-the-medias-fault.cnn.

Gupta, Sanjay. 2014b. "Will a Travel Ban Help Contain Ebola?" CNN, October 21, 2014. https://edition.cnn.com/videos/bestoftv/2014/10/21/exp-ac-will-a-travel-ban-stop-ebola.cnn.

Halldorsson, Vidar. 2021. "National Sport Success and the Emergent Social Atmosphere: The Case of Iceland." *International Review for the Sociology of Sport* 56 (4): 471–92. https://doi.org/10.1177/1012690220912415.

Hallett, Tim. 2003. "Emotional Feedback and Amplification in Social Interaction." *The Sociological Quarterly* 44 (4): 705–26.

Harlow, Roxanna. 2003. "'Race Doesn't Matter, but . . .': The Effect of Race on Professors' Experiences and Emotion Management in the Undergraduate College Classroom." *Social Psychology Quarterly* 66 (4): 348–63. https://doi.org/10.2307/1519834.

Hartman, C. W., G. Squires, G. D. Squires, and D. R. C. Hartman. 2006. *There Is No Such Thing as a Natural Disaster: Race, Class, and Hurricane Katrina*. New York: Routledge.

Hays, Rebecca, and Gavin Daker-White. 2015. "The Care Data Consensus? A Qualitative Analysis of Opinions Expressed on Twitter." *BMC Public Health* 15: 838. https://doi.org/10.1186/s12889-015-2180-9.

Heaney, Jonathan G. 2019. "Emotion as Power: Capital and Strategy in the Field of Politics." *Journal of Political Power* 12 (2): 224–44. https://doi.org/10.1080/21583 79X.2019.1618485.

Heilbron, Johan, and George Steinmetz. 2018. "A Defense of Bourdieu." *Catalyst* 2 (1): 35–49.

Hinton, A.L., D. Fessler, and N. Quinn. 1999. *Biocultural Approaches to the Emotions*. Publications of the Society for Psychological Anthropology. Cambridge: Cambridge University Press.

Hobfoll, Stevan E. 1989. "Conservation of Resources: A New Attempt at Conceptualizing Stress." *American Psychologist* 44 (3): 513–24. https://doi.org/10.1037/0003-066X.44.3.513.

Hochschild, Arlie Russell. 1979. "Emotion Work, Feeling Rules, and Social Structure." *The American Journal of Sociology* 85 (3): 551–75.

Hochschild, Arlie Russell. 1983. *The Managed Heart: Commercialization of Human Feeling*. Berkeley: University of California Press.

Hochschild, Arlie Russell. 2012. *The Managed Heart: Commercialization of Human Feeling*. Berkeley: University of California Press.

Hochschild, Arlie Russell. 2016. *Strangers in Their Own Land: Anger and Mourning on the American Right*. New York: New Press.

Höijer, Birgitta. 2004. "The Discourse of Global Compassion: The Audience and Media Reporting of Human Suffering." *Media, Culture & Society* 26 (4): 513–31. http://mcs.sagepub.com/content/26/4/513.short.

Holbrook, Colin, and Jennifer Hahn-Holbrook. 2022. "Evolved to Learn: Emotions as Calibrational Adaptations." In *The Oxford Handbook of Emotional Development*, edited by D. Dukes, A. Samson, and E. Walle, 3–17. Oxford: Oxford University Press.

Holmes, Mary. 2015. "Men's Emotions: Heteromasculinity, Emotional Reflexivity, and Intimate Relationships." *Men and Masculinities* 18 (2): 176–92. https://doi.org/10.1177/1097184X14557494.

Holton, Avery E., and Seth C. Lewis. 2011. "Journalists, Social Media, and the Use of Humor on Twitter." *The Electronic Journal of Communication* 21 (1–2): 1–20.

hooks, bell. 2000. *Feminist Theory: From Margin to Center*. Cambridge, MA: South End Press.

Hordge-Freeman, Elizabeth. 2015. *The Color of Love: Racial Features, Stigma, and Socialization in Black Brazilian Families*. Austin: University of Texas Press.

Hughley, D. L. 2018. "D.L. Hughley—Racially Charged Police Violence and 'How Not to Get Shot'—Extended Interview." The Daily Show with Trevor Noah. August 16, 2018. http://www.cc.com/video-clips/bx3334/the-daily-show-with-trevor-noah-d-l--hughley---racially-charged-police-violence-and--how-not-to-get-shot----extended-interview.

Ihekweazu, Chioma. 2017. "Ebola in Prime Time: A Content Analysis of Sensationalism and Efficacy Information in U.S. Nightly News Coverage of the Ebola Outbreaks." *Health Communication* 32 (6): 741–48. https://doi.org/10.1080/10410236.2016.1172287.

Illouz, Eva. 1997. *Consuming the Romantic Utopia: Love and the Cultural Contradictions of Capitalism*. Berkeley: University of California Press.

"Implicit Bias in Health Care." 2016. Quick Safety. The Joint Commission, Division of Health Care Improvement. Oakbrook Terrace, IL. https://www.jointcommission.org/-/media/tjc/documents/newsletters/quick-safety-issue-23-apr-2016-final-rev.pdf.

"Intense Training for Ebola Caregivers." 2014. CNN. https://edition.cnn.com/videos/world/2014/10/29/pkg-robertson-switzerland-ebola-caregiver-training.cnn.

Jacobs, Michelle R. 2014. "Race, Place, and Biography at Play: Contextualizing American Indian Viewpoints on Indian Mascots." *Journal of Sport and Social Issues* 38 (4): 322–45. https://doi.org/10.1177/0193723514530568.

James, William. 1907. *Pragmatism: A New Name for Some Old Ways of Thinking*. New York: Longmans, Green.

Jasper, James M. 2014. "Feeling-Thinking: Emotions as Central to Culture." In *Conceptualizing Culture in Social Movement Research*, edited by B. Baumgarten, P. Daphi, and P. Ullrich, 23–44. London: Palgrave Macmillan.

Jenkins, Jimmy, and Matt Katz. 2020. "'A Ticking Time Bomb': Advocates Warn COVID-19 Is Spreading Rapidly Behind Bars." *National Public Radio*, April 28, 2020, sec. Morning Edition. https://www.npr.org/2020/04/28/846678912/a-ticking-time-bomb-advocates-warn-covid-19-is-spreading-rapidly-behind-bars.

Jenkins, Richard. 1982. "Pierre Bourdieu and the Reproduction of Determinism." *Sociology* 16 (2): 270–81.

Johnson, A. 2006. "Steelers Couple Competes for ESPN Wedding." *Pittsburgh Tribune Review*, March 15, 2006.

Johnson, Norris R. 1988. "Fire in a Crowded Theater: A Descriptive Investigation of the Emergence of Panic." *International Journal of Mass Emergencies and Disasters* 6 (1): 7–26.

Julien, Chris. 2015. "Bourdieu, Social Capital and Online Interaction." *Sociology* 49 (2): 356–73. https://doi.org/10.1177/0038038514535862.

Jurgenson, Nathan. 2011. "Digital Dualism and the Fallacy of Web Objectivity." *Cyborgology* (blog). 2011. https://thesocietypages.org/cyborgology/2011/09/13/digital-dualism-and-the-fallacy-of-web-objectivity/§.

Jurkowitz, Mark. 2014. "What the Digital News Boom Means for Consumers." *Pew Research Center*. http://www.journalism.org/2014/03/26/what-the-digital-news-boom-means-for-consumers/.

Kaner, Jolie, and Sarah Schaack. 2016. "Understanding Ebola: The 2014 Epidemic." *Globalization and Health* 12 (53): 1–7. https://doi.org/10.1186/s12992-016-0194-4.

Kang, Miliann. 2003. "The Managed Hand: The Commercialization of Bodies and Emotions in Korean Immigrant–Owned Nail Salons." *Gender & Society* 17 (6): 820–39. https://doi.org/10.1177/0891243203257632.

Katz, Jack. 2012. "Emotion's Crucible." In *Emotions Matter: A Relational Approach to Emotions*, edited by D. Spencer, K. Walby, and A. Hunt, 15–39. Toronto: University of Toronto Press.

Kemper, Theodore D. 1981. "Social Constructionist and Positivist Approaches to the Sociology of Emotions." *American Journal of Sociology* 87: 336–62.

Kesteren, Manja van. 2020. "Sign Language Interpreter Goes Viral." *I Am Expat*. March 16, 2020. https://www.iamexpat.nl/expat-info/dutch-expat-news/sign-language-interpreter-goes-viral.

Kilgo, Danielle K., Joseph Yoo, and Thomas J. Johnson. 2019. "Spreading Ebola Panic: Newspaper and Social Media Coverage of the 2014 Ebola Health Crisis." *Health Communication* 34 (8): 811–17. https://doi.org/10.1080/10410236.2018.1437524.

Kilgore, Adam. 2020. "For Many Fans, the Absence of Sports Feels Like a Loss. Psychologists Say That's Normal." *The Washington Post*, May 21, 2020, sec. Sports. https://www.washingtonpost.com/sports/2020/05/21/sports-fans-withdrawal/.

Kinateder, Max T., Erica D. Kuligowski, Paul A. Reneke, and Richard D. Peacock. 2015. "Risk Perception in Fire Evacuation Behavior Revisited: Definitions, Related Concepts, and Empirical Evidence." *Fire Science Reviews* 4 (1): 1–26. https://doi.org/10.1186/s40 038-014-0005-z.

Klemm, Celine, Tilo Hartmann, and Enny Das. 2019. "Fear-Mongering or Fact-Driven? Illuminating the Interplay of Objective Risk and Emotion-Evoking Form in the Response to Epidemic News." *Health Communication* 34 (1): 74–83. https://doi.org/10.1080/10410236.2017.1384429.

Kloppenberg, James T. 1996. "Pragmatism: An Old Name for Some New Ways of Thinking?" *The Journal of American History* 83 (1): 100–138.

Kraszewski, Jon. 2008. "Pittsburgh in Fort Worth: Football Bars, Sports Television, Sports Fandom, and the Management of Home." *Journal of Sport and Social Issues* 32 (2): 139–57. https://doi.org/10.1177/0193723508316377.

Krishnan, Rekha, Karen S. Cook, Rajiv Krishnan Kozhikode, and Oliver Schilke. 2021. "An Interaction Ritual Theory of Social Resource Exchange: Evidence from a Silicon Valley Accelerator." *Administrative Science Quarterly* 66 (3): 659–710. https://doi.org/10.1177/0001839220970936.

Kuipers, Giselinde. 2005. "'Where Was King Kong When We Needed Him?' Public Discourse, Digital Disaster Jokes, and the Functions of Laughter after 9/11." *The Journal of American Culture* 28 (1): 70–84. https://doi.org/10.1111/j.1542-734X.2005.00155.x.

Kuipers, Giselinde. 2008. "The Sociology of Humor." In *The Primer of Humor Research*, edited by V. Raskin, 361–98. Berlin: Walter de Gruyter.

LaDow, J., J. L. Sherman, E. Blazina, A. Sostek, and B. Donaldson. 2009. "Fandemonium Greets Steelers Parade." *Pittsburgh Post-Gazette*, February 3, 2009. https://www.post-gazette.com/sports/2009/02/03/Fandemonium-greets-Steelers-parade/stories/20090 2030217.

Lange, A., E. M. Meyers, B. H. Reynolds, and R. Styers, eds. 2011. *Light Against Darkness: Dualism in Ancient Mediterranean Religion and the Contemporary World.* Göttingen, Germany: Vandenhoeck & Ruprecht.

Lapchick, Richard. 2012. "The 2012 Racial and Gender Report Card: National Football League." UCF: Institute for Diversity and Ethics in Sport. https://www.sportandsocial justice.org/wp-content/uploads/2012/09/2012-NFL-RGRC1.pdf.

Lareau, Annette, and Elliot B. Weininger. 2003. "Cultural Capital in Educational Research: A Critical Assessment." *Theory and Society* 32 (5–6): 567–606. http://link. springer.com/article/10.1023/B:RYSO.0000004951.04408.b0.

Lavis, T. 2007. "Wedded Bliss: Gobs of Fun, Steelers Polka." *The Tribune Democrat*, July 13, 2007. https://www.tribdem.com/news/local_news/wedded-bliss-gobs-of-fun-steel ers-polka/article_73bae58e-22c1-5c45-b560-d417fc25ac6e.html.

Le Bon, Gustave. 1896/1996. *The Crowd: A Study of the Popular Mind.* https://www.gutenb erg.org/ebooks/445.

Leahy, Sean. 2011. "Hospital in Pittsburgh Wrapping Babies in Terrible Towels." *USA Today*, January 31, 2011. http://content.usatoday.com/communities/thehuddle/

post/2011/01/hospital-in-pittsburgh-wrapping-babies-in-terrible-towels/1#.Xt4X
ZsZS9mB.

Lewis, C. S. 1939. "Learning in War-Time." A sermon preached in the Church of St. Mary the Virgin, Oxford, UK. https://bradleyggreen.com/attachments/Lewis.Learning%20 in%20War-Time.pdf.

Lipsky, Michael. 1980. *Street-Level Bureaucracy: Dilemmas of the Individual in Public Services.* Thousand Oaks, CA: Russell Sage Foundation.

Lively, Kathryn J. 2000. "Reciprocal Emotion Management." *Work and Occupations* 27 (1): 32–63. http://journals.sagepub.com/doi/abs/10.1177/0730888400027001003.

Lois, Jennifer. 2001. "Managing Emotions, Intimacy, and Relationships in a Volunteer Search and Rescue Group." *Journal of Contemporary Ethnography* 30 (2): 131–79. https://doi.org/10.1177/089124101030002001.

Lois, Jennifer. 2010. "The Temporal Emotion Work of Motherhood: Homeschoolers' Strategies for Managing Time Shortage." *Gender & Society* 24 (4): 421–46. https://doi. org/10.1177/0891243210377762.

Lois, Jennifer. 2013. *Home Is Where the School Is: The Logic of Homeschooling and the Emotional Labor of Mothering.* New York: NYU Press.

Lopez, Steven H. 2006. "Emotional Labor and Organized Emotional Care." *Work and Occupations* 33 (2): 133–60. http://journals.sagepub.com/doi/abs/10.1177/073088840 5284567.

Lord, Rich. 2009a. "Council Changes City's Name to Sixburgh." *Pittsburgh Post-Gazette*, February 3, 2009. https://www.post-gazette.com/breaking/2009/02/03/Council-chan ges-city-s-name-to-Sixburgh/stories/200902030162.

Lord, Rich. 2009b. "Super Bowl Parade Costs City $79,500." *Pittsburgh Post-Gazette*, February 4, 2009. https://www.post-gazette.com/breaking/2009/02/04/Super-Bowl-parade-costs-city-79-500/stories/200902040205.

Lorde, Audre. 2019. *Sister Outsider: Essays and Speeches.* New York: Penguin.

Loseke, Donileen R. 2009. "Examining Emotion as Discourse: Emotion Codes and Presidential Speeches Justifying War." *The Sociological Quarterly* 50: 497–524.

Luciew, John. 2011. "Pittsburgh Steelers Fans Make Themselves Part of the Team." *PennLive*, January 6, 2011. https://www.pennlive.com/midstate/2011/01/pittsburgh_ steelers_fans_make.html.

Lutz, Catherine A. 1998. *Unnatural Emotions.* Chicago: University of Chicago Press.

Madden, Pete, Cho Park, and Ryan Smith. 2021. "Clinicians Fear NFL's Concussion Settlement Program Protocols Discriminate against Black Players." *ABC News*, February 3, 2021, sec. Sports. https://abcnews.go.com/Sports/clinicians-fear-nfls-con cussion-settlement-program-protocols-discriminate/story?id=75646704.

Maher, Victor. 2019. "A Timeline of Colin Kaepernick vs. the N.F.L." *The New York Times*, February 15, 2019. https://www.nytimes.com/2019/02/15/sports/nfl-colin-kaepern ick-protests-timeline.html.

Mair, Peter. 2013. *Ruling the Void: The Hollowing of Western Democracy.* London: Verso.

Mao, Frances. 2020. "Coronavirus Panic: Why Are People Stockpiling Toilet Paper?" BBC News, March 4, 2020. https://www.bbc.com/news/world-australia-51731422.

Marres, N. 2017. *Digital Sociology: The Reinvention of Social Research.* Hoboken, NJ: Wiley.

Marwick, Alice E., and danah boyd. 2011. "I Tweet Honestly, I Tweet Passionately: Twitter Users, Context Collapse, and the Imagined Audience." *New Media & Society* 13 (1): 114–33. https://doi.org/10.1177/1461444810365313.

McCarthy, E. Doyle. 1989. "Emotions Are Social Things: An Essay in the Sociology of Emotions." In *The Sociology of Emotions: Original Essays and Research Papers*, edited by D. D. Franks and E. D. McCarthy, 51–72. Greenwich, CT: JAI Press.

McCarthy, E. Doyle. 2017. *Emotional Lives: Dramas of Identity in an Age of Mass Media*. Cambridge: Cambridge University Press.

McIntyre, Lee. 2018. *Post-Truth*. MIT Press Essential Knowledge Series. Cambridge, MA: The MIT Press.

McKee, Rebecca. 2013. "Ethical Issues in Using Social Media for Health and Health Care Research." *Health Policy* 110 (2): 298–301.

McKenzie, Germán. 2016. *Interpreting Charles Taylor's Social Theory on Religion and Secularization: A Comparative Study*. Sophia Studies in Cross-Cultural Philosophy of Traditions and Cultures. Berlin: Springer.

McKinnon, J. 2009. "More Than 100 Arrested in Post-Game Celebration." *Pittsburgh Post-Gazette*, February 2, 2009.

McMarlin, Shirley. n.d. "Couples Set Their 'Sites' on Something Different." *Pittsburgh Tribune Review*, n.d.

McPherson, Miller, Lynn Smith-Lovin, and James M. Cook. 2001. "Birds of a Feather: Homophily in Social Networks." *Annual Review of Sociology* 27: 415–44.

Mead, George Herbert. 1934. *Mind, Self, & Society*. Chicago: Chicago University Press.

Merchant, Raina M., Stacy Elmer, and Nicole Lurie. 2011. "Integrating Social Media into Emergency-Preparedness Efforts." *New England Journal of Medicine* 365 (4): 289–91. https://doi.org/10.1056/NEJMp1103591.

Mesquita, Batja, Michael Boiger, and Jozefien De Leersnyder. 2017. "Doing Emotions: The Role of Culture in Everyday Emotions." *European Review of Social Psychology* 28 (1): 95–133. https://doi.org/10.1080/10463283.2017.1329107.

Mills, C. Wright. 1959. *The Sociological Imagination*. Oxford: Oxford University Press.

Mohanty, Chandra Talpade. 1988. "Under Western Eyes: Feminist Scholarship and Colonial Discourses." *Feminist Review*, 30: 61–88. http://www.jstor.org/stable/10.2307/1395054.

Mosley, Matt. 2008. "NFL's Best Fans? We Gotta Hand It to Steelers (Barely)." ESPN, August 11, 2008. https://www.espn.com/nfl/preview08/columns/story?id=3530077.

Murdock, Graham. 2010. "Pierre Bourdieu, Distinction: A Social Critique of the Judgement of Taste." *International Journal of Cultural Policy* 16 (February): 63–65. https://doi.org/10.1080/10286630902952413.

Näring, Gérard, Mariette Briët, and André Brouwers. 2006. "Beyond Demand–Control: Emotional Labour and Symptoms of Burnout in Teachers." *Work & Stress* 20 (4): 303–15. https://doi.org/10.1080/02678370601065182.

Nathanson, John T., James G. Connolly, Frank Yuk, Alex Gometz, Jonathan Rasouli, Mark Lovell, and Tanvir Choudhri. 2016. "Concussion Incidence in Professional Football: Position-Specific Analysis with Use of a Novel Metric." *Orthopaedic Journal of Sports Medicine* 4 (1): 2325967115622621–2325967115622621. https://doi.org/10.1177/2325967115622621.

Newman, Nic. 2015. "Reuters Institute Digital News Report." Oxford: Reuters Institute for the Study of Journalism and University of Oxford. http://www.digitalnewsreport.org/.

"NFL Positional Payrolls." n.d. Accessed June 21, 2021. https://www.spotrac.com/nfl/positional/.

Nixon, Darren. 2009. "'I Can't Put a Smiley Face On': Working-Class Masculinity, Emotional Labour and Service Work in the 'New Economy." *Gender, Work &*

Organization 16 (3): 300–322. http://onlinelibrary.wiley.com/doi/10.1111/j.1468-0432.2009.00446.x/full.

Nowotny, Helga. 1981. "Austria: Women in Public Life." In *Access to Power: Cross-National Studies of Women and Elites*, C. F. Epstein and R. L. Coser, 147–56. London: George Allen & Unwin.

"Number of Monthly Active Twitter Users Worldwide from 1st Quarter 2010 to 1st Quarter 2019." n.d. Accessed June 21, 2021. https://www.statista.com/statistics/282087/number-of-monthly-active-twitter-users/.

"Number of Social Network Users Worldwide from 2017 to 2025." n.d. Accessed June 21, 2021. https://www.statista.com/statistics/278414/number-of-worldwide-social-network-users/.

O'Connor, Kathryn L., Melissa M. Baker, Sara L. Dalton, Thomas P. Dompier, Steven P. Broglio, and Zachary Y. Kerr. 2017. "Epidemiology of Sport-Related Concussions in High School Athletes: National Athletic Treatment, Injury and Outcomes Network (NATION), 2011–2012 Through 2013–2014." *Journal of Athletic Training* 52 (3): 175–85. https://doi.org/10.4085/1062-6050-52.1.15.

Odlum, Michelle, and Sunmoo Yoon. 2015. "What Can We Learn about the Ebola Outbreak from Tweets?" *American Journal of Infection Control* 43 (6): 563–71. https://doi.org/10.1016/j.ajic.2015.02.023.

Oh, Sang-Hwa, Seo Yoon Lee, and Changhyun Han. 2021. "The Effects of Social Media Use on Preventive Behaviors during Infectious Disease Outbreaks: The Mediating Role of Self-Relevant Emotions and Public Risk Perception." *Health Communication* 36 (8): 972–81. https://doi.org/10.1080/10410236.2020.1724639.

Oremus, Will. 2020. "What Everyone's Getting Wrong About the Toilet Paper Shortage." *Medium*, April 2, 2020. https://marker.medium.com/what-everyones-getting-wrong-about-the-toilet-paper-shortage-c812e1358fe0.

Ost, David. 2004. "Politics as the Mobilization of Anger: Emotions in Movements and in Power." *European Journal of Social Theory* 7 (2): 229–44.

Pager, Devah. 2008. *Marked: Race, Crime, and Finding Work in an Era of Mass Incarceration*. Chicago: University of Chicago Press.

"Panicdemic." 2009. *Urban Dictionary* (blog). May 7, 2009. https://www.urbandictionary.com/define.php?term=Panicdemic.

Parsons, Talcott. 1951. *The Social System*. London: Routledge.

Pew Research Center. 2012. "In Changing News Landscape, Even Television Is Vulnerable." http://www.journalism.org/media-indicators/digital-news-sources-for-americans-by-platform/.

Pierce, Jennifer. 1995. *Gender Trials: Emotional Lives of Contemporary Law Firms*. Berkeley: University of California Press.

Plessner, Helmuth. 1970. *Laughing and Crying: A Study of the Limits of Human Behavior*. Northwestern University Studies in Phenomenology & Existential Philosophy. Evanston, IL: Northwestern University Press.

Polletta, Francesca, Pang Ching Bobby Chen, Beth Gharrity Gardner, and Alice Motes. 2011. "The Sociology of Storytelling." *Annual Review of Sociology* 37 (1): 109–30. https://doi.org/10.1146/annurev-soc-081309-150106.

Porter, Cornelia P., and Evelyn L. Barbee. 2004. "Race and Racism in Nursing Research: Past, Present, and Future." *Annual Review of Nursing Research* 22 (1): 9–37.

Poulton, Emma. 2008. "Toward a Cultural Sociology of the Consumption of 'Fantasy Football Hooliganism.'" *Sociology of Sport Journal* 25 (3): 331–49. https://doi.org/10.1123/ssj.25.3.331.

Qin, Jie. 2015. "Hero on Twitter, Traitor on News: How Social Media and Legacy News Frame Snowden." *The International Journal of Press/Politics* 20 (2): 166–84. https://doi.org/10.1177/1940161214566709.

Quarantelli, E. L. 2001. "Sociology of Panic." In *International Encyclopedia of the Social & Behavioral Sciences*, edited by N. J. Smelser and P. B. Baltes, 11020–23. Amsterdam: Elsevier.

Quotes.net. n.d. "Star Trek: The Next Generation Quotes." Accessed April 2, 2020. https://www.quotes.net/mquote/864248.

Rampton, Roberta. 2014. "Americans 'Can't Give in to Hysteria or Fear' over Ebola: Obama." *Reuters*, October 18, 2014. https://www.reuters.com/article/us-health-ebola-usa-idUSKCN0I61BO20141018.

Rao, Nandita. 2014. "Public Ignorance and Ebola." *Princeton Public Health Review* (blog). November 30, 2014. https://pphr.princeton.edu/2014/11/30/public-ignorance-and-ebola/#comments.

Räsänen, Keijo, and Ilkka Kauppinen. 2020. "Moody Habitus: Bourdieu with Existential Feelings." *Journal for the Theory of Social Behaviour* Online first. https://doi.org/10.1111/jtsb.12234.

Reay, Diane. 2000. "A Useful Extension of Bourdieu's Conceptual Framework? Emotional Capital as a Way of Understanding Mothers' Involvement in Their Children's Education." *The Sociological Review* 48 (4): 568–85.

Reay, Diane. 2015. "Habitus and the Psychosocial: Bourdieu with Feelings." *Cambridge Journal of Education* 45 (1): 9–23. https://doi.org/10.1080/0305764X.2014.990420.

Reckwitz, Andreas. 2002. "Toward a Theory of Social Practices: A Development in Culturalist Theorizing." *European Journal of Social Theory* 5 (2): 243–63.

Recuber, Timothy. 2013. "Occupy Empathy? Online Politics and Micro-Narratives of Suffering." *New Media & Society* 17 (1): 62–77. http://nms.sagepub.com/content/early/2013/10/06/1461444813506971.abstract.

Recuber, Timothy. 2016. *Consuming Catastrophe: Mass Culture in America's Decade of Disaster*. Philadelphia, PA: Temple University Press.

Reid, Jason, and Jane McManus. n.d. "The NFL's Racial Divide." Accessed June 21, 2021. https://theundefeated.com/features/the-nfls-racial-divide/.

Remillard, Arthur. 2013. "Steelers Nation and the Seriously Religions Side of Football." *Marginalia: Los Angeles Review of Books* (blog). https://marginalia.lareviewofbooks.org/steelers-nation-and-the-seriously-religious-side-of-football/.

Ren, Jingqiu, and Joe Feagin. 2021. "Face Mask Symbolism in Anti-Asian Hate Crimes." *Ethnic and Racial Studies* 44 (5): 746–58. https://doi.org/10.1080/01419870.2020.1826553.

Reuters Staff. 2020. "Dutch PM Tells Citizens to Relax, Saying There's Enough Toilet Paper for 10 Years." *Reuters*, March 19, 2020, sec. Healthcare and Pharma. https://www.reuters.com/article/us-health-coronavirus-netherlands-toilet/dutch-pm-tells-citizens-to-relax-saying-theres-enough-toilet-paper-for-10-years-idUSKBN21627A.

Ribes, Alberto J. 2010. "Theorising Global Media Events: Cognition, Emotions and Performances." *New Global Studies* 4 (3): 1–20. https://doi.org/10.2202/1940-0004.1113.

Ridgeway, Cecilia. 2011. *Framed by Gender: How Gender Inequality Persists in the Modern World*. New York: Oxford University Press.

Roberts, Andrea L., Herman A. Taylor, Alicia J. Whittington, Ross D. Zafonte, Frank E. Speizer, Alvaro Pascual-Leone, Aaron Baggish, and Marc G. Weisskopf. 2020. "Race in Association with Physical and Mental Health among Former Professional American-Style Football Players: Findings from the Football Players Health Study." *Annals of Epidemiology* 51 (November): 48-52.e2. https://doi.org/10.1016/j.annepidem.2020.07.013.

Rodd, Isabelle. 2020. "Coronavirus: Violinists Play Titanic Hymn in Front of Empty Toilet Paper Aisle." BBC, March 18, 2020. https://www.bbc.com/news/av/world-us-canada-51942217.

Rogers, Kimberly B., and Dawn T. Robinson. 2014. "Measuring Affect and Emotions." In *Handbook of the Sociology of Emotions: Volume II*, edited by J. E. Stets and J. H. Turner, 283–303. Dordrecht: Springer.

Ronchi, Enrico, and Daniel Nilsson. 2013. "Fire Evacuation in High-Rise Buildings: A Review of Human Behaviour and Modelling Research." *Fire Science Reviews* 2 (1): 7. https://doi.org/10.1186/2193-0414-2-7.

Rose, Diana. 2004. "Analyses of Moving Images." In *Approaches to Qualitative Research*, edited by S. N. Hesse-Biber and P. Leavy. Oxford: Oxford University Press.

Rosenthal, Joseph A., Randi E. Foraker, Christy L. Collins, and R. Dawn Comstock. 2014. "National High School Athlete Concussion Rates from 2005–2006 to 2011–2012." *The American Journal of Sports Medicine* 42 (7): 1710–15. https://doi.org/10.1177/0363546514530091.

Rothman, Naomi B., Michael G. Pratt, Laura Rees, and Timothy J. Vogus. 2017. "Understanding the Dual Nature of Ambivalence: Why and When Ambivalence Leads to Good and Bad Outcomes." *Academy of Management Annals* 11 (1): 33–72. https://doi.org/10.5465/annals.2014.0066.

Rothschild, Anna. 2020. "Dr. Fauci Has Been Dreading a Pandemic Like COVID-19 for Years." *FiveThirtyEight*, April 7, 2020. https://fivethirtyeight.com/features/dr-fauci-has-been-dreading-a-pandemic-like-covid-19-for-years/.

RTL Nieuws. 2020. "Rutte in Supermarkt: 'Genoeg Wc-Papier Voor 10 Jaar Poepen,'" March 19, 2020. https://www.rtlnieuws.nl/nieuws/video/video/5062691/rutte-supermarkt-genoeg-wc-papier-voor-10-jaar-poepen.

Russell, James A. 1991. "Culture, Scripts, and Children's Understanding of Emotion." In *Children's Understanding of Emotion*, edited by C. Saarni and P. L. Harris, 293–318. Cambridge: Cambridge University Press.

Saldaña, Johnny. 2013. *The Coding Manual for Qualitative Researchers*. Thousand Oaks, CA: Sage.

Sarbin, Theodore R. 1995. "Emotional Life, Rhetoric, and Roles." *Journal of Narrative and Life History* 5 (3): 213–20. https://doi.org/10.1075/jnlh.5.3.03emo.

Sastry, Shaunak, and Alessandro Lovari. 2017. "Communicating the Ontological Narrative of Ebola: An Emerging Disease in the Time of 'Epidemic 2.0.'" *Health Communication* 32 (3): 329–38. https://doi.org/10.1080/10410236.2016.1138380.

Scales, Kezia, and Michael J. Lepore. 2020. "Always Essential: Valuing Direct Care Workers in Long-Term Care." *Public Policy & Aging Report* 30 (4): 173–77. https://doi.org/10.1093/ppar/praa022.

Schachter, Stanley, and Jerome Singer. 1962. "Cognitive, Social, and Physiological Determinants of Emotional State." *Psychological Review* 69 (5): 379–99.

Schackner, Bill. 2009. "Pitt Plans to Discipline Those Arrested after Super Bowl." *Pittsburgh Post-Gazette*, February 4, 2009. http://old.post-gazette.com/pg/09035/946 710-53.stm.

Scheer, Monique. 2012. "Are Emotions a Kind of Practice (and Is That What Makes Them Have a History)? A Bourdieuian Approach to Understanding Emotion." *History and Theory* 51 (2): 193–220. http://onlinelibrary.wiley.com/doi/10.1111/j.1468-2303.2012.00621.x/full.

Scheff, T. J. 1979. *Catharsis in Healing, Ritual, and Drama*. Berkeley: University of California Press.

Seery, Brenda L., and Elizabeth A. Corrigall. 2009. "Emotional Labor: Links to Work Attitudes and Emotional Exhaustion." *Journal of Managerial Psychology* 24 (8): 797–813. https://doi.org/10.1108/02683940910996806.

Shah, Megha K., Nikhila Gandrakota, Jeannie P. Cimiotti, Neena Ghose, Miranda Moore, and Mohammed K. Ali. 2021. "Prevalence of and Factors Associated with Nurse Burnout in the US." *JAMA Network Open* 4 (2): e2036469. https://doi.org/10.1001/jamanetworkopen.2020.36469.

"Share of African Americans in the National Football League in 2019, by Role." 2019. https://www.statista.com/statistics/1154691/nfl-racial-diversity/.

Sherlaw, William, and Jocelyn Raude. 2013. "Why the French Did Not Choose to Panic: A Dynamic Analysis of the Public Response to the Influenza Pandemic." *Sociology of Health and Illness* 35 (2): 332–44. http://onlinelibrary.wiley.com/doi/10.1111/j.1467-9566.2012.01525.x/full.

Shilling, Chris. 2012. *The Body and Social Theory*. Published in Association with Theory, Culture & Society. London: Sage.

Shott, Susan. 1979. "Emotion and Social Life: A Symbolic Interactionist Analysis." *American Journal of Sociology* 84 (6): 1317–34. http://www.jstor.org/stable/10.2307/2777894.

Shropshire, Kenneth L. 1996. *In Black and White: Race and Sports in America*. New York: NYU Press.

Silverman, Alex. 2020. "Demographic Data Shows Which Major Sports Fan Bases Are Most Likely to Support or Reject Social Justice Advocacy." September 10, 2020. https://morningconsult.com/2020/09/10/sports-fan-base-demographic-data/.

Simon, Robin W., and Leda E. Nath. 2004. "Gender and Emotion in the United States: Do Men and Women Differ in Self-Reports of Feelings and Expressive Behavior?" *American Journal of Sociology* 109 (5): 1137–76. http://www.jstor.org/stable/10.1086/382111.

Sinclair, Shane, Kate Beamer, Thomas F. Hack, Susan McClement, Shelley Raffin Bouchal, Harvey M. Chochinov, and Neil A. Hagen. 2017. "Sympathy, Empathy, and Compassion: A Grounded Theory Study of Palliative Care Patients' Understandings, Experiences, and Preferences." *Palliative Medicine* 31 (5): 437–47.

Slaby, Jan, and Christian von Scheve. 2019. *Affective Societies: Key Concepts*. Routledge Studies in Affective Societies. Philadelphia: Taylor & Francis.

Slisco, Aila. 2020. "Watch: Netherlands Coronavirus Healthcare Workers Receive Nationwide Standing Ovation for Tackling Pandemic." *Newsweek*, March 17, 2020. https://www.newsweek.com/watch-netherlands-coronavirus-healthcare-workers-receive-nationwide-standing-ovation-tackling-1492856.

Sloan, Melissa M., Murat Haner, Amanda Graham, Francis T. Cullen, Justin T. Pickett, and Cheryl Lero Jonson. 2021. "Pandemic Emotions: The Extent, Correlates, and

Mental Health Consequences of Fear of COVID-19." *Sociological Spectrum* 41 (5): 369–86. https://doi.org/10.1080/02732173.2021.1926380.

Smith, Pam, and Maria Lorentzon. 2008. "The Emotional Labor of Nursing." In *Common Foundation Studies in Nursing*, 4th ed., edited by J. Spouse, M. Cook, and C. Cox, 67–88. Philadelphia, PA: Elsevier.

Smydo, J. 2009. "City Schools to Have 2-Hour Delay Day after Super Bowl." *Pittsburgh Post-Gazette*, January 29, 2009. https://www.post-gazette.com/breaking/2009/01/29/City-schools-to-have-2-hour-delay-day-after-Super-Bowl/stories/200901290297.

Sohoni, Deenesh, and Salvatore Saporito. 2009. "Mapping School Segregation: Using GIS to Explore Racial Segregation between Schools and Their Corresponding Attendance Areas." *American Journal of Education* 115 (4): 569–600. https://doi.org/10.1086/599782.

Sostek, Anya. 2008. "How the Steelers' Schedule Rules Our World." *Pittsburgh Post-Gazette*, April 20, 2008. https://www.post-gazette.com/life/lifestyle/2008/04/20/How-the-Steelers-schedule-rules-our-world/stories/200804200247.

Sprague, Joey. 1997. "Holy Men and Big Guns: The Can(n)on in Social Theory." *Gender & Society* 11 (1): 88–107.

Stacey, Clare. 2011. *The Caring Self: Work Experiences of Home Care Aides*. Ithaca, NY: Cornell University Press.

Staples, Brent. 1998. "Just Walk On By: A Black Man Ponders His Power to Alter Public Space." *Literary Cavalcade* 2: 38–41.

"Statement on Georgia-Pacific's Response to COVID-19." 2020. October 15, 2020. https://www.gp.com/news/2020/10/statement-on-georgia-pacifics-response-to-covid-19.

"Steelers Tattoos." 2021. *Google Image Search* (blog). June 21, 2021. https://www.google.com/search?q=steelers+tattoos&client=firefox-b-d&hl=en&sxsrf=ALeKk02f-4c4Y-xmh1_YRxjdMaYSM8lkWA:1591606602246&source=lnms&tbm=isch&sa=X&ved=2ahUKEwihmpjR7PHpAhWRyKQKHVElArIQ_AUoAXoECA8QAw&biw=1440&bih=703.

Stets, Jan E., and Jonathan H. Turner, eds. 2014. *Handbook of the Sociology of Emotions: Volume II*. Dordrecht: Springer.

Stevens, Alex. 2020. "Governments Cannot Just 'Follow the Science' on COVID-19." *Nature Human Behaviour* 4 (6): 560. https://doi.org/10.1038/s41562-020-0894-x.

Summers-Effler, Erika. 2006. "Ritual Theory." In *Handbook of the Sociology of Emotions*, edited by J. E. Stets and J. H. Turner, 135–54. Boston: Springer. https://doi.org/10.1007/978-0-387-30715-2_7.

Summers-Effler, Erika. 2010. *Laughing Saints and Righteous Heroes: Emotional Rhythms in Social Movement Groups*. Morality and Society Series. Chicago: University of Chicago Press.

Summers-Effler, Erika, Justin Van Ness, and Christopher Hausmann. 2015. "Peeking in the Black Box: Studying, Theorizing, and Representing the Micro-Foundations of Day-to-Day Interactions." *Journal of Contemporary Ethnography* 44 (4): 450–79. https://doi.org/10.1177/0891241614545880.

Swartz, David. 1997. *Culture & Power: The Sociology of Pierre Bourdieu*. Chicago: Chicago University Press.

Sweet, Paige L. 2019. "The Sociology of Gaslighting." *American Sociological Review* 84 (5): 851–75. https://doi.org/10.1177/0003122419874843.

Swidler, Ann. 1986. "Culture in Action: Symbols and Strategies." *American Sociological Review* 51 (2): 273–86. https://doi.org/10.2307/2095521.

Taylor, Charles. 2002. "Modern Social Imaginaries." *Public Culture* 14 (1): 91–124.

Taylor, Steven, and Gordon J. G. Asmundson. 2021. "Negative Attitudes about Facemasks during the COVID-19 Pandemic: The Dual Importance of Perceived Ineffectiveness and Psychological Reactance." *PLOS ONE* 16 (2): e0246317. https://doi.org/10.1371/journal.pone.0246317.

Tenbarge, Kat. 2020. "The Toilet Paper Shortage Has Become a Meme during the Coronavirus Quarantine, with Posts about Stockpiling or Substituting It Going Viral." *Insider*, March 19, 2020. https://www.insider.com/toilet-paper-memes-coronavirus-quarantine-shortage-tiktoks-2020-3#people-predicted-what-would-happen-once-all-the-toilet-paper-was-gone-4.

Theodosius, Catherine. 2006. "Recovering Emotion from Emotion Management." *Sociology* 40 (5): 893–910. https://doi.org/10.1177/0038038506067512.

Theodosius, Catherine. 2008. *Emotional Labour in Health Care: The Unmanaged Heart of Nursing*. New York: Routledge.

Thoits, Peggy A. 1989. "The Sociology of Emotion." *Annual Review of Sociology* 15: 317–42.

Threadgold, Steven. 2020. *Bourdieu and Affect*. 1st ed. Bristol: Bristol University Press. https://doi.org/10.2307/j.ctv1453m06.

Tierney, Kathleen, Christine Bevc, and Erica Kuligowski. 2006. "Metaphors Matter: Disaster Myths, Media Frames, and Their Consequences in Hurricane Katrina." *The ANNALS of the American Academy of Political and Social Science* 604 (1): 57–81. https://doi.org/10.1177/0002716205285589.

Tiffany, Kaitlyn. 2019. "The Rise and Fall of the Man Cave." *Vox*, March 4, 2019. https://www.vox.com/the-goods/2019/3/4/18246518/man-cave-boom-pre-recession-masculinity-male-friendship.

Timmermans, Stefan, and Iddo Tavory. 2012. "Theory Construction in Qualitative Research: From Grounded Theory to Abductive Analysis." *Sociological Theory* 30 (3): 167–86. https://doi.org/10.1177/0735275112457914.

Tracy, Sarah J. 2010. "Qualitative Quality: Eight 'Big-Tent' Criteria for Excellent Qualitative Research." *Qualitative Inquiry* 16 (10): 837–51. https://doi.org/10.1177/1077800410383121.

"Uganda: West Creating Ebola 'Mass Panic.'" 2014. CNN. https://edition.cnn.com/videos/world/2014/10/28/qmb-uganda-ebola-panic-rose-namayanja-intv.cnn.

Ungar, Sheldon. 1998. "Hot Crises and Media Reassurance: A Comparison of Emerging Diseases and Ebola Zaire." *The British Journal of Sociology* 49 (1): 36–56. https://doi.org/10.2307/591262.

Vance, Karl, William Howe, and Robert P. Dellavalle. 2009. "Social Internet Sites as a Source of Public Health Information." *Dermatologic Clinics* 27 (2): 133–36. https://doi.org/10.1016/j.det.2008.11.010.

Viera, Anthony J., and Joanne M. Garrett. 2005. "Understanding Interobserver Agreement: The Kappa Statistic." *Family Medicine* 37 (5): 360–63.

Wacquant, Loïc. 1995. "Pugs at Work: Bodily Capital and Bodily Labour among Professional Boxers." *Body & Society* 1 (1): 65–93.

Wacquant, Loïc. 2008. "Pierre Bourdieu." In *Key Sociological Thinkers*, 2nd ed., edited by Rob Stones, 261–77. London: Macmillan.

Wamsley, Laurel. 2020. "Coronavirus Fears Have Led to a Golden Age of Hand-Washing PSAs." *National Public Radio*, March 4, 2020. https://www.npr.org/2020/03/04/811609241/coronavirus-fears-have-led-to-a-golden-age-of-hand-washing-psas.

Weiss, Karen G. 2013. *Party School: Crime, Campus, and Community*. Northeastern Series on Gender, Crime, and Law Series. Evanston, IL: Northeastern University Press.

Westbrook, Adam. 2020. "People Around the World Are Panic-Buying . . . Toilet Paper?" *The New York Times*, March 12, 2020, sec. Opinion. https://www.nytimes.com/2020/03/12/opinion/toilet-paper-coronavirus.html.

Wharton, Amy S. 2009. "The Sociology of Emotional Labor." *Annual Review of Sociology* 35 (1): 147–65. https://doi.org/10.1146/annurev-soc-070308-115944.

White, Ismail K. 2007. "When Race Matters and When It Doesn't: Racial Group Differences in Response to Racial Cues." *American Political Science Review* 101 (2): 339–54. https://doi.org/10.1017/S0003055407070177.

"W.H.O. to Review Ebola Response." 2014. CNN. https://edition.cnn.com/2014/10/18/world/who-ebola-response/index.html.

"WHO Warns: Masks May Give False Sense of Security, Lead to Neglect of Proper Hygiene." 2020. February 4, 2020. https://www.gmanetwork.com/news/lifestyle/healthandwellness/724760/who-warns-masks-may-give-false-sense-of-security-lead-to-neglect-of-proper-hygiene/story/.

Williams, Simon J., and Gillian Bendelow. 1998. *The Lived Body: Sociological Themes, Embodied Issues*. London: Routledge.

Wilson, William Julius. 2010. *More Than Just Race: Being Black and Poor in the Inner City*. New York: W. W. Norton & Company.

Wingfield, Adia Harvey. 2009. "Racializing the Glass Escalator: Reconsidering Men's Experiences with Women's Work." *Gender & Society* 23 (1): 5–26. https://doi.org/10.1177/0891243208323054.

Wingfield, Adia Harvey. 2010. "Are Some Emotions Marked 'Whites Only'? Racialized Feeling Rules in Professional Workplaces." *Social Problems* 57 (2): 251–68. https://doi.org/10.1525/sp.2010.57.2.251.

World Health Organization. 2014. "Ebola Virus Disease–Spain." Retrieved from https://www.who.int/csr/don/09-october-2014-ebola/en/.

World Health Organization. 2015. "Ebola Virus Disease Factsheet." Retrieved from http://www.who.int/mediacentre/factsheets/fs103/en/.

World Health Organization. 2016. "Situation Report: Zika Virus Disease, Yellow Fever, Ebola Virus Disease." http://apps.who.int/iris/bitstream/10665/205686/1/WHOsitrep_28Apr2016_eng.pdf?ua=1.

World Health Organization. 2020a. "Report of the WHO-China Joint Mission on Coronavirus Disease 2019 (COVID-19)." https://www.who.int/docs/default-source/coronaviruse/who-china-joint-mission-on-covid-19-final-report.pdf.

World Health Organization. 2020b. "State of the World's Nursing 2020." https://www.who.int/publications/i/item/9789240003279.

World Health Organization. 2020c. "WHO Director-General's Opening Remarks at the Media Briefing on COVID-19—24 February 2020." https://www.who.int/dg/speeches/detail/who-director-general-s-opening-remarks-at-the-media-briefing-on-covid-19--24-february-2020.

World Health Organization. 2020d. "FIFA/COVID-19 Virtual Press Conference." March 23. who.int/docs/default-source/coronaviruse/transcripts/who-audio-emergencies-coronavirus-press-conference-full-23mar2020.pdf?sfvrsn=846ecb41_4.

Young, Kevin. 2002. "Standard Deviations: An Update on North American Sports Crowd Disorder." *Sociology of Sport Journal* 19: 237–75.

Young, Virginia Alvino. 2020. "Nearly Half of the Twitter Accounts Discussing 'Reopening America' May Be Bots." Carnegie Mellon University. May 20, 2020. https://www.cs.cmu.edu/news/nearly-half-twitter-accounts-discussing-%E2%80%98reopening-america%E2%80%99-may-be-bots.

Zemblyas, Michalinos. 2007. "Emotional Capital and Education: Theoretical Insights from Bourdieu." *British Journal of Educational Studies* 55 (4): 443–63.

Index

For the benefit of digital users, indexed terms that span two pages (e.g., 52–53) may, on occasion, appear on only one of those pages.